A Lady's
Honor

Also by Laurie Alice Eakes

The Daughters of Bainbridge House Series

A Reluctant Courtship

A Flight of Fancy

A Necessary Deception

The Midwives Series

Choices of the Heart

Heart's Safe Passage

Lady in the Mist

A Lady's Honor

A CLIFFS OF CORNWALL NOVEL

Laurie Alice Eakes

ZONDERVAN

A Lady's Honor
Copyright © 2014 by Laurie Alice Eakes

This title is also available as a Zondervan ebook.
Visit www.zondervan.com/ebooks.

Requests for information should be addressed to:
Zondervan, *Grand Rapids, Michigan 49530*

Library of Congress Cataloging-in-Publication Data

Eakes, Laurie Alice.
 A lady's honor / Laurie Alice Eakes.
   pages cm.
 ISBN 978-0-310-33206-0 (trade paper)
 1. Royal houses--Fiction. I. Title.
 PS3605.A377L34 2014
 813'.6--dc23
                               2013041268

All Scripture quotations are taken from the King James Version of the Bible.

Any Internet addresses (websites, blogs, etc.) and telephone numbers in this book are offered as a resource. They are not intended in any way to be or imply an endorsement by Zondervan, nor does Zondervan vouch for the content of these sites and numbers for the life of this book.

Publisher's Note: This novel is a work of fiction. Names, characters, places, and incidents are either products of the author's imagination or used fictitiously. All characters are fictional, and any similarity to people living or dead is purely coincidental.

Cover design: Kristen Vasgaard
Interior design: James A. Phinney
Printed in the United States of America

14 15 16 17 18 19 20 / RRD / 21 20 19 18 17 16 15 14 13 12 11 10 9 8 7 6 5 4 3 2 1

To my aunt Alice.

*So many of my happy childhood
memories include you.*

For where your treasure is, there will your heart be also.

MATTHEW 6:21

CHAPTER I

Cornwall, England
April 1811

"FASTER. FASTER." ELIZABETH TRELAWNY LEANED FORward on the edge of the carriage seat as though the angle of her body could bring the impossible out of the coach and four—more speed. "This pace will never do."

"It will g-get us all killed." Her middle-aged companion, Miss Pross, stammered one more protest to the breakneck pace Elizabeth demanded of her coachman. "It's d-dark out."

Indeed it was—too dark. The three-quarter moon Elizabeth counted on to guide her escape floated somewhere above a layer of black clouds rolling in from the English Channel and threatening rain at any moment.

Rain would be her undoing, making narrow, winding roads too slick for speed.

"But the marquess is right behind us." He had been since he caught up with them at an inn outside Plymouth. Only the freshness of Elizabeth's horses and the fatigue of the marquess's, coupled with her coachman's quick thinking, had gotten them way ahead of Elizabeth's would-be fiancé. With the size of Romsford's entourage and the ability to send men across

Cornwall on horseback or to sail along the coast in a fishing boat, Elizabeth's slight advantage wouldn't last for long.

"I must reach Bastion Point before he blocks our way in all directions."

Bastion Point, perched on the cliffs along the north coast of Cornwall and still twenty miles away, had represented safety for Trelawnys for the past one hundred and fifty years. Elizabeth Trelawny was one more generation seeking shelter behind its gray stone walls.

"But this p-pace isn't dece— Ooph."

Brakes squealed. The carriage slewed sideways and jarred to a halt.

"No." Elizabeth shot up and rapped on the hatch. "Do not stop. Coachman—"

Shouts and the sound of galloping hooves surrounded the vehicle. A shot roared like thunder for the approaching storm. A man yelled. Another one laughed.

"Highwaymen," Miss Pross cried.

"Romsford." Elizabeth nearly sank to her knees. If only she knew something more than the liturgical recitations she performed with the congregation at St. George's Hanover Square every Sunday morning.

"At least we've stopped." Miss Pross sounded calm, her usual self-possessed person of governess turned companion. "You will see that the marquess will not harm you. His intentions are completely honorable."

"Then why does he seem incapable of listening when I say no?" Elizabeth knocked on the hatch again. "Coachman, stop this nonsense and get moving."

The hatch remained closed, the coachman silent, others unnaturally quiet, the hiss of their whispering voices not much louder than the sea a hundred yards away. Those murmurs rose and fell close to the carriage door, but not close enough for more than a word or two to penetrate the enameled panels as though the wind snatched a fragment of conversation here and there to throw it against the window.

"...boat..."

"...never do..."

"...circle around..."

Her heart beating hard enough to break through to her stomach, Elizabeth pressed her face to the glass. Despite her eyes adjusting to the darkness inside the carriage, she could see little beyond the window, as though a curtain had been drawn across the outside of the pane.

Yet the subdued argument continued, and this time she heard her name. Her name. No highwayman would have her Christian name.

She grasped the handle. "I'm going out there."

"You cannot." Miss Pross clutched Elizabeth's shoulder. "They could be—"

The carriage door burst open. Strong hands grasped Elizabeth by the waist and swung her from the coach. A scream rose in her throat, but she choked it back. *Souvenez qui vous etes.* She recited the family motto in her head. *Remember who you are.*

Trelawnys didn't scream; they fought.

She kicked the shin of the man who held her. Pain shot through her toes in their kid slippers. She sucked in her breath. The man merely laughed as he slung her over his shoulder and started carrying her away from her carriage.

Miss Pross was screaming as she scrambled out behind them. She carried no family motto demanding a certain type of behavior. "You let my lady go, you brute, you beast." She ran after them, brandishing her umbrella.

The man ignored her and instead picked up his pace, striding forward as though Elizabeth weighed no more than her velvet cloak.

That same velvet cloak imprisoned her arms so she couldn't beat on his back and twisted around her knees so she couldn't jab him in the middle. Her hood tumbled over her face, smothering her and muffling the sobs pressing at her lips.

I'll not cry. I'll not cry. I. Will. Not—

Tears burned in her eyes. She struggled in the man's hold, trying to loosen it.

He held on to her more tightly. "Stop it, Elys. You're safe now."

Elys?

She went limp over the man's shoulder. Only four people in the world called her by her Cornish name. Grandpapa, Grandmama, Conan, her childhood friend, and—

"Drake?" Her soft exclamation of her brother's name became lost in Miss Pross's shout of protest.

"I'll not go back to the carriage without my lady. You cannot make me."

Apparently they could. A door slammed and the protests grew muffled. A whip cracked. With a crunch of wheels on roadbed and the flicker of swaying carriage lamps, the coach began to move.

The man holding Elizabeth, the brother she hadn't seen in six years, set her atop a horse. "Grab the reins," he commanded in an undertone, a gentle voice just above a murmur. "You can still ride astride?"

"Yes, of course, but where—"

"Later." He released her.

As bidden, she caught up the reins with one hand, then tried to smooth her skirts over her legs as far as possible with the other. Darkness, if not the fabric of her narrow skirt, preserved her modesty. As though allowing anyone to see her stocking-clad ankles mattered when Drake had not failed her after all but had come to her rescue in the spectacular way she expected of her daredevil elder brother.

She nearly laughed aloud.

"Let's ride." Drake rode up beside her on another horse. "I've got a lead rope. You just stay in the saddle. We're going to go fast to beat this rain."

He clicked his tongue at his mount, and both horses sprang into action, heading west toward the narrow track that led over the spine of Cornwall to Bastion Point. Elizabeth held on with hands and knees, bent low over the horse's neck, her hair flying loose of the last of its pins. Behind them, the rumble of the carriage and other horses faded away to the east, back toward Falmouth. Romsford would catch up with Miss Pross, not Elizabeth.

As long as his men hadn't managed to ride cross-country or take a boat and get ahead of her.

She was free, flying through the night toward Bastion Point, toward home at last.

Except they continued west instead of taking the road—such as it was—north. Elizabeth smelled the sea on the rising wind before she heard the crash of waves against the rocky shore to her left instead of the quiet of the moorland at night.

Nearly breathless, she tried to rein in. But Drake with the lead rope kept her mount going, galloping despite the darkness, despite the danger.

"Wait," she shouted above hoofbeats and surf. "This is wrong."

"No!" Drake's shout sailed back to her on the wind. "This is best."

He must know what he was doing. He knew Cornwall better

than she, having never left it save for his illegal forays to France for silk and tea. He knew more than she of why she should not allow their parents to force her to marry the Marquess of Romsford. After all, it was Drake who had written to warn her against the nobleman even before his lordship's behavior made his repulsiveness quite, quite clear to her.

She shuddered, sick at the memory, and concentrated on maintaining her seat atop the galloping horse. She would be sore in the morning, but what matter as long as she suffered in her old room under her grandparents' care?

Laughter bubbled to her lips again, worry fleeing on the Channel gales.

"Home. Home. Home," she called out.

Lightning forked across the obsidian sky. Her mount shied, then skidded to a halt just as the sky opened with a torrent of rain.

"All right?" Drake dropped back beside her.

"Yes." Her legs ached from the unfamiliar position of gripping the horse with her knees, but it had saved her from sliding to the ground.

Drake squeezed her arm. "Good girl. We're almost there."

"Almost where?"

He either did not hear or chose not to answer her. No matter. He'd suggested that he help her get home safely, escape the man their parents insisted she marry after her three—to her parents, anyhow—unsuccessful seasons. They didn't believe the rumors about the Marquess of Romsford. They saw his title and his ten thousand pounds of income a year. Elizabeth saw the look in his one good eye when it fell upon her. A patch covered his other eye. A quantity of scent failed to cover up less pleasant odors on his person. His title and money didn't stop him from attempting liberties no gentleman should take.

She would endure a hundred miles in the driving rain to get away from him.

She had endured perhaps one, although it felt like a hundred with rain soaking through her cloak, sarcenet pelisse, and gown to pebble her skin with gooseflesh. She couldn't feel her cold fingers inside her leather gloves. Presumably she still clutched the reins. She couldn't tell until after Drake finally slowed them and led her mount into a cobbled yard, the horses' shoes ringing on the stones. He dismounted to help her down.

"Let go." He tugged the reins from her frozen hands. "We'll be inside in a moment."

"Inside w-what?"

She sounded like Miss Pross with her chattering teeth.

"The inn. Or what used to be an inn. No one comes here anymore except a few locals on Saturday nights. But there's an old innkeeper here. He'll give us shelter until the rain stops and we can take a boat around Land's End to the Point."

"A fire?"

Drake lifted her to the ground. "I expect so, but wait beneath the eaves until I am sure none of Romsford's men have gotten ahead of us and sheltered here first."

Elizabeth started forward toward the dark bulk of the inn that couldn't boast more than a common room and one or two rooms to let for wayfarers not wanting to stay in Falmouth five miles behind. Perhaps a fisherman or two.

Above the roar of the rain and wind, the sea's deep boom crashed against the rocky shore a hard stone's throw away. The inn lay silent and dark. She hesitated beneath the eaves. They afforded little cover from wind and rain. Drake had said to wait there. But surely she would be all right to step over the threshold. If she was wrong and someone was inside, she could dash into the night again, hide . . . somewhere.

She groped for the dagger she kept in her pocket. Drake had given it to her when she left for London at fifteen. A lady couldn't be too careful.

She lifted the handle and nudged open the door, then poised on the threshold. She'd never walked into an inn alone in her life. No matter that this one appeared deserted, a hollow blackness reeking of spilled ale and vinegar. Twenty-one years of training told her entering a common room on her own just would not do. Yet her hands, toes, lips, and chin had gone numb. She smelled no smoke to suggest the innkeeper was present and had built a fire. But at the same time, a roof, walls, and air warmer than what blew off the sea beckoned. And Drake would join her in a moment.

In a flash of lightning through a window, she caught a glimpse of tables and chairs, black humps rising from the dark chasm of the floor. Nothing moved save for a piece of paper skittering off one of those tables and into a distant corner. Beyond the deserted chamber, most likely where the kitchen lay, a streak of light shone from beneath a door.

Fire. Hot water. A cup of tea.

Elizabeth started forward, her kid slippers a mere whisper on the dusty floorboards, her sodden skirt clinging to her legs. And then she stopped. She must appear disreputable, worse than something the cat would think to drag in, with her hair tumbling down her back as though she'd been swimming in the sea and her clothes clinging to her in a most unsuitable fashion. Even if one or more of Romsford's men hadn't managed to get ahead of her and seek her in the first shelter the bleak coast offered . . .

She finger combed her hair away from her face and twisted it into a knot at the base of her neck where her hood held it in place. She could do nothing about her sodden clothing.

Whether the enemy or an innkeeper, his wife, or his maiden aunt sat behind the door with the promising light, she couldn't walk in there alone. The mahogany color of her hair and ice-blue eyes would give her away as a Trelawny. By morning her reputation would be in tatters. She must, at the least, be accompanied by her brother. Drake's behavior wasn't always the most respectable, but he was beloved in the county. If he told the innkeeper to remain silent about her presence, then the innkeeper would remain silent about her presence.

Romsford's men wouldn't remain silent if it would serve their master's purpose. The marquess was determined enough to wed the last female in London whose parents were desperate enough to be rid of their obstinate and unpopular daughter to accept his offer. Especially after that unfashionable daughter had been caught kissing a dance partner in one of the ballroom bowers. A stupid schoolgirl stunt to play, but she had been so weary of society—and hoping to be returned to Cornwall once and for all—that a stupid action seemed the right course to take.

She'd been hoisted on her own petard, giving her parents reason to marry her off as soon as possible.

Of late, she'd made too many mistakes. She didn't need to risk making one more.

She remained where she was in the middle of the floor, motionless, listening. The wind was shifting, carrying the spring storm west to the Atlantic. Waves still slammed against the shore. Storm and surf blotted out all other sounds from outside or in, and Drake reappeared beside her with no more warning than the absence of cold air from the still-open door as it clicked shut.

"You should have waited outside as I told you to." Though he spoke in the undertone that suggested he didn't want anyone to hear him more than a yard or two away, an edge of anger tinged his voice. "This innkeeper has always been a friend to . . .

a Trelawny, but one never knows when someone with the marquess's rank comes along."

"I know. I was thinking Romsford or his men could have come by sea and gotten ahead of me." She held out her hand, still shaking from the cold and perhaps more, needing reassurance. "He couldn't have, could he?"

"I'd like to say no." He took her hand and tucked it into the crook of his elbow. "I haven't seen any sign of another boat or horses present, but we'll proceed with caution. Shall we?" He led the way across the common room, his booted feet making less sound than her slippers and dragging gown.

At the inner door, he released her and raised his hand to his neck. When he brought his fingers in front of him again, light flashed off the blade of a knife.

Elizabeth raised her own knife and stepped back.

"One can't be too careful." His teeth flashed in the faint light, and then he lifted the door latch with his free hand.

Light flared from a single candle guttering on a deal table in the center of the kitchen. Cold air swirling around them suggested an open door beyond the stacks of barrels lining the walls and forming a divider against one end of the room. Despite the candle, the room appeared deserted.

"Where's the innkeeper?" Elizabeth asked.

"I don't know. I thought he would be in here by a fire." He glided away from her, moving through the shadows cast by the flickering tallow dip on the table. "I'll secure this back door and then build a fire."

Teeth clenched against their chattering, Elizabeth huddled by the door to the common room, her dagger drawn, her gaze fixed on her brother.

He prowled around the periphery of the room, looking behind the stores too plentiful for an inn with little business, a clear sign of a man in league with smugglers. He moved with grace and stealth for such a big man. And a man he was now, not the youth of nineteen she'd left in Cornwall. He'd grown brawnier, seemed a bit taller. And he apparently cared little for the fashion of shorter hair; his own fell in loose waves around his ears and collar. Such pretty, dark hair for a man to possess.

Too pretty. Too dark.

He glided out of the shadows behind a stack of barrels. The candlelight fell full on his face for the first time, and Elizabeth pressed a hand to her lips to stifle a scream, her heart battering against her ribs like the sea beating at the rocky shore outside. She managed to choke out, "You're not my brother."

CHAPTER 2

HER ONE BREAK FOR FREEDOM FROM THE CONFINES OF her parents' strictures and she'd played the fool, trusted without thinking. Simply because the man used her Cornish name, she'd presumed he was Drake. She should have made him stand in the carriage lamps. She should have insisted he speak to her in his normal voice. She should have done anything but let him drag her across Cornwall to this remote inn. Now she must be twenty miles from Bastion Point in the middle of the night. No matter. She must get away before Romsford arrived.

She whirled toward the common room and grabbed on to the open door's edge.

"Don't go out there, Elys." He spoke louder this time, his real accent clear, not the broad vowels of the West Country, nor the clipped accents of an educated Englishman. Something soft and slow and a little mesmerizing. "You might not be safe." Despite herself, she turned to look at him, gazing into his eyes shining with candlelight.

"Better 'might not be safe' out there than 'most certainly not safe' in here." She was shaking again, but not from cold. Looking into his eyes, like the deep blue of the sea on a clear day, sent warmth spreading through her despite her wet cloak and gown.

He started toward her. "You're safe in here."

"I can't be. You lied to me." She released her hold on the door.

"I didn't lie. I let you think I was Drake so you'd come with me."

"To turn over to your master." Her throat closed and her eyes burned.

He reached out a hand with long fingers bronzed from exposure to sunlight—a worker's hand, not the hand of a gentleman. "If you mean the marquess, he's not my master. My master—"

"What have you done with my brother?" She lashed the question at him. "If you've harmed him . . ." She lifted her dagger.

The stranger smiled. "Drake was just fine about three hours ago. He just ran into a bit of trouble with some excise men and needed someone to come fetch you."

"Excise men? Oh, Drake." Instantly deflated, Elizabeth covered her eyes with one hand.

Her brother was forever taking risks with the revenue service. Grandpapa kept warning him he wouldn't continue to free Drake from his follies. One day he would go too far and find himself transported to New South Wales.

Elizabeth groaned. "Why would he risk it tonight of all nights?"

"He found it necessary to move goods for Conan Lord Penvenan."

Elizabeth lowered her hand and looked at the man. With his back to the candle now, his face lay in shadow, all chiseled planes and angles forming a rather rugged beauty like the West Country moors. The harsh features didn't go well with the gentle voice. But the information that he knew of the nighttime activities of Drake and their nearest neighbor, Conan Penvenan, eased the knot of apprehension in her middle.

And yet . . . he had tricked her once, and he might know just enough to do so again in order to deliver her to the Marquess of Romsford.

She opened the door. "Just the same, I think I'll be better off—"

A pistol cracked. Elizabeth staggered as though the ball had struck her.

"The landlord. The double-crossing—"

The stranger lunged for the rear door, then stopped, his head tilted, his face hard.

More shots rang out, two in the distance, one closer.

"I was told I could trust him, but he hid himself from us good."

Elizabeth tensed all her muscles to keep herself calm. "He isn't trustworthy if that is him signaling"—she gulped—"someone."

As if she didn't know it was Romsford on her trail. With the storm blowing itself out to sea, the hoofbeats and rumble of carriage wheels surged through the night. Apparently the marquess had gotten his men along the coast ahead of her this far west on the track north to Bastion Point.

If this stranger truly was from Drake and not in Romsford's pay, whatever he claimed, he was helping her.

He grasped her arm and spun her away from the door. "Hide yourself. I'll try to divert them."

She nodded and ran for the nearest stack of barrels. The instant she crouched on the floor behind the pillar of wooden crates, she wished she hadn't. The odors of spirits and worse tickled her nostrils. Something scurried across her foot, and a spiderweb trailed over her shoulder like a boa.

Drake would be ashamed of her cowering like a craven. *Souvenez qui vous etes.*

Trelawnys didn't hide like mice behind the wainscoting. She should race into the night, hide herself amidst the trees and rocks and blackness of the night. Yet she huddled, shaking, sobs clogging her throat.

If only her family allowed her to do anything for herself, she might know how to make wiser choices.

A draft to her left suggested another door. She might have been able to reach it before anyone entered the inn if the stranger hadn't positioned himself between her hiding place and both doors. To keep others away? Or her trapped?

A scream gurgled in her throat.

"Shh." The stranger rested his hand on her shoulder.

Heavy footfalls rang on the floorboards. "Where is she?" Romsford's gravelly voice rang through the common room.

Elizabeth shoved the side of her hand between her teeth.

The stranger raised his hand from her shoulder. His fingertips barely skimmed across her cheek, but Elizabeth felt a peculiar kind of reassurance, as if he said, "Trust me," and gave her irrefutable reason to do so.

Oh, how she wanted to trust . . . someone!

"Where is she?" Romsford shouted. "Where is my wife?" Elizabeth stiffened, grinding her teeth. His wife, indeed! Over her dead body!

As the sound of footsteps came toward the room, the stranger squeezed her shoulder. Then he stepped forward and propped his own shoulder against the barrels. He rested one hand on his hip, the thumb looped through his waistband. "You don't have a wife, Romsford."

"Who the devil are you?" Romsford demanded as he entered the room.

Tension eased from Elizabeth; Romsford didn't know him.

"Who I am isn't important," the stranger said. "You being here is."

"You're right, it is," Romsford said. "I'm looking for my wife. I've reason to believe she's here."

"You don't have a wife," the stranger repeated. "Miss Trelawny is not your concern."

"In her parents' absence, she most certainly— How do you know about her?"

The stranger didn't answer.

"I asked you a question, man," Romsford barked.

The stranger remained silent.

"Answer me." Heels pounded on the floor as Romsford advanced toward the stranger—and Elizabeth's hiding place. She shook hard enough for the chattering of her teeth to be heard on the other side of the Tamar River despite biting through her leather glove.

The stranger didn't move.

"She's here!" Romsford shouted. "Take her."

More feet pounded across the floorboards, and Elizabeth sprang to her feet. Romsford's men would capture her in a moment, drag her out to his carriage, and carry her to a clergyman more interested in money than obeying the strictures of the marriage laws.

Unless her parents had signed a special license.

Please, Lord, no. She managed a prayer at last.

The stranger stood poised between her and her enemies. Elizabeth didn't notice him moving so much as a fingertip. Yet the tower of barrels crashed to the floor. Wood splintered. Tea sailed into the air like autumn leaves on a gale. Billows of flour formed choking clouds of dust. Men shouted and began to cough.

Under cover of the chaos, the stranger grabbed Elizabeth's hand and they raced out the back door.

"After them," Romsford bellowed.

His men would have to run around the inn. Not much time

wasted. Perhaps enough to give Elizabeth and her escort a head start.

To where?

Nowhere if she couldn't run faster. Her wet skirt and petticoat clung to her legs, hobbling her like a pony in a paddock. Throwing caution to the wind, she caught up her skirt in one hand and sprinted after the stranger. Deceitful and untrustworthy as he might be, he was getting her away from Romsford, which was all that mattered for now.

Rocks bruised her feet. Sharp little stones cut through her delicate slippers. Stifling exclamations of pain, she stretched out her long legs in a way her mother had always abhorred, the way she'd grown up racing along the beaches below Bastion Point.

But six years of sitting in London drawing rooms and sedate walks in Hyde Park had taken their toll. Across a field, with Romsford's men too close behind, she began to gasp for air. Her lungs seized up, and she stumbled over a tussock and landed on her knees.

"I cannot." She gasped out the two words on panting breaths. Her lungs heaved like a blacksmith's bellows. "Can-not."

"I can." He stooped beside her, then lifted her into his arms and slung her over his shoulder.

"I'm too . . . heavy."

"You're not small." His soft voice held a smile.

She suppressed the urge to knee him in the middle. "Can we hide?"

"Not fast enough." He set out at a lope, not the flat-out run of before, but eating up the ground.

Not fast enough. At a shout, she raised her head. Through the tangle of her hair, she caught a glimpse of a man racing with a torch, sparks flying out behind him like the trailing vapors of fireworks. He'd soon see them. He must already hear them. The open fields and rocky shoreline offered no shelter. Soon, too soon, she'd find herself caught, this stranger caught and likely punished, and she'd become the fourth wife of a man whose other wives had died violent deaths.

A sob rose in her chest, crowded her throat. The sob broke free. Another followed. Tears blurred her sight of the men in pursuit.

The stranger tightened his hold. "Soon. You'll be all right soon. Hold on tight."

She gripped the back of his coat as he slid to a halt, then veered to the right and began to walk in that near soundless way of his. Walked. Walked. Walked, with the marquess's men too close.

She did knee him this time, pushed against him.

And he let her go. She slid to the ground in an ignominious heap and with an *ooph* their pursuers should have heard.

Except they were shouting, bellowing, saying words she rarely heard even on the London streets. Their torches dipped, flared, extinguished.

The stranger crouched beside Elizabeth. "There's a ditch there. They'll have a time getting themselves out."

"You led them— Why? Why are you helping me like this? Surely you never expected—"

"Later." He helped her to her feet. "Quietly."

They moved slowly this time, creeping along the ha-ha ditch that separated two fields, then into a copse of trees stunted from the constant wind off the sea. A thousand questions ran through Elizabeth's head, but she clamped her lips against any of them bursting forth. From the sound of things, Romsford's men were sorting themselves out. They were still too close.

In the same county was too close for her.

The inn was certainly too close for her, but they left the

trees a mere dozen yards from the hostelry's rear door, where Romsford stood near the opening, a torch in his hand.

"You brought us back! What—"

The stranger laid a finger across her lips. "Stubble it for now. We need horses. We'll never get to the boat and cast off before they catch us, if they don't already have someone on the dock to stop us."

"I should think Romsford's men will be watching the stable as well."

"But their own horses are near the road with only one guard." As easily as a man would stroll into a chophouse for a late supper, he disappeared around the stable and into the court-yard in front of the inn, where more than half a dozen horses stood, four of them hitched to the coach. Equines whinnied. A man shouted, and then hoofbeats slammed against the muddy ground. A moment later, he cantered up to her hiding place in the ha-ha. "Need help mounting?"

She needed help climbing from the ha-ha.

He dropped down beside her and lifted her out, again as though she weighed no more than a peck of apples. "Hurry. We only have a moment's advantage."

She slipped her foot into the stirrup, and he tossed her onto the saddle fast and hard enough that only a lifetime of experi-ence kept her from flying off the other side. She grasped the reins and kneed the mount to go. A glance behind told her the stranger followed. Beyond him, across the field, Romsford's men seemed to be in confusion as to where to look next. Their torches bobbed along the tree line, the ditches between fields, and the shore. None of them looked toward the road.

Elizabeth and the stranger had chosen the most visible route of escape, hiding in plain sight. Drake had done that more than once when eluding the excise men.

Drake. She grimaced. Wherever he was, hopefully he had managed to do so once again. She didn't want him jailed, especially not before she had a chance to give him a piece of her mind. She would only be able to scold her brother if she escaped.

Someone near the inn called out, "They're escaping."

"Yes, sir, we are," her companion said. "Let's ride."

Elizabeth leaned forward to coax more speed from her mount. She wasn't on a leading rope this time. She could head up the track over the spine to the north coast, possibly lose her companion. If she headed for Penmara, the estate next to Bastion Point, she could get Conan and his sister to help her reach her grandparents. She began peering through the darkness in search of the track.

"Elizabeth, Romsford will likely have sent men in that direction." The stranger spoke as though he knew exactly what she intended as he spurred up beside her and leaned over to take her reins. "We're safer staying on this road."

"We don't have that much of a lead on them. We have two of their horses, but they have ours."

"We should have enough of a lead. Their horses are as tired as ours, and Romsford will have to send one or two men north. It should delay them long enough to let us reach our contingency plan."

"What is that?" Clutching her horse's mane, Elizabeth glanced over her shoulder.

Lights bobbed directly behind, disappeared around a curve in the road, then appeared again. They were too close for comfort, but not gaining . . . she hoped.

"Return to Falmouth."

"Return—" She glanced around, weighing the potential injury she would suffer if she simply leaped from her horse to escape over the hills.

Not a good notion. The countryside was too open. Even if she didn't sprain or break an ankle, she couldn't run faster than these men. Even if she did, the land farther north was riddled with mines, and a body could fall into one in the dark.

She made herself breathe calmly for several moments. "If I thought Falmouth was safe, I would have stayed there in the first place. But when we encountered Romsford's men at the inn and Drake wasn't there yet, I knew we had to keep going. That still seems like the best course—keep going and hide if we can't make it to Bastion Point tonight."

"Not without fresh horses." And nearly impossible to acquire at all that time of night, impossible with Romsford and his men sure to swarm over every hostelry in Falmouth the minute they arrived.

"A boat?" Elizabeth suggested. "The storm's gone."

Her companion—her benevolent captor—glanced behind them this time. "He's going to look on the wharves as well."

"Why me?" Elizabeth closed her eyes, fighting the pain in her belly that assaulted her every time she asked herself this question. "I'm not that good a catch for him to go to all this trouble."

"An excellent question."

Elizabeth winced at the insult, but kept her voice steady. "So if inns are unacceptable and make me too easy to find, and the harbor is the same, but we cannot go north because of the horses, what are we doing back in Falmouth?"

"Where we would have gone had we caught up with you and your companion sooner."

"Conan was with you, but you took me away instead of him doing so? Why?"

"He said he couldn't risk getting caught with you. Your grandparents are too interested in the two of you marrying."

That her grandparents were interested in her marrying Conan was news to Elizabeth.

"And if I'm caught with you by someone who has interest in marrying me himself?"

The stranger said nothing. The horses began to slow, their sides heaving with exertion. Hoofbeats behind them sounded closer, and the stranger released Elizabeth's reins. "Ride ahead of me. If they catch up with us, I'll do my best to slow them."

"But where am I going?" A note of panic tinged her voice.

"Straight into town, then right at the first turn."

"Then where am I going?" She would have reined in if the thunder of hooves and rumble of wheels didn't vibrate the air like an explosion.

"There's a house that belongs to a friend of Conan's. We can hide there until the coast has cleared to leave."

She wanted to stop. She wanted to slide to the ground and run. But she kept going, marking the beginning of houses that indicated the town lying quiet and dark in the night. She made herself speak with calm. "I can't do that. It's wrong. It's indecent. I don't even know you."

"I know you, Miss Elys Trelawny."

"Nonsense. I don't even know your name."

"Rowan Curnow."

A good Cornish name, even if his speech said someplace most likely not even British.

"I am certain I've never met you."

"Not . . . formally, but—" He hesitated. "It's no doubt rude of me to remind you of this, Miss Trelawny, but you danced with me at the Drummonds' masquerade ball last month. I was the one dressed as the Marquis de Lafayette."

The masquerade ball in London three weeks earlier, two weeks before she began her mad dash for Cornwall. The man who had drawn her attention, a rare man taller than she was and dressed like a French soldier of the *Ancient Regime*. The only gentleman dressed like the Marquis de Lafayette.

Like the gentleman she'd been so unwise as to kiss in the ballroom bower.

CHAPTER 3

Worse and worse and worse.

Elizabeth wanted to set her mount from their present canter to a gallop and vanish somewhere in the warren of streets opening around them. Better yet, she should disappear into a larger city like Plymouth. She could reappear in about a decade when too many other scandals large and small would have blotted out memories of her folly.

Unfortunately, she needed to ride around the first right-hand turn in the lane, a narrow alleyway. The sounds of pursuit faded beyond high garden walls, but not enough that she dared to venture forth on her own. She was stranded with the stranger and her shame.

"I was feeling desperate," she began. "That is to say, I've never before . . . I take being a Trelawny and a lady quite seriously . . ." She stumbled over her confused and mumbled excuses for what had simply been an act of rebellion, a kick against restraints too long in place.

She'd never been kissed before that night. Although the humiliating fact was she hadn't been kissed by him so much as done the kissing herself—clumsily, inexpertly, mashing her nose on his before she managed to touch her lips to his. And he'd been such a gentleman about it. He hadn't laughed at her, at least not aloud. He'd held her waist, but whether to set her from him or draw her closer she wasn't given the opportunity to find out before Mama shoved aside the trailing vines forming a curtain to the bower.

No one took that kiss too seriously. Not even Mama. She had been so eager to drag Elizabeth out of the ballroom she hadn't given the man a thought until later when seeking his identity would have brought even more attention to her daughter's outrageous behavior. Wanting Elizabeth married off, Mama ranted about how a gentleman would have owned up to his bad behavior, but the misstep wasn't his; it was Elizabeth's, and she hadn't blamed him for vanishing. He hadn't been eligible. He didn't appear to be eligible now. He had likely sneaked into the ball uninvited and needed to depart before anyone caught him.

"He never should have let me kiss him," had been Elizabeth's only excuse.

"A man will take what you give him, Elizabeth," had been only one line of a lecture that could have rivaled a seven-volume novel. "You go into an alcove with a man, especially when you both wear masks, and the rest is inevitable."

Especially when the female in the duet rose on her toes and set her lips to the man's.

She pressed the back of her gloved hand to her mouth and rubbed, as though she could scrub away the memory, the sensation of that contact. But it clung to her lips and thoughts like the odors of the inn and the mud from their dash through the fields was clinging to her cloak.

Disappearing into the night for a score of years might be long enough to blot out her mortification. She settled for bowing her head and allowing her hood to fall forward and hide her face.

He reached across the space between their mounts and touched her arm. "I wasn't a complete stranger, Miss Trelawny."

No more Elys or even Elizabeth. They had reverted to the formal and proper addresses. This was good. It created distance.

It left her hollow.

"We'd met at Hookham's Library the day before," he continued.

Her head snapped up. "We had? I'm afraid I don't remember."

The ball, the kiss, and the consequences had blotted out all memory of the rest of that first week of the season.

"We were reaching for the same volume of John Locke."

"Nonsense. My mother would never allow me to read John Locke."

"Which is why you were reading it between the stacks, I expect?"

Elizabeth laughed, some of her mortification easing. "So you found me out. I manage to elude her watchful eye upon occasion. Oh, I do remember. But I never saw your face. I mean, I never looked around at you."

She would have remembered a face like his.

"I saw your face when you walked in. You had on a white straw hat with ribbons the color of your eyes. I thought you were the prettiest lady I'd seen in London."

Elizabeth snorted. "You need spectacles, sir."

Despite her derisive words, warmth spread through her at the compliment. It wasn't true, of course. He was simply being a gentleman, trying to make her feel better about having kissed a stranger at a ball.

They lapsed into silence as they rode deeper into town, the broader thoroughfare streets quiet, with lanterns hanging outside inns and homes. The horses' hooves rang like hammer blows upon the cobbles, and any speech between them might have been overheard by someone at an open window or tucked into a doorway.

At one of those doorways, one set into the front of a tall,

narrow house in the middle of a row of tall, narrow houses, Rowan Curnow stopped, dismounted, and reached up his hands to lift her down. "I'll take the horses to the mews, then be back."

"We're staying here?" Elizabeth twisted her hands together in the damp folds of her velvet cloak. "Alone?" With not a whisper of pursuit now, could she dare escape on her own?

"The lantern is hanging on the left side of the door, so I know Conan managed to get Miss Pross here and all is well."

"Conan got her here? What of my coachman?"

She should have thought of him sooner, but he was hired merely for this journey, and she didn't even know his name. Still, he needed to be paid and his transport back to London managed.

"He fell off the box when he tried to shoot us with a blunderbuss, so Conan intended to take him to an apothecary and pay for him to sail back to London."

More difficult for Romsford to find and question if he was on the water. Clever Conan.

Rowan touched a fingertip to her chin. "All is well right now. Let's see it stays that way."

"Yes, of course." Finding her in Falmouth would not be easy for the marquess, but no sense in taking risks.

"I'll escort you and Miss Pross to Bastion Point day after tomorrow."

"What about Conan? Didn't he stay?"

"He said he wouldn't. He wanted to get home and be sure . . . Drake is all right."

She hugged her arms across her middle. "I don't know how to thank you. My parents think I'm mad for so blatantly trying to avoid marriage to Romsford." *Mad enough to kiss a stranger at a masked ball.* "But he was repulsive and . . . and— Well, I thank you."

"You're welcome." He smiled.

Her insides turned to the consistency of a jellied eel. She swallowed against the dryness in her throat. "Shall I knock for Miss Pross?"

"I've a key." He produced it from a coat pocket and opened the door.

Warmth and the scent of apples and spices flowed out like beckoning arms. Elizabeth stepped into that embrace, to the promise of dry clothes and a fire, to candlelight and, suddenly, Miss Pross flying out of nowhere to wrap her plump arms around Elizabeth.

"You're safe. Thank the good Lord. I've been sitting here praying and praying, and is Mr. Drake coming in?"

"No, he—that is—" Elizabeth glanced back at the clop of hooves.

Rowan was already walking the horses away into the shadows of the street between house lanterns.

"He's taking care of the horses."

Her conscience pricked at not confessing the man was not her brother. If they were to hole up for another day, Drake might come to help instead of the stranger.

"Romsford gave us a merry chase," she said instead. "But we managed to circle back here."

"That man." Miss Pross shut the door and threw the bolt with a decisive click. "He and his men were most rude to me and Lord Penvenan. Were I not so much shorter than you, I think he would have pulled off my garments to prove I wasn't you in disguise. Something is wrong with a man who is so desperate for a bride."

"He still doesn't have an heir and has three dead wives." Dead, rumors had it, by his hand when they produced only daughters, two of whom were older than Elizabeth.

She shivered.

"You're wet and cold. Let's get you up to your room. There's a fire, and I can fetch up hot water." Miss Pross tucked her arm through Elizabeth's and bustled her toward the staircase.

She not only set Elizabeth down before a fire and produced cans of hot water for washing, she provided her with bread and cheese and an apple pie. Elizabeth ate every crumb and drank an entire pot of tea with it. She snuggled in the brocade dressing gown trimmed with swansdown Miss Pross produced from the luggage, a fur blanket from the back of a bedchamber chaise, and the drying and brushed cloak of her hair before she finally stopped shivering.

Returning from the kitchen with another steaming pot, this one smelling of hot chocolate, Miss Pross sat opposite Elizabeth, poured out two cups of the dark, spiced liquid, and fixed Elizabeth with her piercing dark eyes. "A handsome young man has taken up residence in the kitchen. Let himself in with a key. Quite unexceptionable behavior, but not truly a gentleman."

"Indeed?" Elizabeth hid behind her chocolate cup.

"Indeed." Miss Pross's mouth set in a thin line for a moment. "He has a peculiar way of speaking, so I asked him where he's from. He says South Carolina. That's in the colonies, isn't it? Or rather, *states*, I think they call them now."

"Is that what his accent—" Elizabeth sank her teeth into her lower lip—too late.

Miss Pross set down her cup. "You weren't with Drake tonight, were you?"

"No." Elizabeth's cheeks burned. "I thought he was Drake when he carried me off, but when we sheltered from the storm in an inn before Romsford caught up with us, I realized— You won't . . . tell anyone, will you? I'd be quite, *quite* ruined if anyone found out." Elizabeth's hands shook.

"Which, of course, would make you unacceptable to the marquess." Miss Pross's eyes gleamed.

"Miss Pross, you would never betray me." She paused, considering the ramifications of creating a greater scandal than kissing a masked man at a ball. She watched firelight shimmer in her cup and set it down before her shaking spilled the dark liquid on her dressing gown. "If necessary—*only* if necessary—let me tell the grandparents myself. They will decide what to tell my parents."

"That seems well enough, though I would prefer not to keep things from Sir Petrok and Lady Trelawny. And he seems like a nice young man. Not good enough for a Trelawny of Bastion Point, of course, but a treat to the eyes."

Elizabeth laughed. "Miss Pross, for shame."

They finished their chocolate over a discussion of the best way to reach Bastion Point the following morning. By then morning had come. As Miss Pross gathered up the chocolate cups and set them on the tray for delivery to the kitchen, the first streaks of dawn began to light the bedchamber window.

Elizabeth rose and picked out clothes to wear for a day of hiding. It must be something nice after her disheveled appearance Mr. Curnow had seen the night before. She also chose garments to wear for seeing the grandparents for the first time in six years. The last time they had seen her, she'd been a gawky fifteen, too tall, too thin, too inclined to turn her gowns into rags by the end of a day riding, fishing, or exploring the caves beneath the cliffs on which the ancestral home had been built.

Now she was twenty-one, still too tall, taller than most men, and far from too thin. The high waist and narrow skirt of her blue cambric gown and pelisse emphasized her height and curves, not at all acceptable traits for fashion or beauty. Likewise, her hair was so straight it refused all attempts to curl it as other young ladies did, swept to one side of their faces or caught up in back. She was lucky if her heavy mahogany tresses remained in pins for an entire evening. She wanted to braid it and wrap it around her head, but that would have increased her height.

She braided it that day, though. Mr. Curnow wouldn't care about how tall she was, especially since she saw nothing of him throughout the hours that dragged past with too much inactivity. After some much-needed sleep, she read. She plied her needle to a strip of embroidery for a gown, and she climbed up and down the steep staircase to work knots loose from her legs, cramping from riding as far and as fast as she had the night before. Mr. Curnow didn't return until sometime that night when she startled awake to the click of a closing door below stairs and then heard only silence.

The silence assured her Romsford had not found her. He would have charged up the steps to carry her away. Likewise, Drake hadn't come to fetch her. He, too, would have cared nothing for her being asleep.

Disappointment over her brother's continuing absence warred with curiosity about the stranger and kept her awake through two rounds of a distant church bell ringing. Dawn was turning the square of window from black to gray before she finally slept again.

Miss Pross, not looking rested from the week's mad dash across the country, woke Elizabeth and presented her with a neatly pressed rose jacquard gown. "We will be heading for Bastion Point today."

"Wonderful." Feeling as though she would fly out of the door screeching if she had to remain inside another day, Elizabeth barely managed to stand still as Miss Pross hooked up the back of Elizabeth's gown and pinned up her hair.

"There's tea and toast in the kitchen." Miss Pross walked to the door. "Mr. Curnow says we will leave in half an hour from now."

For the duration of their stay, he had made himself scarce. He wasn't in the kitchen, where Elizabeth and Miss Pross seated themselves at the table to sip at cups of tea and nibble on slices of toast. Neither said much. Miss Pross kept glancing toward the window, and Elizabeth was thinking of what lay ahead. Now that she was about to see the grandparents and brother, her insides had begun a twisting, turning motion like cream beneath the paddle of a butter churn. Excitement. Anxiety. The wish to tell Drake what she thought of him abandoning her.

Then Mr. Curnow walked through the kitchen door, and the churning in her middle turned to a lump of lead in the pit of her stomach. Her mouth went dry, and the toast in her hand crumbled to dust between her fingers.

He looked even finer by the light of day. Imposing and strong.

She offered him a tentative smile.

He didn't smile back. As he shut the door behind him and closed the distance between entry and table, sunlight fell on his face, emphasizing pallor beneath his sun-bronzed skin, especially a whiteness around his lips.

She surged to her feet, knocking her chair over. "What's wrong?"

"Conan . . . and your brother . . ." He took her hand, toast crumbs and all, in both of his. "I just learned in the mews stable—" A tremor ran through his hands to hers.

She swallowed a cry. "What about my brother and my friend?"

"Mr. Trelawny was nearly caught by the revenue officers and has gone into hiding, and Conan—" He took her other hand in his. "Conan is dead."

"Dead?" Elizabeth and Miss Pross chorused.

Elizabeth's grip tightened on Mr. Curnow's. "There must be some kind of mistake."

"He was well night before last." Miss Pross clutched at the edge of the table. Her eyes widened, the pupils dilating.

"How?" Elizabeth kept hold of Mr. Curnow's hands for balance in a world that had begun to spin out of control. "Di-did the revenue men shoot him? I've always feared either Conan or Drake would end up—"

"No, it wasn't the excise officers who killed him." Mr. Curnow released her fingers and closed his hands over her shoulders. "He was murdered."

CHAPTER 4

ROWAN STEPPED CLOSER SO HE COULD SLIP HIS ARMS around Miss Trelawny if she fainted. Her face had drained of color, her already creamy skin becoming so pallid her ice-blue eyes shone as vividly as the sky.

Shone . . . and remained open and clear. Her shoulders, broad for a female's, straightened. Her chin elevated and grew a hint firmer, and her lips, though bloodless, betrayed only the merest quiver.

Miss Elys Trelawny possessed too much of a backbone to faint.

More than a twinge of disappointment pinched Rowan's middle. He'd have welcomed the opportunity to hold her again, kiss the quiver from her lips, bring color rushing to her mouth and cheeks like that glorious night in the bower. Lilies had made the ballroom smell more like a funeral than a festival, yet the sweet innocence of her kiss had tasted like the elixir of life itself for those precious moments.

Tamping down the disappointment, Rowan released her, shoved his hands into his salt-stained coat pockets, and addressed the two females with as much cool indifference as he could produce around the lady who had piqued his interest the minute he found her surreptitiously reading John Locke in the lending library.

"I'm sorry, Elys—Miss Trelawny." He must remember to be formal with her in Cornwall, where he was just short of being a gentleman, unlike in London, where his quest for information had necessitated he play a different role. "I know Conan Lord Penvenan was your friend."

"And yours." Compassion shown through the tears in her eyes.

Rowan inclined his head. "And mine."

For too short a time, but they had liked one another.

Guilt twisted Rowan's gut. If he had created a better plan for helping Elizabeth escape, if he had done more in the week he had been in Cornwall, he might have been able to help Conan more, extricated him from the smugglers, kept him alive.

"He was such a dear boy." Miss Pross's moan rose like wind around a house corner.

Miss Trelawny gripped her elbows, but not hard enough to stop her shaking. "Who? Why?"

The answer wasn't pleasant, but she might as well know since her brother was quite likely involved. "A falling out amongst the smuggling gang. The revenue men got information when to be on the beach. But Conan shouldn't have been there. He said he wouldn't after recent events."

"Lawlessness." Miss Pross wiped her eyes with a stiff linen handkerchief. "He never should have smuggled."

"He thought he had no choice to save his estate. He's been trying to break away, but they've threatened him and his sister." They, the anonymous smugglers who lived and worked and attended church services side by side with those who never dared tell anyone if they noticed a neighbor slipping off at the dark of the moon.

"Those who snitch die." Miss Trelawny spoke as though she was reciting something she'd heard. "If Conan was the informant, they would kill him. Drake might even be tempted to do so. But Conan wouldn't inform on his fellow Cornishmen."

"No." Rowan wished he could wrap her in something warm—like his arms—to thaw that frosty façade she had donned. "He wouldn't do that even with the threats."

"Who would threaten Lord Penvenan?" Miss Pross made her enquiry in a quiet wail.

"How?" Miss Trelawny asked. "Is Senara safe?"

"His sister is safe. As for the threats, they didn't seem particularly dangerous at the time—a message chalked on the front door of the house, a dead bird on the doorstep . . . Almost child-prank stuff." Rowan clenched and unclenched his fists. "Maybe his dog."

Her face paled. "Someone hurt his old dog? That's unconscionable."

"We don't know. It simply vanished from his rooms one day."

If only he had been around when the messages were left. He knew a little of tracking and might have been able to trace the originator—and gotten his throat cut.

Rowan rubbed his thumb along a crust of sea salt on the pocket of his wool coat and turned away from Miss Trelawny. "We can bemoan Lord Penvenan's smuggling all we like, but it doesn't get you ladies safely to Bastion Point today. There's been no sign of Romsford or his men since yesterday morning, but the sooner I get you home, the better."

"Romsford. I'd have been home if he hadn't caught up with us, and then perhaps Drake and Conan . . ." Miss Trelawny trailed off, spun on her heel, and strode across the room so fast the bottom frill on her skirt swung up to reveal trim ankles in white silk stockings and the pink ribbons from her shoes. Not fashionable, dainty ankles. Nothing about Elys Trelawny was dainty, from her name, to her height, to her masses of mahogany hair. She was slender and strong, Boadicea in pink muslin.

And like a queen, she wasn't for a peasant like him to take an interest in.

Rowan suppressed a sigh and fixed his gaze on a row of nails pounded into the plaster wall to hold a motley collection of pots and pans. "The weather is calm this morning. I can get you onto a boat up the Fal River to Truro. I'll send someone with a message overland to Bastion Point to have you met there by a carriage and outriders." He let himself gaze upon her straight back and the proud carriage of her head. "Without Conan, I don't think you want to arrive with me."

"And have them think I traveled all this way with you?" Miss Trelawny gave her head a hard shake. "Certainly not." She faced Rowan, her face cold. "Why didn't Drake come to help me?"

"If he's wise," Rowan said, settling on evasion, "he's already out to sea."

Lightning flashed in Miss Trelawny's eyes. "He will still be here in Cornwall. Trelawnys know who we are. We do not run." Her voice rang as hard and cold as a steel blade on a frozen pond.

Rowan paused, seeing for the first time that rumors of this lady's great-great-something grandmother being a pirate were quite possibly true. A man tended to forget her family history when he had witnessed her surreptitiously trying to read Locke behind a bookshelf at Hookham's Lending Library, and her desperate, "I am twenty-one and never been kissed" before she—

"You ran." Rowan spoke the truth with as much of a chill as Miss Trelawny to counter a flash of warmth in his middle— a memory of that kiss and a flash of anger for her arrogant assumption her brother could smuggle and go unscathed while Conan got his throat cut and common folk went to prison, got transported, or lay shot down on the beach like mad dogs.

She glanced at him with dislike narrowing her eyes, yet with a hint of vulnerability in the quiver of her lower lip, a touch of humor in the slight lift to one corner of her lush mouth. "You're not intimidated by my family, are you?"

"No, ma'am, I'm not."

"No wonder Drake entrusted my safety to you."

Rowan shifted from one foot to the other, clasped his hands behind his back, and strode to the door. "I'll get that message sent and ensure the boat is ready."

He opened the door. Chilled, damp air drifted into the kitchen, too cold for late April, as far as he was concerned. But a profusion of wildflowers in the narrow strip of overgrown garden and birds merrily singing behind the cottage belied the idea that the weather was unseasonable. A narrow beam of sunlight struggled to slice through the clouds. He stepped toward it, reaching for the promise of warmth—any kind of promise for a future that had become all too uncertain in the past twenty-eight hours.

He closed the door on the lady the murder of Conan Lord Penvenan had placed beyond his reach and headed into the mews. A number of lads lounged about seeking work. He chose two at random to take separate messages to Sir Petrok Trelawny in the event Romsford had sent his minions around the coast in search of his would-be bride to waylay her on the road to Bastion Point.

Had Romsford, the marquess no one had considered, ordered Penvenan killed for taking the Trelawny lady out of his clutches? No, Rowan decided. It was unlikely, even for a man with too many dead wives in his past. He'd never order the death of a peer.

Rowan, on the other hand, wasn't even an Englishman. He watched his back on his way to the harbor in the event Romsford or his men had returned to Falmouth in the past hour. He watched his back while arranging for transport to carry the ladies upriver. He watched his back on his return to the cottage where the ladies waited.

He noticed no one interested in his activities. More than likely, the marquess had gone on to the north to keep an eye out for his prey where he knew she'd end up—Bastion Point, the three-hundred-year-old house perched on a cliff above the sea, owned by the Chinoweth family until the English Civil War, then claimed by a Trelawny ancestress when the Restoration came. A house Rowan had heard of all his life but never seen.

He reached the borrowed house to find the ladies had barred the door. Good thinking on their part. Miss Trelawny opened it to show Miss Pross still seated at the table with a cup of tea and her crumpled handkerchief, then stood waiting for news.

Miss Trelawny's tresses would be so glorious fanned around her shoulders . . .

He focused on her ice-blue eyes. "All the arrangements are made, and I saw no sign of anyone too interested in this house. There's just one difficulty."

"What is that?" the ladies asked together, Miss Pross anxious, Miss Trelawny cool.

He smiled. "I hope you like the smell of fish."

❧

Elizabeth stared at the single-masted fishing boat bobbing on the Fal River and wrinkled her nose. She liked fishing. She did not like the smell of fish in this strong a compote. Even though no one could know she had been with Rowan Curnow, she did not like the notion of him leaving them on their own.

"These men won't let anything happen to you." He had touched her arm as though he read her mind. "They won't let anyone near you whom you don't wish near you."

Elizabeth brushed at her arm, trying to remove the sensation of warmth his touch left behind. "But what if Romsford or his men are there instead of someone from Bastion Point?" Her voice held a note of panic, remnants of the tension with which she had struggled for the past week. "They could overpower these men or bribe them or—" She pressed the back of her hand to her lips.

"I'm expected elsewhere . . ." He glanced from Elizabeth to the boat, then back to Elizabeth. "All right. A few more hours won't matter now that Conan's gone."

Her knees wobbled under the strength of her relief. "Thank you."

"May the Lord bless you." Miss Pross bowed her head as though praying for that then and there.

He tipped his hat to her. "He has blessed me. Shall we go now?" He shepherded them onto the boat, to a stretch of open rail near the prow, and said, "I won't make myself too familiar in public like this." With that pronouncement, he strode aft to join the fishermen by tiller and taffrail.

Elizabeth stood on the deck of the fishing smack that reeked of its recent catch and fixed her gaze on the throng of fisherfolk and townspeople along the wharf, the former selling, the latter buying. For a while, even as the fishing boat cast off its mooring and headed against the river current, she remained motionless and silent, glad Mr. Curnow was with them, wishing she hadn't so desperately wanted him to abandon whatever work he had to come along. She stood at the rail until a warehouse blocked her view of the town, then she turned to Miss Pross. "I won't feel safe until I'm inside Bastion Point."

"I do not believe I'll ever eat fish again." Her normally pink and white complexion tinged with green, Miss Pross leaned on the rail and pressed her handkerchief to her lips. "If I cast up my accounts in front of these young men, I'll never forgive that Mr. Curnow."

He wasn't the one who needed forgiving. Elizabeth was for setting this entire debacle into motion with the man she had just persuaded to risk compromising her even more than the past day and a half already had, more than her behavior in London had, if anyone learned the truth of that masked man's identity.

"No wonder he does not treat a Trelawny with any deference." Elizabeth dropped her hand to the rail and gripped it hard enough to split the seam on her right ring finger where a silver knot ring graced her hand. "I made a fool of myself with him."

"Not at all, my dear." Miss Pross covered Elizabeth's hand with hers. "You acquitted yourself most appropriately this morning. I thought for a moment you might faint when you heard the news of Lord Penvenan's . . . demise, but you neither swooned nor resorted to histrionics."

"I was too stunned to do either. But that's not what I am speaking of." Elizabeth gazed at the tree-clad riverbank slipping past, the sun-dappled water, the pale blue sky with its remaining wisps of cloud drifting toward the sea, and swallowed against a dry throat.

Miss Pross peered up from beneath the brim of her hat. "What then, child? His dress might be rough and his speech odd, but he conducted himself with—"

"He kissed me in London," Elizabeth blurted out. "No, it is worse than that. I kissed him in London. He kissed me back. The masquerade . . . the bower . . . it was him." She slumped as though the confession weakened her spine, and cast a glance aft.

Miss Pross dropped her handkerchief into the river. Her very silence spoke volumes more than the preface of the lost square of linen.

Overhead, the single sail snapped in the wind, and the boom

slid above their heads like a pointing finger. Someone shouted a command, the Cornish accent so strong Elizabeth barely understood the words after a six-year absence from her beloved homeland. The boat heeled to starboard. Miss Pross staggered away from the rail, and Elizabeth caught her around the waist, steadying her.

"Thank you. I never have been much of a sailor." Miss Pross seized hold of the rail. "But I am a good judge of character, and I've a difficult time believing that young man is anything less than honorable. After all, he could have taken advantage of you, so I cannot see him taking advantage of you in a London ballroom. Besides—well, this sounds horribly snobbish, I know, but he does not look the sort to be attending London balls, even masquerades."

"It was him." Elizabeth toyed with the great-great-great-great-grandmother's ring fashioned from captured Spanish silver. "Remember, I made the overture. Pushing me away would have made more of a scene than . . . than what happened. At least it would have been less of a scene if Mama had not found us and shrieked like a banshee."

"Are you saying kissing you was the gentlemanly thing to do?"

"I am."

"But why would he be ungentlemanly enough to remind you of your folly?"

Elizabeth winced at the reminder of such. "So I'd trust him with my safety. He is trustworthy."

"Trying to convince me or yourself?" Miss Pross asked the question in the gentlest of tones.

"It does not matter. Once we reach Truro, he'll be gone."

A hollowness yawned inside her.

"So do we still tell your grandparents as little as possible?"

"Yes. I'd rather they not know I was alone with a stranger for hours."

"I'd still rather not deceive Sir Petrok and Lady Trelawny, my dear." Miss Pross curled her hands around the rail. "Even lies of omission are wrong."

"You can say that even after six years in London?" Elizabeth snorted. "Then say nothing at all, if it pricks your conscience. It does not prick mine to keep my family from making even more excuses for marrying me off to the murdering marquess. I am free of him and intend to stay that way."

But she was not free of him. The Fal bent eastward at King Harry's Reach, and the fishing smack continued up the Truro River with its banks wooded in stunted oaks, to the Truro quayside, and when they moored, two men stood awaiting them on the wharf, one with an erect posture and mostly black hair that made him appear two decades less than his seventy-five years, the other with sagging jowls and lines of dissipation making him appear two decades beyond his fifty years.

Her grandfather, Sir Petrok Trelawny, and the Marquess of Romsford, standing side by side.

CHAPTER 5

THE TEMPTATION TO BEG THE FISHERMEN TO RETURN her to Falmouth ran so high Elizabeth spun away from the rail and headed aft two steps.

"Trelawnys don't run." Rowan Curnow's voice rose from the hatchway. A reminder. A taunt.

She faced the dock, her hands buried deep inside the sleeves of her cloak so no one could see them shaking. "It seems that all this was for nothing." Her voice emerged a bit steadier than her hands.

Or her middle. Her insides felt as though she rode on a hurricane-tossed sea.

She'd eluded Romsford for a week crossing England, had risked ruin spending hours alone with a stranger, and ended up landing at Romsford's feet. At Romsford's feet with Grandpapa's blessing, apparently. They were standing close enough to have been engaged in dialogue. Dialogue about what? If Romsford had told Grandpapa about Elizabeth being alone in that inn with a stranger, she may as well start planning how to be the first of Romsford's wives to stay alive for more than a pair of years. Kissing a stranger was bad enough, but being alone with him at night was social suicide.

Mouth set in a hard, thin line to keep her chin from quivering, Elizabeth preceded Miss Pross down the gangway, pressed a guinea into the fisherman's gnarled hand, and glided to Grandpapa as though Romsford did not exist. She dropped a curtsy. "You need not have come all this way to meet me, sir, but I thank you for doing so."

"Of course I came to meet you." Sir Petrok Trelawny, once condemned as a pirate and ending up knighted for his heroic deeds—or the depth of his coffers—tucked his walking stick under one arm and gripped Elizabeth's hands with a strength belying his seventy-five years. He held her gaze with eyes as black as Welsh coal. "I couldn't entrust your safety to anyone else."

Her safety?

She flicked a glance toward Romsford.

"Your parents expected me to ensure your safety," the marquess said.

"As you see, your assistance was wholly unnecessary." She smiled.

He scowled.

She held her breath, waiting for Romsford to proclaim victory or mention her escapade with Rowan Curnow. Waiting for Grandpapa to tell her she was in a depth of trouble.

"We shall collect your luggage and be on our way." Grandpapa spoke first.

He did not so much as glance at Romsford.

"I requested a word with Miss Trelawny." The marquess enunciated as though he believed Grandpapa was deaf.

"Do you wish to speak with him?" Grandpapa asked Elizabeth.

She shook her head. "I've told him all I wish to." She started to turn away with Grandpapa, who was already signaling two footmen from Bastion Point to collect the baggage.

Romsford grasped her arm. "I, my dear, am not the untrustworthy one." His voice was a murmur, his person close enough for her to catch his odor of linens not changed often enough. "Or do you think my being on the quayside here with Sir Petrok is mere coincidence?"

Her lips parted on a gasp. She tried to gather her spinning thoughts enough to ask a coherent question about Curnow and the messages he said he'd sent north, but Romsford was already striding away. A glance back at the boat told her Curnow was nowhere in sight, or she would have flung accusations at him regardless of the consequences to her reputation.

A reputation Romsford could destroy if he chose to disgrace the bride he wanted with such desperation—desperation beyond reason. And unreasonable people took drastic measures.

"Do not look so frightened, child." Miss Pross tucked her hand into the crook of Elizabeth's elbow. "He cannot harm you now that Sir Petrok is with us."

She shook her head and allowed her companion to nudge her toward Grandpapa and the Bastion Point traveling coach, though how her legs worked when they had turned to the consistency of spun sugar she didn't know. Her brain, unfortunately, was not a weak froth. It brought her ideas all too clearly.

Mere coincidence. Mere coincidence. Mere coincidence. Romsford's words began as a murmur and ended in a shout ringing in her ears as though the marquess followed her with his repetitive Greek chorus.

Rowan had sent out two messengers, he said, in the event Romsford intercepted one. But perhaps he meant he had also sent a messenger to Romsford as to where to find her. Perhaps Curnow had come along so readily to ensure Romsford caught her and her pretend rescuer got paid well for—what?

No. He could have simply turned her over to the marquess the night before last and saved much trouble. She would not allow a seed of doubt against Mr. Curnow to creep into her head.

Drake had sent him. Conan knew him. Romsford had merely followed Grandpapa or intercepted one of the messages.

Unless they wanted her alone with Rowan to ruin her if—when—the truth emerged. Emerged due to Conan's death.

She clamped down her whirling thoughts and clambered into the carriage. Because Miss Pross tended toward travel sickness if she took the rear-facing seat, Elizabeth settled onto that one before her companion could object. Miss Pross, however, tried to sit beside her charge.

Grandpapa held out a staying hand. "I wish to sit beside my granddaughter. You won't mind us talking, will you, Miss Pross?"

"No, sir." Miss Pross opened her reticule. "I'll simply read my New Testament. I need some spiritual refreshment after that boat journey."

"Ah, yes, refreshment." Grandpapa plied his walking stick to the roof of the coach. "The hamper, John."

A moment later, a footman handed in a basket. It held nothing fancy—a bottle of lemonade, bread and butter, slices of ham.

"I thought you ladies would be hungry after your unconventional means of transport home." Grandpapa gave Elizabeth a twinkling glance. "You do know how to make a grand entrance, do you not?"

"I had no intention of doing so." Elizabeth took the food he gave her, but wished to eat none of it. "I simply had to get to Bastion Point, to you and Grandmama."

"And you do not wish to be a marchioness." Grandpapa leaned back against the squabs as though he settled in his favorite chair before the library fire.

Elizabeth removed the basket from his lap, returned her

viands, and slid the hamper onto the seat beside Miss Pross before she faced the grandfather. "I do not wish to be the Marchioness of Romsford."

"Ah, so you do not object to marriage?"

"Of course not. It is simply that . . ."

Images of a hundred balls, dinner parties, soirees, and other entertainments swirled through her head, partners foisted upon her. No, more like she was foisted upon her escorts. Those partners slipping away even before doing so could be considered polite, even her dowry not enough to counteract her height and her desire for intelligent conversation. Other couples slipped off for walks along the private paths at Vauxhall Gardens, at country house parties, at picnics. She never had been invited by anyone she'd dare spend a few moments alone with, until she took matters into her own hands.

No one she should have been alone with.

She stared out the carriage window to a countryside alternating between newly tilled fields and the detritus of the copper and tin mines. She couldn't see the sea, but she could smell it above smoke from the steam engines pumping water from the mines, crisp and clean, a balm to her aching soul.

"No one ever asked me to marry him who wasn't either a fortune hunter or a knock-in-the-cradle," she said, making the admission without a flicker of emotion.

"Except for Romsford." Grandpapa covered her hand with his.

She nodded, still not looking at him. "He is precisely the same height as I, so does not appear to care that I am so tall and taken with talking about, um, philosophy."

Rowan Curnow was half a head taller. She'd had to rise up just a little to touch her lips to his.

"If you wanted to wed him," Grandpapa began, "I'd have

looked into these rumors of his other wives dying so rapidly after producing only two girls; however, I'd not have encouraged the match in any way. Even if he were innocent of their deaths, he's not the right man for you, and I do not understand why your parents cannot see that."

"They only see a daughter who is becoming an embarrassment. Mother is still so beautiful, and Father—well, he looks like an older version of Drake."

"Do not," Grandpapa bit out, "mention your brother's name to me at the moment."

Elizabeth flinched, started to ask a question, then chose silence instead.

"You're beautiful, Elizabeth." Grandpapa nodded to Miss Pross. "Do you not agree?"

The companion glanced up from her New Testament. "Indeed. I know many a young lady who would give dearly for those cheekbones."

Those cheekbones grew overly warm, and Elizabeth squirmed on her seat. "Even if I agreed with you two old flatterers, it does not diminish the fact that I did not take in three seasons, and was not likely to take this season. The older I get, the less desirable I am."

"So you decided to kiss a stranger." Grandpapa's tone was stern, but the corner of his mouth twitched suspiciously.

Elizabeth ducked her head. "Mama wrote you that too?"

"She did. Is it true?"

"It's true. I kissed a stranger. He was taller than I am."

"Scarcely a reason for such behavior, child." Grandpapa flicked a finger against her chin. "But you're a Trelawny, and we are known for stepping over the bounds of proper behavior from time to time. If that is the worst you have done, there is nothing to concern us, unlike your brother and cousin."

"Drake and Morwenna?" Elizabeth straightened and turned to face Grandpapa. "What has Morwenna done now?"

"She's, ehem, gotten herself into trouble and refuses to say who the father is."

Elizabeth gasped. Morwenna, four months younger than she, had been the rebellious daughter of a rebellious son, scaring off governesses, getting herself expelled from schools for sneaking out after curfew, choosing friendships amongst the daughters and sons of the miners rather than the gentry. But, as much as the dark-eyed beauty flirted, she'd never so much as hinted at being the sort to overstep the boundaries of propriety that far.

"Is he—" Elizabeth swallowed. "Is it likely the son of some miner? Sam Carn, perhaps? They were always . . . close."

Grandpapa sighed. "Sam Carn is the constable this year and courting Alis Bell, so I doubt as much. I expect the father is wholly unsuitable, and she fears I'll have him dismissed from whatever is his position if she says."

"You would not, though."

"No, I'd not. Nor would I allow them to marry."

"Is she still living at Bastion Point, or have her parents returned from Brazil?"

Elizabeth's uncle, her father's younger brother, had become an explorer and married a woman just as interested in traveling the globe as was he. But they had left their daughter behind.

Grandpapa's face hardened. "I could not have her living at Bastion Point. It wouldn't be seemly. She's living with a hired companion in a cottage I've rented from the Penvenans, and is banished from Bastion Point until she's willing to be honest with us." Steel edged his tone. "Besides, now she couldn't live at Bastion Point with you there. It would sully your reputation."

Elizabeth shivered. Although she'd kept herself pure, Grandpapa might exile her too, if he learned how she could be ruined by gossip about her being alone with a stranger in the night.

Miss Pross caught her eye across the carriage and gave her a half smile and a nod before returning to her Bible. The reassurance that her secret was safe with her companion didn't warm Elizabeth much, not with Romsford knowing. Not with Rowan himself knowing. And Drake and Conan—

Oh, she was a self-centered beast.

"What about Drake? Is he—did you—"

"Exile him too?" Grandpapa's hands curled into fists on his knees. "Your brother was warned if he went out with the smugglers once more I'd not help him escape any consequences. I do not care if a bit of lawlessness seems to be a family inheritance; I intend for it to stop with my grandchildren, and he, above any of the three of you, has known it for some time now. And with Conan's murder—" His voice suddenly sounded old and quavery. "I do not know what has happened to my beloved Cornwall when someone dares murder a peer."

"But it was not Drake. You know he would never do such a thing."

"Of course he would not. That is the only reason I've not turned him over to the riding officers myself—I do not want him accused of murder and the real culprit allowed to get away because they think they have their man."

A man the officers had wanted to catch and make an example of for years—the grandson of the richest man and one of the most powerful men in the county.

"And I do not need him leading you into temptation either." Grandpapa gave Elizabeth a stern look.

"He already did, encouraging me to run away from Romsford."

"Perhaps that is one good thing he has done of late." Grandpapa leaned back and closed his eyes for a moment. Lines of fatigue etched his face and shadowed his dark eyes. All of a sudden he looked old and tired and sad.

Elizabeth's throat closed. "Grandpapa? Is something more wrong?"

Do not let me be the next of your grandchildren you condemn. I need your approval and love. You and Grandmama are the only ones who have ever given it to me.

He took her hand in his, squeezed hard for a moment, then sighed and opened his eyes. "I was not a good father to my sons. I let them have too much money and gave them too little discipline. Nor did I bring them up in the ways of the Lord. I did not know him myself then, and now I've lost your father to political and social ambitions and your uncle to explorations that will likely kill him before I go to my reward."

"Grandpapa—"

"Do not interrupt. I need to say this." He rubbed at a crease between his eyes. "I want things to be different for my grandchildren, but am afraid I've let it go too late there as well. At least with Drake and Morwenna. But you, child, you're the only one who has done nothing that can be construed as ruinous behavior."

"I kissed a stranger at a ball."

Grandpapa smiled and waved his hand like erasing a slate. "Youthful high spirits at a masquerade, nothing more. And I've been tempted to give you Bastion Point outright—"

"What?" Elizabeth jumped. "You cannot. You would not. That's Drake's inheritance as the only grandson. I have my dowry and—"

"Hush, child. I haven't done it for the very good reason that you should have to do what young people of our class never have to do and yet *should* have to do—earn something, be worthy of the wealth and privilege you enjoy."

"I—well, I . . . I can never earn even half of Bastion Point's worth."

"You can. And so can your brother and cousin if they repent of their behavior."

"H-how?" Elizabeth hugged her arms across her roiling middle.

"This family's wealth was built on other people's treasure. I want it to be maintained by treasure of your own. In this world, I've found treasures that money and wit and strength cannot buy. They have brought your grandmother and me great joy despite our mistakes and sorrow over having made those mistakes."

Grandpapa smiled at her. "Whichever grandchild finds that treasure first shall inherit Bastion Point and the bulk of its wealth."

CHAPTER 6

Elizabeth stared at Grandpapa in the growing gloom of twilight. "You're saying I've a chance to inherit Bastion Point?"

"I am."

"But . . . but . . ." Words eluded her. Her head spun. Her heart leaped.

Owning Bastion Point lay within her grasp—if only she worked out what Grandpapa meant by the sort of treasure he wanted her to find. If only he didn't learn that she'd essentially ruined her reputation in her determination to elude Romsford.

With Bastion Point in her possession, she need not marry. She would have wealth and prestige all on her own. She wouldn't be allowed to sit as the local justice of the peace like Grandpapa, but she could give house parties and invite enlightened ladies and gentlemen, men and women of science and letters, and they would come. She could create space for them to work and study. And if this war with France ever ended, she could travel to Paris and Vienna and Italy, Greece and Russia, and India, perhaps even America, or Brazil like her aunt and uncle.

"I . . . I do not know what to say," she murmured.

"You need not say anything, child. It is what you must do."

"But how?"

"Your grandmother and I'll do our best to help. Perhaps we

will not fail with you as we did with the others. And speaking of the others . . ." He glanced at Miss Pross.

"I hear nothing, Sir Petrok," Miss Pross said without looking up. "I say even less."

"She's completely trustworthy, Grandpapa. It's why I keep her in my employ instead of a customary lady's maid."

"I wish to keep my post. I do not indulge in servants' gossip." Miss Pross turned another page of her Testament.

Grandpapa nodded, apparently deciding she and Elizabeth spoke the truth, and looked at Elizabeth. "You may wish to say good-bye to Drake. He sails on the next ebb tide."

"You will allow that?"

"If you tell him what I just told you." Grandpapa patted her hand, then released it. "I've already told Morwenna in the hope it will persuade her to speak of her baby's father."

The carriage slowed and turned between two serpentine stone pillars topped with carved granite tigers, crouched as though ready to spring down upon hapless visitors. To Elizabeth they spelled welcome, safety, their mouths grinning, not growling. Were she a child, she would have sprung from the carriage and raced through the parkland of ancient, gnarled trees beyond them until she reached the front steps.

But she remained where she was, hands clasped in her lap, gaze fixed on the passing scenery of budding tree limbs lifting high against the gray-blue sky of dusk, thoughts racing ahead to where she'd find her brother.

The carriage swept around a curve, with a fountain in the shape of a leaping dolphin burbling in its center. Before the granite front steps of the magnificent stone edifice beyond it, the coach halted. Toe tapping, Elizabeth waited for Grandpapa and then Miss Pross to alight. Once her feet touched the ground, she scarcely managed a polite greeting to the ancient family butler and two footmen who emerged to carry luggage before she slipped inside the entryway and into Grandpapa's study.

The door closed and locked behind her. She crossed the room to a single column of books, removed the fifth book from the left on the third shelf—a translation of *Don Quixote* this year—and pressed on the paneling behind. The bookcase swung toward her. She leaped back, then rounded the shelves to step into a room barely tall enough for her to stand upright in and neither wide nor long enough to lie down, should the need arise. Another press of her fingers on the back wall of this room set the bookshelves swinging into place with a click that indicated a well-oiled mechanism. By feel from long practice since the day Drake showed her the secret room, she found the shelf with its candles and tinderbox. Once a flame glowed from a taper, she made a third press on the side wall. It opened the rear wall of the room to reveal a flight of steps descending into blackness, smelling of the sea.

They smelled of the sea because those steps led directly to a cave accessible only by boat at high tide, a hiding place and a bolt hole created by a family that had more often than not operated outside the laws of the realm until Grandpapa saw the error of his ways and the benefits of serving his king.

A trait he had failed to pass along to his grandson.

In a deeper subterranean chamber and behind another panel with a hidden opening, the glow of light led her to her brother. A brazier lent warmth to the chamber, a lantern gave him light, a blanketed cot some comfort. The scent of tea and a savory stew suggested Grandpapa wasn't allowing Drake to starve while he awaited exile.

He didn't look comforted. Elizabeth stood in the opening for several moments, watching him slumped forward, his elbows on his knees, his hands buried in his thick, mahogany hair.

"Praying or meditating on your misdeeds," she spoke at last.

He sprang to his feet, a pistol appearing in one hand like a conjurer's trick. "Elys, you startled me. I could have shot you."

"Not likely." She grinned, then flew into his arms.

For several minutes, they simply clung to one another. She didn't even try not to weep. His body trembled as though he was struggling to keep his own tears at bay. After a while, he spoke her name again and again and hugged her hard enough to bruise a rib or two.

"Give over." Laughing through her tears, Elizabeth tugged herself free. "I can't breathe."

"You won't want to if Grandfather finds you here."

"He knows. He gave me his blessing on a visit."

"Did he now?" Drake stepped back, his face, with all its proud Trelawny bones, twisting to one side as though he smelled something awful. "At what cost to you?"

"Drake, be nice. He isn't mercenary."

"Hmph. Even when I told him why I went out with the gang night before last, he still wouldn't forgive me disobeying him."

"Then why did you go out instead of coming to help me?"

Drake glared at her. "Do not you too start flinging accusations at me. I sent Conan to help you because I thought, if all else failed, he could whisk you off to Guernsey and marry you to keep you out of Romsford's clutches." He narrowed his eyes. "Since you're here, I presume you did keep out of Romsford's clutches, even if Conan let me down after what I risked—and am suffering—to help him."

"But he did not let you down. He did come, along with—"

"Then how could he have gotten himself killed on the beach here?"

"I do not know." Knees weak, Elizabeth sank onto the cushioned bench against one of the cave's surprisingly smooth, paneled walls. "I did not know he was killed on the beach here.

I thought . . . I do not know what I thought. I . . . Tell me what all happened."

"Tell me why Grandfather let you come down here."

She set her lips in a firm, stubborn line. Drake did the same. They glared at one another in the latest skirmish of a lifelong battle of wills as to who would get his own way first.

The roar of the incoming tide reminding Elizabeth of the passage of time, she gave in first. "Grandpapa wants me to tell you that if I can find a treasure worth more than Bastion Point, he will let me inherit."

Drake's jaw dropped. "Instead of me? But I'm the only male in our generation. It is my right."

"Not if Grandpapa says it is not. The land isn't entailed. Besides, he said the first of us who finds it . . ."

If only she knew what Grandpapa meant by treasures that money and wit and strength cannot buy. That was the only clue he had seemed willing to give her. But in the world she had always known, that sort of treasure sounded too elusive to discover.

"First. As though I have a chance now to get what's rightfully mine—" Drake drew back his arm, fist clenched as though he were about to punch the wall of the cave.

Elizabeth grasped his wrist with both hands to stop him from surely breaking all of his fingers. "Do not be a fool, Drake. Hurting yourself will not hurt Grandpapa."

"Nothing hurts that hardhearted old man. I help a friend, and he exiles me to the plantation on Barbados like I am some sort of criminal."

"It's not exile forever, and you know I've no idea what he means by a treasure worth more than Bastion Point. I thought Grandpapa had invested all his ill-gotten gains in legitimate investments."

"They were not ill-gotten—exactly. And, yes, he has. But

lately . . ." Drake jerked his hand free of Elizabeth's grip and turned away. "You cannot expect me to help you find the way to inherit Bastion Point out from under me after what I sacrificed to help you."

Guilt stabbed Elizabeth for a moment, then she stiffened her spine. "No one forced you to go out with the smugglers. You did not need to send Conan to me. I'd not have married him under any circumstances, and he took great pains to keep from being compelled to marry me since I never actually saw him."

"You never saw him?" Drake dropped onto the bench beside her. "But you knew he came to help ensure Romsford did not catch up with you before you got here. At least I'm assuming you know, since you're here and not wed to the murdering marquess. Do tell me what happened."

"We nearly got caught by Romsford on the east side of Falmouth, and then managed to get just beyond Falmouth, as you recommended we go, when horsemen stopped us. Conan left with Miss Pross in the carriage as a decoy and took her back to a house in Fal—"

"What?" Drake's hand clamped on her forearm. "Conan never stayed with you?"

"N-no. He took Miss Pross to Falmouth and left her there."

"And he left you on your own?" His hand tightened so hard she feared a bruise would form. "If he were not already dead, I'd kill him myself. How could he? How dare he? I give up my inheritance and possibly my life in exchange for him helping you, and he—"

"Drake, ease over." The childhood expression slipped from Elizabeth's lips.

At once he released her arm and smoothed his fingers over it as though doing so could erase the hurt he caused. "My dastardly temper. I am so sorry, Elys, but truly a man never had such a disloyal friend. That is, I thought he would do this for your friendship with him and his sister, if nothing else, and—"

"But I was not alone." She spoke loudly to drown Drake's tirade. "Your friend Rowan Curnow took me on to an old inn. We were going to wait for the weather to clear to take a boat from there to here, but Romsford caught up with us, so we had to escape him and— What is wrong?"

Drake was staring at her, his face white.

"Go on," he commanded in a hoarse voice. "What did you do?"

Elizabeth swallowed against the dryness in her throat. "We circled back to Falmouth to where Miss Pross was waiting."

"So you were with Curnow until Falmouth?"

"I was with him until he put us on a boat up the Fal this morning. I mean . . . That is—"

"You were alone with a stranger more than half the night?"

"He was not precisely a stranger. We had, um, met in London." Her ears burned. "In Hookham's Library and at a ball. And— Why are you looking at me like that?"

"You know Grandfather will never approve of you spending all that time alone with a man at night, especially now that Morwenna has gotten herself into trouble. He has become such a high stickler in his old age and—"

"But Rowan Curnow is your friend. Indeed, I went with him to begin with because he called me Elys like you do and . . ." She trailed off as Drake shook his head once, twice, three times, then stared at her with a blend of pity and concern.

"Elys, I've no idea what went on the other night with Conan and you, or what you even did to escape from Romsford. I do not know what happened to Conan after he left Miss Pross in Falmouth that got him killed on our beach. But I can be sure of one thing—I've never heard of Rowan Curnow."

CHAPTER 7

Surely the unthinkable had occurred and the tide had fully sealed off the opening to the cave, sucking all the air from the chamber, all the air from Elizabeth's lungs. She opened her mouth to speak and ended up gasping like a fish tossed onto the deck of a smack.

"What's amiss, Elys?" Drake crouched before her. "Did this man take advantage of you? You know I'll risk all of Grandfather's wrath and the revenue men and go after him if he did. No man harms my sister—"

"No." Elizabeth managed to croak the single word, then drag in a breath and add more. "He was a perfect gentleman."

Except perhaps in reminding her how she'd kissed him.

"And you never saw him before that?" Drake persisted.

"No. Yes. Drake, he's the man I kissed at the ball that set Mama's back up so much she and Papa decided I must marry Romsford at once and— What are you about?"

Drake had surged to his feet and begun to pace the cave. "The rogue, the roué, the— I'll darken his daylights. I'll teach him a thing or two about Cornish wrestling. He dared . . . My little sister . . ." His fists clenched. His jaw tensed. "Where is he?"

"I've no idea. But, Drake, it was my fault—the kissing, I mean."

"Did he stop you? Did he push you away?"

"No, he, um, kissed me back." Heat washed over her at the memory—heat and a restlessness that made her want to find what stock Grandpapa kept in the stable and ride along the beach at a gallop, her hair flowing freely behind her. "When he admitted it was he, I did not mind being so foolish because he said he was your friend. I figured you approved."

"He said he was my friend and I approved of him touching you?"

"Well, no, he did not precisely say so. I presumed because he knew so much about you and Conan smuggling and your friendship and . . . and—"

"He let you think he's my friend."

"He—well, I just assumed it. He said he had seen you hours before." She pressed the heels of her hands to her eyes. "I am such a fool. If word gets about that I was alone with a stranger night before last, even Grandpapa will wish to marry me off at once."

"Then he must never know. You cannot marry in haste now that you could inherit Bastion Point. You will have every fortune hunter in England after you."

"I already did with my dowry. Besides, I have to work out this treasure." She gave Drake a hopeful glance.

He looked away, the message clear—he would defend her honor, but not help her rob him of what he thought was his by right of birth and being male.

She would just have to work hard to please Grandpapa and ensure she was the one who inherited Bastion Point. Drake was to have the Barbados plantation, which had been in the family for over a hundred years, and Morwenna would have a family of her own.

And speaking of pleasing Grandpapa . . .

She rose and shook out her skirt. "I must go, Drake. You will be careful, will you not? And write to me."

"I'll do my best." He hugged her close, kissed the top of her head, and led her back to the door at the foot of the steps. "Do not fret about me. Perhaps I'll turn pirate like Grandfather did in his youth."

"You must not. He'd never buy you a pardon."

"No, I expect he wouldn't." Sadness clouded the bright pale blue of his eyes. "All he's inclined to buy me is passage west. Away from the revenue men."

"Oh, Drake." She blinked hard to hold back tears. "I came home at last to see you, and now— Why has everything gone so terribly wrong?"

"Not all." He gave her a bracing smile. "You're free of Romsford. Think of that. You're safe at Bastion Point."

Yes, she was safe.

She clung to that notion all the way up the winding staircase to the secret room. Romsford couldn't touch her at Bastion Point. Her parents' machinations couldn't touch her at Bastion Point.

Rowan Curnow couldn't touch her at Bastion Point.

She reentered the study and ascended to her room, the same one that had been hers when they left for London. Before greeting Grandmama, she needed to change her gown. Grandmama was always such an image of perfection and elegance that Elizabeth never liked appearing before her in less than her best possible looks.

Miss Pross knew it and awaited Elizabeth in the corner chamber overlooking Grandmama's garden on one side and the cove below Bastion Point on the other. A froth of wind-ruffled waves drew Elizabeth to the window like a thirsty man to fresh water, but Miss Pross caught her arm and gently turned her toward the dressing table.

"You must not keep them waiting longer, child. They have guests."

"Guests?" Elizabeth glared at her reflection, noting her red-rimmed eyes and worse-than-usual pallor. "I am unfit for greeting guests."

"But it's Lord Penvenan's sister and a guest of hers."

"Senara is here? The day after her brother's death? One would think decency would insist she stay home and receive callers."

"With her brother gone, who does she have to turn to but Sir Petrok and Lady Trelawny?" Miss Pross began to remove hairpins and brush out sections of Elizabeth's hair with a speed that belied laws of physical science. Each stroke of the brush should have sent the rest of her hair cascading down her back. Instead, the twists and coils slid neatly into place.

"I had your blue silk pressed." Miss Pross gave the last pin a gentle push into place. "It will do for guests and carry you on to dinnertime."

"Perfect, of course." Elizabeth rose and allowed her companion and, when not in London, lady's maid to help her out of the rose muslin gown and into one of blue silk with a double row of lace-trimmed flounces at the hem. The dressmaker had assured Elizabeth it would diminish her height to widen the dress. It didn't work, but the effect was pretty with the froth of lace against the sea blue fabric. It lent Elizabeth a measure of confidence in front of strangers and Senara Penvenan, the childhood friend she hadn't seen in more than half a decade.

Senara ventured out only to visit Bastion Point or attend church. Her life centered on her home, Penmara—keeping the crumbling old house looking as well as possible with the family's limited funds, and helping feed herself and her brother and their few servants from her extensive and flourishing garden.

❧

Plump and pretty and wearing a black dress that appeared twenty years out of date, Senara sprang from her chair the instant Elizabeth stepped into the drawing room and flung herself into her old friend's arms.

"Elizabeth, you don't know how happy I am that you're here now. I could never bear this alone." A sob racked her body, and she drew back long enough to press a black-bordered handkerchief to her swollen eyes. It, like her gown, reeked of lavender and camphor as though they had been stowed away for two decades. "I know you loved him too."

"Yes, Conan was my friend too." Elizabeth patted Senara's shoulder and stared past her friend's glossy black curls with a plea for help to the grandparents.

Instead of meeting either Grandpapa or Grandmama's eyes, she met those of a stranger—a stranger with gray eyes, silver-streaked black hair, and the patrician features of an aristocrat. He smiled at her from where he stood and offered her a bow.

Elizabeth flicked her gaze to Grandpapa, who stood beside the stranger, for an explanation or introduction.

"Elizabeth, allow me to present Austell Penvenan, the heir presumptive to Penmara," Grandpapa announced.

Senara shuddered.

Elizabeth stared. "I had no idea—that is to say, I did not realize—"

The new Lord Penvenan—if his claim was legitimate—smiled. "My branch of the family has been in America for the past hundred years." He spoke in a rich, drawling voice that seemed to omit the use of the letter *r*. "A visit has been long overdue, but Conan Lord Penvenan thought—"

"How convenient you reached here just in time for Conan's

death." Senara turned on the newcomer. "Or should I call it what it is? Conan's murder. A coincidence—"

"Senara, that is quite enough," Grandmama interjected in her light, low voice.

Elizabeth, Grandpapa, and Austell Penvenan stared at Senara.

"Cousin Senara," Penvenan began.

"No, it is not enough." Senara continued as though no one had spoken. "My brother is dead by foul play, and this man and his henchman—"

"Senara, cease at once." Grandpapa never raised his voice, but the quiet command brought a halt to Senara's tirade.

Elizabeth took her friend's hand and led her to a chair close to the low fire burning on the hearth. "Shall I send for tea?"

"It's been sent for." Grandmama held out her hands to Elizabeth. "Why do you not greet me properly, then sit so the gentlemen may do the same?"

With a quick glance to Grandpapa and Penvenan, Elizabeth closed the distance between herself and Grandmama and laid her hands in the older woman's and kissed her on the cheek. Later, when they were alone, she would embrace her and indulge in a few tears upon Grandmama's shoulder, though those tears pricked the backs of her lids at that moment.

Afraid they would spill over right then and there, Elizabeth backed up to lower herself onto a chair from the previous century with legs so spindly she feared she'd shatter the carved wood if she moved too far to right or left. Under normal circumstances, she never would have chosen that seat. Its carved arms rose too high for her to rest her elbows upon them, yet were not far enough apart for her to hold her arms neatly at her sides. The back, designed with flowers, leaves, and trailing vines that bore no resemblance to anything appearing in nature, prohibited leaning back. Feeling as though her bony knees jutted through the filmy fabric of her petticoat and gown and into the center of the room, she perched on the edge of the chair—

And for the first time, noticed a third man in the room. Unlike Austell Penvenan and Grandpapa, he remained standing with his back to the chamber, his attention apparently fixed on the panorama of sea and sky beyond the terrace, a tall, broad-shouldered figure silhouetted against that breathtaking view. A man with hair that shone in the glow of the candles. Unkempt dark chestnut hair that appeared wind-blown even in the still atmosphere of the parlor.

The too-still atmosphere. As in the cave, Elizabeth believed no oxygen filled the room. It certainly left her lungs, as the blood left her head. For a moment, she thought she might faint. She thought she'd be better off if she did. She could escape before she'd had her suspicions confirmed.

But Mr. Penvenan was speaking. "Miss Trelawny, allow me to introduce my secretary, Rowan Curnow."

CHAPTER 8

Miss Elizabeth Trelawny's already creamy complexion turned the color of skimmed milk. She didn't rise to offer him a curtsy, which wasn't expected for a mere secretary anyway. Even if it were, she appeared incapable of moving from the chair that looked more like an instrument of torture than a seat of repose.

Rowan waited for her to acknowledge that she knew him. When she did not, she merely inclined her head scarcely far enough to say she acknowledged he existed and he offered her a bow a little too deep not to hold a hint of mockery.

"Miss Trelawny, your servant."

No, another man's servant, once and for all announced that he was not good enough for Elizabeth of Bastion Point. If anyone outside her family learned the identity of the man she'd kissed in that ballroom bower, or if anyone learned she'd spent hours alone with him in the night, her humiliation would be complete. Her ruin would be complete.

But he would be there to pick up the pieces and help restore her reputation. If only she'd look at him with those beautiful, ice-blue eyes, he could reassure her.

She looked at Miss Penvenan instead and started to say something. A tap at the door and entrance of two footmen bearing trays interrupted her.

"Set those here." Lady Trelawny indicated the low table before her. "Elizabeth, will you serve our guests?"

"Yes, ma'am." Elizabeth rose with alacrity and began to pour tea into cups of china as thin as eggshells. Her hands, slender and long-fingered, moved with a dancer's grace, lifting the steaming silver pot, sending black tea jetting into the cups, exchanging pot for sugar tongs or milk pitcher according to each person's wishes.

Each person except for Rowan. She pointedly did not ask him his preference. Maybe she would ignore him altogether. He settled himself on the window seat and watched her, waiting for how she'd manage that without insulting his employer, the new Lord Penvenan.

She carried a cup to him first, then to Miss Penvenan, who sipped hers immediately and grimaced. "You did not put in enough sugar, Elizabeth. You know I always take two lumps."

"Of course I did not forget, my dear." She gave Miss Penvenan a gentle smile and proceeded to serve the grandparents.

"I really dislike bitter tea," Miss Penvenan pronounced. "At least my brother was able to provide us with good tea, if nothing else."

No one else spoke as Miss Penvenan babbled about tea, and Elizabeth finished serving the important people.

At last, with only two cups left on the tray, she turned toward Rowan. "Mr. Curnow, is it? Milk? Sugar?" She kept her gaze downcast as she posed the question.

"Nothing, thank you." He willed her to look at him.

"You must have used small lumps of sugar," Miss Penvenan persisted. "Will you bring me another one, please?"

Elizabeth hesitated. For a moment, Rowan thought she'd set down his cup and take the sugar to Miss Penvenan first.

"Senara," Lady Trelawny said, "why do you not stir your tea and try it again? Elizabeth has another guest to serve."

"Guest." Miss Penvenan sniffed, but she stirred her tea.

Elizabeth crossed the red-and-gold carpet to Rowan, her head bent over his cup as though she needed to watch it or her footsteps. Lamplight gleamed in the rich coils of her mahogany hair held with gold pins he so wished to tug loose.

The silver spoon upon the saucer tinkled like tiny bells announcing that her hands were not quite steady. But the gaze she shot his way held that cool reserve that had enchanted him from the first time he saw her.

He smiled and took the cup from her. "Thank you, Elizabeth. I—"

She turned away from him before he could speak further, leaving him holding a cup of tea he didn't want. He detested tea. He wanted coffee, strong and black, hot and bitter. Nor did he want any of the delicacies arranged on the serving plates—sweet biscuits and tiny cakes with candied flowers on top. He preferred the hardy fare of men who labored for a living—the substantial Cornish pasties with their potato and gravy filling, or pork pies and thick stew.

He accepted an offer of the sweets for another chance to say something to Elizabeth. But this time she looked through rather than at him, as she offered him a tiny plate with one hand and the platter of refreshments with the other.

"Miss Trelawny . . . ," he began.

Again, she walked away from him, set the remaining delicacies on a table beside Miss Penvenan, and took her own cup of tea back to her chair.

"You're so thoughtful, Elizabeth." Miss Penvenan slid three more cakes onto her already empty plate. "You know we can never afford to make sweets at Penmara. Sugar is just too dear."

"I am quite certain Cook can send a basket home with you." Elizabeth glanced at Penvenan. "I am certain you have already told the grandparents of how your arrival came about, so do please forgive me for asking out of my own curiosity, but when did you reach Cornwall?"

"Yesterday morning, coincidentally." Miss Penvenan spoke around a bite that took up half of one of the cakes. "Do you not think that—"

"Senara," Sir Petrok interrupted, "refrain from making even slanted accusations against Lord Penvenan."

"Lord Penvenan, indeed." Senara's lower lip, dusted with sugar crystals, jutted like a chicken roost.

"Mr. Penvenan will do." Penvenan smiled. "I was in truth in Truro night before last and the week before that, but have been in England for several months. Rowan and I were residing in London to take care of business there."

"Or send threats to us here," Senara Penvenan muttered.

"And I never met you?" Elizabeth turned her head, no doubt so she couldn't accidentally glance at him out of the corner of her eye.

His lips twitched, and he stiffened the corners to stop himself from smiling or, worse, laughing aloud at her endeavors to pretend he wasn't present.

Penvenan chuckled. "We didn't move in such exalted circles as you, Miss Trelawny, though I believe we attended a ball or two together. We simply did not have the privilege of being introduced."

"She would never consider it a privilege." Senara grumbled around a bite of cake, then stuffed another piece into her mouth, only to begin choking, as tears ran down her face.

"Shall I take her to my room?" Elizabeth offered.

"I'll take her to a guest chamber." Lady Trelawny rose with a rustle of silk and the grace her granddaughter had inherited.

Rowan stood with the other two men.

"I want to know what is being done to find my brother's killer." Still seated, Senara fixed a ferocious glare upon Sir Petrok.

He nodded. "Of course you do. As magistrate, I will ensure that the coroner makes enquiries of anyone who might have been out and about; however, those involved in the trade aren't likely to talk for fear of prosecution, and those who are not won't talk for fear of retribution."

And now without Conan, discovering which was which was nigh on impossible.

Rowan raised his teacup to mask his lips tight with anger.

"As magistrate," Miss Penvenan was saying, "you should already know who the criminals are."

"Conan didn't even know for certain who the smugglers are," Penvenan began. "What one doesn't know—"

"I don't think it was one of them anyway." Miss Penvenan's voice rose on a note of hysteria.

Lady Trelawny held out her hand to Miss Penvenan. "Do come with me, Senara. I think you should perhaps stay with us until matters surrounding Conan's death are settled."

"Stay here at Bastion Point?" Miss Penvenan's eyes widened, and she sprang to her feet, amazingly not spilling a drop of tea or crumb of a cake. "May I take my tea?"

"I'll send for fresh." Lady Trelawny clasped Miss Penvenan's elbow with a grip that appeared kindly, but from the set of her jaw, only a little softened with her advanced years, suggested defying her was unwise.

Elizabeth got to her feet. "Shall I join you?"

"Remain and take care of our guests," Lady Trelawny flung over her shoulder.

The door opened at her approach, no doubt a footman lingering in the corridor for just such an operation, and closed behind them with only a flash of a dark blue livery-clad arm and gloved hand.

The men sat. This time Elizabeth reseated herself on the settee beside her grandfather, lifted the teapot, then glanced at Sir Petrok as though not certain what to do with the silver jug.

"I think we could all use a little more tea, my dear." Sir Petrok turned to Penvenan. "Do not hold Miss Penvenan's behavior against her. She's overset by her brother's death and the potential loss of the only home she has ever known, for all it is falling down about her ears."

Elizabeth filled Penvenan and Sir Petrok's cups.

"Even when Conan Lord Penvenan wrote to us," Penvenan said, "I never realized in what terrible straits he found himself. Our branch has prospered so, I never thought the English branch would not also."

Sir Petrok sighed. "I am afraid Conan's late father made some unwise investments in ships that were not insured. If he had not, Conan would not have smuggled, and would likely still be with us."

"So you think smugglers killed him, sir?" Rowan asked.

"I do. My grandson does." Sir Petrok's lips thinned at the mention of his grandson. "I know Conan wished to stop the trade, and they may have feared he would betray them if he did."

"He did wish to stop." Penvenan began to stir his tea, *chime, chime, chime* of silver on china, a sound that set Rowan's teeth on edge. "That is why he sent for me."

"You were brave to make the crossing," Sir Petrok said. "Were you not concerned your secretary would be taken up for a British subject and pressed into the navy?"

"I was born after 1783, sir." Rowan glanced at Elizabeth, who had returned to her seat, ignoring him. "By three years. But it was close. The captain who stopped our brig wasn't much inclined to accept my papers as legitimate proof of my citizenship being American and not English."

Penvenan smiled. "I think it was his uncouth way of speaking that convinced the man in the end."

"That Brown University education wasted." Rowan made the claim in another effort to garner Elizabeth's attention.

She didn't so much as hesitate in lifting her cup to her lips, let alone flick him even half a glance.

"This impressment of Americans," Penvenan continued, "is a practice that needs to cease or there will be trouble between our countries."

"Another conflict is the last thing Great Britain needs." Sir Petrok set his empty cup aside. "But that is incidental to what is about here. You say Conan asked you to come?"

"Yes. He hoped for assistance to save Penmara." Penvenan gave Rowan a look he well understood—say nothing more than essential.

The reminder was unnecessary. With Conan Lord Penvenan dead by foul play, the stakes increased on Penvenan's and potentially Rowan's lives.

"He said he hoped to marry in the next year." Penvenan smiled at Elizabeth. "And he didn't want to have nothing but the lady's dowry to start their new life."

"We had hoped for a union between Elizabeth and Conan," Sir Petrok admitted.

Elizabeth shook her head. "I could never have wed Conan. He was like a brother to me."

"Your friendship is why we thought it would be an excellent match, considering . . ." Sir Petrok hesitated.

"Considering I never took in London?" Elizabeth grimaced, but cast her grandfather an affectionate look. "I expect you're correct in that. We would have gotten along better than most.

But now . . ." Her face crumpled, and two tears chased down her pale cheek.

Rowan had his handkerchief in his hand before he realized he intended to offer it to her. But she was too far away from him, and Penvenan reached her first with his own linen. "We're all distressed."

Elizabeth flashed him a warm smile and accepted the handkerchief.

"Sir Petrok," Rowan ventured to break the awkward silence, "Lord Penvenan and I understand you have a fine stable here. Would you be willing to lend us horses until we are able to procure our own?"

It didn't work. She smiled at Penvenan instead of him. "You ride, my lord?"

"Please, Mr. Penvenan will do. And, yes, Rowan and I are used to riding nearly every day. We have a fine string of horses on the South Carolina plantation and a horse farm in Virginia."

"Then you, sir, are more than welcome to join us. We ride on the beach when the tide is out." She turned her smile on her grandfather. "At least we used to. Do you still?"

"We do, though at a more sedate pace than you prefer. Ah, I believe that is my bride approaching." Sir Petrok rose.

Rowan heard the footfalls then, as light and quick as a girl's. He stood, taking the opportunity to dump his tea into the pot of an unsuspecting plant.

Of course Elizabeth chose that moment to look his way. He grinned at her before she turned to address her grandmother.

"Is Senara all right?"

"She's resting. I admit I slipped a drop or two of laudanum into her tea." Lady Trelawny grimaced. "She never noticed the taste with all that sugar she likes, the poor child. Losing her brother has overset her greatly, and she always overindulges in sweets when she's overset. Lord Penvenan, do you have all you need at Penmara? I'd invite you to stay here, but under the circumstances, I think the less Senara sees of you, the better, if you feel safe at Penmara."

Penvenan bowed. "We will be safe enough. I've ordered a number of provisions to be sent out from Truro once I saw the state of things in the house, and the housekeeper assures me she's a passable cook."

"Indeed she is." Lady Trelawny nodded. "Plain but edible fare."

Rowan's stomach twinged at that notion. Hardy fare, he hoped, as he had eaten nearly nothing for the past day.

"Then we will take our leave." Penvenan bowed to her ladyship and shook hands with Sir Petrok. He clasped Elizabeth's hand far too long—long enough for her color to heighten into a beautiful pale pink that enhanced the icy blue of her eyes.

Rowan's stomach decided it wasn't hungry after all. With a brief nod to his host and hostess and what might be construed as the cut direct to Miss Elys Trelawny, he followed Penvenan from the parlor.

A footman directed them to the massive front door, where their carriage awaited departure.

"How did she manage that?" Rowan asked as soon as a footman slammed the door behind them.

Penvenan laughed. "The skill of breeding and fifty years as chatelaine of this great house, I expect. No doubt she sent for the carriage before returning to the parlor."

"Overstayed our welcome?"

"I expect so, but we're uncouth Yankees and can get away with a little rudeness. I didn't want to leave without working out how to see Miss Trelawny again. Fine maneuver with the horses."

"Fine for you." Rowan doubted he kept the bitterness from his tone.

Penvenan gave him what could only be construed as a pitying glance. "As things stand right now, Rowan, Miss Elizabeth Trelawny is above your touch."

"And you're going to take advantage of that fact." Rowan's hands balled into fists. "You know, and yet you—" He ground his teeth together.

If he said more of what he thought of the older man, he would only make matters worse between them than they had been for the past ten years.

"My dear boy," Penvenan said, "she might have kissed you when she thought you were some lordling at a ball, but now she knows who you are, she didn't even look at you. I'd say a lady who is that high in the instep isn't worthy of your attention."

"So you intend to spare me by courting her yourself? And what about her safety if she's associated with you?"

"Do you honestly believe the smugglers will care whom I court simply because I am Conan Penvenan's heir?"

"Conan believed so. He warned us—"

Penvenan laughed. "No one will dare harm a Trelawny lady, and I will have need of her dowry to restore Penmara properly."

Her dowry, the immoveable barrier between Rowan and Elizabeth. She believed every poor man who courted her wanted her inheritance. She would never believe it of a rich man like Austell Penvenan.

Many times over the past decade Rowan had found himself despising Austell Penvenan, but not so much as he did in that moment of the older man being absolutely right about Miss Elizabeth Trelawny.

CHAPTER 9

Senara's circumstances were dreadful, yet Elizabeth found herself wishing Grandmama hadn't been quite so inclined to offer their neighbor shelter in these troubling times. Between the coroner's inquest regarding the cause of Conan's death—by person or persons unknown—the graveside funeral service attended only by the men, and Senara's frequent histrionics over the loss of her brother to the knife of a murderer and her home to a suspicious cousin who was a stranger to her, Elizabeth saw little of either of the grandparents during the next few days. When she did see them, Senara or another neighbor was also present.

"I've served more tea in the past three days than I served in a week in London." Elizabeth glared at the decimated tray that had contained tea and yet more sweet biscuits after visits from the vicar's wife and several other ladies. "Cook has likely gone through an entire cargo-load of sugar cones."

"Even I think I've had enough cakes for a while." Senara brushed sugar crystals off the skirt of the black dress Grandmama had unearthed from the Bastion Point attics and had her own lady's maid alter to fit the shorter female. "Perhaps Cook should serve some of those cheese biscuits instead."

"Or nothing at all," Elizabeth muttered.

Grandmama shot her a sharp glance, a warning to be nice.

Teeth clenched, Elizabeth strode to the window to take a good look at the sky and the beach below.

Rain every day, though not stopping the endless stream of callers, had prevented her from riding on the beach—or anywhere else. It had kept her from going for walks along the cliffs. Either activity would have gotten her away from Senara's constant accusations against Austell Penvenan, as exercise was not an activity Senara enjoyed. Instead, to keep her quiet, Elizabeth provided Senara with tales of London and an ever-present supply of Minerva Press novels unearthed from the bottom of one of Elizabeth's trunks that had reached her with a cryptic note from her mother.

You've made your bed. You can lie in it. I doubt Romsford will want you now.

If only Mama were right. Unfortunately, she'd heard the marquess remained in Truro, though he had made no attempt to see Elizabeth.

Suddenly, the empty stretch of beach no longer appealed. Nor did walking anywhere but inside Grandmama's walled garden draw her interest now that she realized how easily, in this remote county, Romsford could take her away, carry her off to Guernsey or even Scotland by boat where no one was likely to catch up with them.

Yet surely the man didn't want or need her that badly. He couldn't need the money. His wealth, garnered from the dowries of his previous wives, was legendary.

And so was hers. So was the connection of her family.

Senara should recognize that she was the fortunate one. If a man of wealth asked her to marry him, she'd know it was because of who she was, not because she brought anything but herself to the marriage.

She stared at her reflection in the glass and the darkening sky beyond. "I think we will have fine weather tomorrow."

A banal thing to say. If she and Grandmama were alone, she'd have asked about family history and treasures worth more than Bastion Point and why Grandpapa had suddenly decided to place Bastion Point on the family auction block instead of passing it to Elizabeth's father and then Drake in the normal scheme of inheritance when a male heir was present.

Not that Drake was present. He'd sailed four days earlier, headed for the West Indies, provided a French ship didn't capture his vessel along the way. He'd promised to write. He'd left a note for her in the cave, telling her to be wary of the stranger Rowan Curnow.

For all you know, he works for Romsford.

That, at least, she didn't believe against him. Too easily, he could have turned her over to the marquess between meeting her on the road and seeing her safely into Grandpapa's care. He worked for Austell Penvenan. Lord Penvenan, apparently, since the man held an unbreachable alibi for the night of Conan's murder. Not that he couldn't have hired someone to do it. Considering how much money he was already spending on Penmara and workmen to repair the old manor house, hiring an assassin seemed a trivial expense. The rumors circulated around the neighborhood like a hurricane wind, growing stronger with each passing day, according to the callers at Bastion Point.

Sick to her stomach all of a sudden, Elizabeth drew the curtains closed against the dying light and headed for the parlor door.

"Where are you going?" Senara pushed herself out of her chair like an old woman with rheumatism.

Elizabeth took a deep breath to master her impatience, trying to think how lost she'd feel without her brother, even if they had seen nothing of one another over the past six years. "I am going to my room to lie down before dinner. I am afraid I've the headache."

Senara's countenance drooped from her eyelids, to the corners of her mouth, to her chin that was threatening to become a double one soon. "I am so used to talking to Conan in the evenings, I feel quite lonely."

Elizabeth cast Grandmama a helpless glance.

"Why do you not rest also, Senara." Grandmama rose. "We will put together a puzzle game after dinner. I just received a shipment of new ones."

Senara's face lit. "I do love puzzles. But I am used to having a household to take care of." Senara's lower lip protruded.

"I am afraid the housekeeper would not appreciate me having you dust the library shelves." Grandmama smiled. "But if work is what you would like . . ."

Elizabeth escaped, slipping down a back passageway to side steps so Senara wouldn't catch her on the main staircase. If she left her room dark and locked the door, perhaps she could have a few minutes of peace and truly rest.

Her first hint that this wouldn't happen struck her before she reached her door. A veritable gale of cold air flowed from beneath the portal, strong enough to flip up the flounce at the hem of her dress. If Grandpapa had been home, she'd have gotten him to go into the chamber. But he was in the village hearing cases as his responsibility as justice of the peace. A footman stood at the top of the steps awaiting anyone's command to have an errand run, but Elizabeth didn't like to call him to her room over something likely nothing more than a window left open.

By whom? With rain still falling earlier, she hadn't opened the windows before descending to the parlor to attend to the guests. Miss Pross disliked the cold air off the Bristol Channel and wouldn't have opened a window. Perhaps a maid . . .

Even as she lifted the door handle and flung the panels wide, Elizabeth knew no maid would dare open the closed window over the garden and forget to shut it again. Yet she didn't know why anyone else had. Though clearing, the air held a biting chill and strong aroma of the sea softened with a hint of lilac from Grandmama's walled garden. Elizabeth's nostrils flared, catching another scent she didn't immediately recognize, though instinct told her it should be familiar.

She paced the room. She saw nothing out of the ordinary. The wind fluttered the pages of a book left open on her desk and billowed out the bed curtains. She slammed the window closed, rattling the diamond panes. Needing more light against the grayness cast by the ancient glass, she picked up the tinderbox from her desk and attempted to light a candle. Not until she failed to hold steel to flint hard and long to catch a spark in the oiled waste did she realize her hands were shaking. She set the tinderbox down, commanded herself to be calm, and tried again. This time the flame caught and held long enough for her to set fire to the wick. This time she saw why someone had ventured into her chamber.

Gleaming in the yellow candle flame, the mother-of-pearl head of a hatpin jutted from one of her pillows, its point jabbed through a length of ice-blue satin ribbon encircling a rolled sheet of parchment.

Her hands trembling once more, Elizabeth set down the candle and slipped the ribbon off the scroll. The parchment unfurled, suggesting it hadn't been in its tubular form long. Nor had the parchment held the ink for long, as its sharp scent stung her nose.

The words burned her eyes.

The sun rises at six o'clock tomorrow. I'll meet you on the beach with your horse.

The message bore no signature. She'd never seen his handwriting, but she knew who had dared to sneak the missive into her bedchamber in broad daylight.

"The rogue. The unconscionable . . ." She ran out of epithets.

The parchment tore between her hands. She balled up the scraps and threw it against the wall as hard as she could. It bounced off the beak of a parrot molded into the plaster, struck the bedpost, and dropped to the floor. Elizabeth kicked it under the bed, thought about a maid finding it, and dove beneath the frame to retrieve the note. The man had gotten into her bedchamber and taken one of her hatpins!

If only she could ride then, she'd send the horse flying across the sand or countryside, chase the wind, as she and Rowan Curnow had the night they fled from Romsford.

The night he duped her into thinking he was Drake.

She jammed the hatpin into its cushioned holder only to realize it wasn't her pin at all. She didn't own one of mother-of-pearl. Mama would consider that too common. Yet it didn't look common laid across her palm. It shimmered and glowed as though holding its own light. The surface slid through her fingers as smooth as scented oil.

Scent. Ah, now she knew it. He'd left his scent behind—leather and the sea, a sailor's aroma, a countryman's aroma.

She opened a vial of violet perfume and inhaled deeply enough to numb her nostrils.

She shouldn't have been able to catch his scent with all that wind blowing through unless he hadn't departed but seconds before she opened the door. Heaven forfend, if Senara had come with her . . .

Her heart clenched. "Are you trying to ruin me, Rowan Curnow?"

She tore the note into pieces and tossed them on the hearth.

A touch of the candle and the note vanished with a curl of smoke that cleansed the room of all scent of him as well. If only she could as easily banish him from her life. But if she wanted to ride, she'd be on the beach to meet Rowan Curnow at first light.

CHAPTER 10

WALKING THE HORSES ALONG THE BEACH TO PREVENT them from standing in the misty morning chill, Rowan kept his gaze on the cliff path. At a quarter past six o'clock, she hadn't arrived for his proposed rendezvous. He couldn't wait much longer for the sake of the livestock and the quality of the beach itself. In another half an hour, the tide would turn. A half hour after that, the half-moon cove below Bastion Point would be cut off from the rest of the beach.

He turned his mount, a fine roan gelding, and cantered to the far side of the cove, where an arm of the cliff jutted into the water so far that reaching the beach on the other side was impossible at any level of the tide. When he turned back, she'd appeared on the cliff path, statuesque and shapely in her fitted riding habit of dark blue velvet.

His mouth went dry. His eyes burned from staring at her with the brisk wind blowing into his face. Only the pressure of willpower kept him from touching his heels to the gelding and sending him and the mare swooping across the tide-packed sand toward Elizabeth, to Elizabeth. He rode at a sedate walk, never taking his gaze off her, drinking in the way she descended the path with her smooth, long-legged gait. By the time he met her at the base of the cliff, his heart pounded as though he had run the quarter mile instead of riding like a novice on a job horse.

"You came." It was all he could think to say as he dismounted and gave her a bow.

"You have the only mounts Grandpapa says are suitable for me." Though the blue of her habit had darkened her eyes to aquamarine, the glare she shot his way held shards of blue ice. "I'd report the stable hands you bribed if it would not get them dismissed, though why you would waste your wages on bribing stable hands is beyond my comprehension."

Rowan winced at her use of wages. He smiled into her eyes. "I had to find some way to talk to you."

"I cannot imagine why. I've nothing to say to you."

"Not even 'help me mount, you scrub'?"

She gave him a blank look.

"A man of low work, though playing your groom this morning does not fall into that category."

One corner of her mouth twitched—a good sign. "You have a smooth tongue for a . . . a—"

"Mere secretary? An uncouth American?"

"A man who—" She snapped her teeth together, then sighed. "It's untrue that I've nothing to say to you. I've a great deal to say to you, none of it complimentary. But I wish to ride the beach while I still can."

"Then ride the beach you shall."

Rowan stroked the mare's nose, told her to stand, and rounded to the left side of the horse.

Elizabeth followed. The excess fabric of her habit looped over her arm. She grasped the reins in one hand. "She's absolutely perfect. What's her name?"

"Grisette."

"Of course. Little gray one." Elizabeth stroked the mare's mane, then stepped into the cup of his hands he braced on his bent knee.

"Ready?" He grinned up at her.

"I am."

"One. Two. Three."

On the count of three, he lifted. She bounced off her right foot at the same time. In one smooth motion, she landed on the saddle, her right knee hooked around the saddle horn, her skirt draped over her legs to preserve her modesty.

For the first time since she noticed him in the grandparents' parlor, she cast him an approving glance and something he could call a smile. "Thank you. That was well done."

"The fault is all yours." Feeling as though someone were tossing him into the air, he returned to the gelding and leaped into the saddle.

She said she wanted to talk to him, and she'd smiled at him.

And he was a fool to care so much about either from her.

He backed his mount out of her path. "You lead."

She led, walking Grisette at first, settling into the gray's gait. Once around the outcropping of rock that separated Bastion Point beach from Penmara land, she increased her speed to a trot, then a canter, and with two miles of open, hard-smooth sand before her on the beach below Penmara, she let Grisette have her head.

And she could ride. He'd known as much already. Conan had assured him of the fact when they made their mad-dash escape from Romsford's men six nights ago, telling him how Elys—what he and Drake called her—used to ride astride her horse as a child. But he had never seen her ride in the daylight, in the open. Her hat blew off in the wind off the sea. One by one, her hairpins worked loose. Freed from its moorings, her hair flowed behind her in a long, silken curtain glinting with coppery highlights in the slanting rays of the morning sun.

Rowan leaned low and scooped up her hat by its plumes without missing a stride in the gelding's gait, then sent his own mount racing after her. She glanced over her shoulder, saw him gaining on her, and leaned over Grisette's neck, apparently coaxing a little more speed from the gray. Rowan did the same with his gelding. Such speed wasn't safe. He shouldn't encourage it, but when her laughter rippled behind her brighter than the morning, he couldn't resist the lure, the chase that brought such joy springing forth.

It ended all too soon. A tumble of rock from a cliff collapsed in some storm decades earlier created a hazard on the beach. She drew up her mount, then wheeled her around to walk her back to where Rowan paused to stroke the gelding's neck.

"Thank you." She looked at him with genuine warmth.

"For what?" He turned so they walked their mounts side by side, cooling them down.

"Not stopping me." She turned her face away. "I've been unable to ride like that for years—other than the other night, and that was different. I was not . . . free."

"And you are now?"

She didn't respond. Face turned away from him and toward the waves rolling in from a sea the color of a slate roof tile, she rode at an easy trot back to the half-moon cove below Bastion Point before she spoke again. "You were guiding my mount." She slid to the ground and glared at him over the back of the mare. "You duped me and then dragged me into the night."

"I never said I was your brother." He held her gaze.

She narrowed her eyes. "You knew I thought you were. And when I discovered you were not, you told me you knew Drake and had just seen him hours before."

"I did lead you to think I knew Drake and he'd sent me." His conscience pricked his heart. "I am guilty on both accounts. I thought it was the right thing to do at the time, as I didn't think you'd come with a perfect stranger otherwise."

"Stranger, yes. Perfect?" Her nostrils pinched.

"All right then, not perfect." He tried not to smile. He only half succeeded in keeping his mouth neutral; one corner curled up, and the other twitched. "I'm a flawed being, but the Lord loves me anyway and has seen fit to forgive me for my lack of judgment, however well it was meant. I can only ask for your forgiveness and hope one day you'll grant it."

Her face twisted as though a pain had stabbed her, and she turned away. Reins in hand, she walked Grisette along the base of the cliff. Sixty feet above her, the gray stone and diamond-paned windows of the oldest part of the house were poised like a sentry guarding the copper mines and farmland beyond. The Trelawny legacy. Elys Trelawny's legacy, at least in part.

Because of his choices, he had too little to offer a lady with so much. Not nearly enough with which to woo a lady with every-thing and more.

But he would try.

He fell into step beside her, leading his horse from the other side so the equine didn't come between them. "We should get off the beach before the tide pins us down here for the next four hours."

"I know, but I'd rather not go back into the house just yet."

"Who said anything about going back into the house? We can't run the horses across the fields, but we can still ride."

"You're willing to do that? You do not wish to return for your breakfast?"

His stomach protested, but he shook his head. "As long as you won't be missed, I'm willing to ride with you."

"I'll be missed, but that is rather the point of being out." Her voice held a hard edge to it.

Something to explore, if she'd tell him, though he suspected he already knew what troubled her at home.

"Shall I help you mount again?"

She nodded, and they repeated the ritual of earlier. It went as smoothly—with one exception. Her loosened hair blew across his face, as soft as a caress brushing his cheekbone. Once perched atop her mount, she brushed the strands behind her ear with a quick, impatient gesture and glanced at the sand as though she believed she'd find her errant pins.

He removed her hat from where he'd hung it over the saddle-bow and gave it to her. She set the velvet confection with its now battered feathers atop her head and wheeled Grisette for the gentler cliff path on the Penmara side of the beach.

They rode in single-file silence, Rowan following like some hired hand. He was a hired hand for now. If Penvenan chose to go riding with her, he got first choice and Rowan got left behind. Penvenan, however, was too thoroughly occupied with solicitors and excise officers—the former explaining succession laws, the latter hunting for clues to who had murdered Conan—builders, and account books to have time to ride or even court. For a while, Rowan could keep her safe and escort her on her rides as long as she allowed it.

"Do you want to stay on Penmara land, or go around the wall to Bastion Point?" Rowan asked.

Bastion Point offered neatly raked paths beneath neatly trimmed trees in the parkland. Penmara offered a tangle of over-grown underbrush and trees, the former able to catch at a horse's legs, the latter at the rider's hair.

She glanced from the upper stories of the house visible above the dividing wall, to the unkempt woodland ahead, then at him. "Stay on Penmara land for now. Otherwise we can be seen from this side of the house, and if Senara sees me with you . . ." She shuddered hard enough for Grisette to toss her head and snort as though in agreement.

"Not a good day awaits you, I presume?" Rowan cast a smile her way.

She laughed without much humor. "I know she's your employer's cousin—"

"Several times removed."

"And she and I grew up here together, but her brother's death has . . . unsettled her."

"Would you not be unsettled if someone threatened your family and then murdered your brother?"

Her chin lifted. Her mouth thinned. "I'd not have histrionics once, let alone several times a day."

"The ice-blue ice maiden," Rowan murmured.

They had reached a meadow fragrant with knee-high grass and pastel wildflowers, and she reined in to glare at him from those ice-blue eyes. "What. Did. You. Say?"

He grinned at her. "The first time I saw you there in the corner of Hookham's, you regained your composure so quickly, I named you the ice-blue ice maiden after the color of your gown."

The glare turned to a stare. A flush anything but icy crept up her cheeks, and her lips parted as though she were about to speak. Or maybe she looked more like she was about to be kissed.

More likely he only *wished* she looked like she was about to be kissed—and like she wanted to be.

"And the way you went all stiff and prim and wouldn't look at me—"

"Stop it." She touched her heel to Grisette's side, sending the mare skimming through the meadow to a path on the other side too overgrown to ride along.

At least the mare thought so. She balked at the woodbine draped over a tree like a snake, dug in her hooves, and ducked her head.

Elizabeth stayed on. She was too good a horsewoman not to.

But her hat tumbled off, and her skirt caught on the thorns of a bramble.

Rowan dropped his horse's reins over his head and sprinted to Elizabeth's side. "Allow me." He reached for her ensnared skirt.

"Do not." She slid to the ground and began to disentangle the fabric. "You have humiliated me enough for one lifetime, calling me an ice maiden, duping me the other night, not warning me before you walked into the grandparents' parlor . . . I'll be ruined if anyone knows how I was alone with you the other night. It's bad enough Romsford knows. If the grandparents find out, I'll lose my chance to inherit Bastion Point."

She could inherit Bastion? The idea made Rowan feel sick. Inheriting the house and land would give her responsibilities she couldn't leave, even if she wanted to.

Penvenan was no doubt right to laugh at Rowan's aspirations. "Would inheriting Bastion Point please you?"

She smiled at him with shining eyes. "I've never wanted anything else. This is where I'm safe. This is the only place I've ever been happy."

⚓

As he went about his work days later, Rowan reflected on what Elizabeth had said. At one time she might have been safe there on the north coast of Cornwall, where Trelawnys had reigned with their wealth for a century. But Rowan was uncertain if that safety continued. It had ceased for the Penvenans, an even older family in the county than the Trelawnys. Someone had suggested Conan should have been dead for weeks before his murder.

Everyone suspected smugglers. They had terrorized the parish for as long as anyone living remembered. Cross them, snub the tea or bolt of fabric they left for payment when they borrowed a pony in the middle of a dark night, and things happened to the family. Stores disappeared. Livestock was butchered, and sometimes people died.

Yet Conan had opened the caves beneath Penmara to the smugglers to hide their boats and contraband. He used the power of his rank as a peer of the realm to protect them from too close inspections by the riding officers. He even sailed with them upon occasion, not for the thrill of risking getting caught as had Drake Trelawny, but because every penny went into holding impoverished Penmara together.

"But now it's tearing it apart," Conan had told Rowan on the first of their very secret meetings. "I've got to stop, but when I left messages that I was closing off the caves, the threats began."

"When was that?"

"The week you and Cousin Austell landed in Plymouth. I came home to find a foul message on the door and Senara having histrionics."

"That entail needs to be broken at once then."

The sooner Conan sold Penmara and moved away, the better. But Rowan and Austell's work on that behalf had failed in London. Entails were sacrosanct in England. Renewed with each generation of heirs to the land to protect it from slipping into the hands of those outside the family, breaking the restriction on the property's ownership took three males in direct succession to the line of inheritance to break the entail. Penvenan and Rowan failed to find more male heirs between Conan and Austell Penvenan and had encountered obstinacy from the courts on severing the title from the land. Rowan traveled to Cornwall to discuss Conan going to London himself to handle the matter and learned of how Elizabeth had pleaded for her brother's help.

"Let's keep her safe from this bounder." Conan spoke of his

childhood friend with great affection that raised the head of envy in Rowan. "We'll ride to meet her."

But the dead bird had delayed them. They didn't get to Elizabeth until nearly too late, and Conan had returned home immediately.

"I have to look after my own," had been nearly the last words Conan spoke to Rowan. The last words had been, "Watch over all three of the young ladies."

Senara, Elizabeth, and Morwenna.

Senara and Elizabeth were well enough inside Bastion Point. Miss Morwenna Trelawny looked a bit more vulnerable in an isolated cottage with a simple gate to lock for protection. Rowan didn't know why or how he should look after this black sheep, and look after her he tried to do, which was not easy when he never even saw her. Still, he patrolled her cottage just after dark either on his way to or from the village. He never saw anything untoward.

He learned nothing in the single smoky room of the village tavern. He pretended to sip from a tankard of ale and listened for snatches of useful conversation spoken in unguarded moments from those who did not pretend to drink.

Except none of the conversation proved useful. Regardless of how many pints of ale some of the men downed, when Rowan walked into the taproom, conversation died, then started up again with only desultory remarks about the fishing or the planting, the mining, and even the latest Sunday sermon.

After a week, Rowan gave up on the tavern visits, if not the patrols of Miss Morwenna's house. Late nights trying to learn something of the threats Conan had received and early-morning rides were taking a toll on his alertness. He would be of no use to anyone if he fell asleep supervising work on the Penmara roof and fell off. So he took to his bed early and went on early-morning patrols before his rides with Elizabeth, that precious hour that made the frustrating humiliation of working for Austell Penvenan tolerable.

Humiliating and potentially dangerous.

One morning when he stepped out the door to go for the morning ride, he found the corpse of a thrush flattened on the step.

❧

Today, two and a half weeks after they began their early morning rides, Rowan determined to put the warning aside until later. He could do nothing about it until Penvenan awakened, and Rowan wanted nothing to marr his ride with Elizabeth. She seemed so happy to be back in Cornwall where she could ride. With her, he could forget murder and threats and be happy in her company. Her London pallor had faded behind delicate bloom in her cheeks, making her eyes even bluer. She simply sparkled in the abandon with which she rode, in the lilt to her voice when she spoke of the land, her childhood, and now, even the writings of Thomas Paine she had managed to spirit out of the library.

"Do you know who he is?" she asked him.

He laughed. "Of course. He influenced our revolution."

"Have you read him?"

"I managed to muddle through a bit of it." He grinned at her across the space between their mounts. "By the time I was fifteen."

"Prove it."

So he did, and she gazed at him with such admiration his heart began to slip from its tenuous hold on not tumbling into love with her.

To give himself a few moments to collect and control his

wayward heart, he asked her for more tales of her childhood. She told him of escapades and frolics with Conan and Drake, Morwenna, sometimes Senara—Hide and Go Seek in the caves, Catch as Catch Can on the beach, swimming in the cove at midnight. They had been undisciplined, unfettered, and left to their own devices far too often. In the end, she drew a picture of five young people with too little responsibility and too much free time, too much money on the part of the Trelawnys, and too little parental guidance or love.

He recognized it because it reflected much of his own childhood.

"Were you able to play much?" Elizabeth asked him as they walked the horses to cool them down and she plucked woodbine from a vine. "I mean, you haven't had to work all your life, have you?"

"I wasn't always poor, no." He found a wild rosebud struggling for life amidst the honeysuckle. Its pale pink reminded him of the color of Elizabeth's cheeks when she blushed. "I had schooling, but in the summer, we spent as much time as we could in or on the water. It's so hot in Carolina."

Elizabeth's eyes lit. "Fishing?"

"Fishing." He smiled down at her eager face. "Would you like to go?"

"I—" She pursed her lips.

He brushed them with the rose. "Speak the truth."

She shook her head. "I cannot go out before dawn."

"No?" He tapped her lips with the rosebud. "Seems to me you can."

The grandparents seemed so occupied with estate business, justice of the peace duties, and charity work for the tenants, miners, and church, Elizabeth still enjoyed perhaps too much freedom.

She puffed out a breath, stirring the petals of the rose. "Take that thing away."

"All right." With her lower lip protruding and her eyes downcast, she looked so adorably sulky he couldn't resist removing the rose and replacing it with his lips.

For one glorious moment, her lips, tasting of salt spray and rose petals, clung to his; then she shoved him away hard enough to stagger him back a pace and ran for her mare.

"Running, Elys Trelawny?" he murmured.

"I won't let you ruin me." She flung the accusation over her shoulder. "I won't let you trick me into needing to wed you. I don't care what Mama says. I am worth more than my fortune."

Before Rowan recovered from his shock enough to know what to say, her momentum carried her up and onto the back of Grisette, and she sped away from the meadow, Rowan's gelding following close behind at a canter.

By the time he caught up with her, she was preoccupied deep in conversation with the other Trelawny lady he was charged to protect—Miss Morwenna Trelawny, a dark-haired, dark-eyed beauty as petite as Elizabeth was statuesque. He welcomed the opportunity to meet Miss Morwenna and regretted he now didn't know when he would have another chance to talk to Elizabeth, for the night before, Penvenan had informed Rowan his two and a half weeks acting as Elizabeth's groom would end.

"Unless you wish me to send you back to Charleston."

That and only that must have prompted Rowan to be stupid enough to kiss Elizabeth and distress her so. He had to acquiesce to Penvenan's command. He needed to convince the older man that the danger had not died with Conan.

CHAPTER 11

MORWENNA WAS THE LAST PERSON ELIZABETH WANTED to see just moments after Rowan Curnow kissed her. She needed time to let her heart cease galloping ahead of her horse and the tingling warmth of that brief contact to fade. But there Morwenna stood, one hand gripping the top rail of the gate onto Bastion Point land, and Elizabeth could not proceed without talking to her or running her over.

"Good morning, Morwenna, you're looking . . ."—it burned her tongue, but it was the truth to say—"beautiful."

Her hair, uncovered, glowed blue-black in the sunlight, and Morwenna's face glowed as though lit from within. Despite her lack of inches in height and the roundness of her middle, she still moved with a kind of rolling grace.

Suddenly conscious of her straight hair, her pale skin, and her too tall, mostly too bony figure, Elizabeth added, "Though I didn't realize you were, ahem, so very much increasing."

"No, I suppose they didn't tell you." Morwenna curled her plump upper lip. "Though I don't think they know. I didn't show until three months ago, but now . . ." Her even plumper lower lip quivered and tears brightened her huge, dark eyes. "You've got to help me."

"I've no idea how I can. I spent all this quarter's pin money on getting to Cornwall."

"Oh, you." She swished her hand through the air like erasing a slate. "Do you think of nothing but money? I don't need that—or not the little you could get your hands on. I've a place to live and enough food. But I need to come back to Bastion Point."

A sharp remark stuck to Elizabeth's tongue, but the desperation on Morwenna's face dissolved the words before they emerged.

"You can," Elizabeth said instead. "All you have to do is name the baby's father."

"I can't do that."

"Or marry him."

"I can't do that either."

"Then how do you expect anyone to help you?" Elizabeth tossed back her head to cast her gaze at the crystal blue heavens, as though God would give her an answer.

When she brought her gaze back to her cousin, she caught site of Rowan emerging from the trees. She shot him a glare, a warning to keep his distance.

Elizabeth gave her head a toss of annoyance—and lost her hat. She sighed.

Morwenna grasped the snaffle and held on as though she could keep motionless a horse ten times her weight. "Please. I've never asked a thing of you. Please ask Grandpapa to relent."

"Morwenna, you have asked a great deal of me over the years. Remember the night you climbed down the ivy to meet Sam Carn and I let you back in?"

One corner of Morwenna's mouth twitched. "I did forget. Poor Sam."

Elizabeth backed her mount. One of the mare's hooves crushed Elizabeth's fallen hat. "But that changes nothing for us. I'd not have helped you with your wanton behavior then. I cannot help you now."

"All right then, do nothing." Morwenna crossed her arms over her rather expanded front. "Do nothing, and I shall see to it Grandpapa learns what you were doing in the meadow just now."

Though she remained upright on her mount, Elizabeth's stomach felt as though it plunged to the ground to be trampled upon like her hat. "I've no idea what you're talking about. You were not in the meadow."

"Ha." Morwenna snorted. "I didn't need to be. I can see into the meadow from the roof of my cottage."

So she could.

Only with great effort did Elizabeth stop herself from clutching her roiling middle. "Why?" She didn't even attempt to make herself speak loudly. "Why would you do that to me?"

"Because I and my baby are in danger."

If Morwenna didn't look so frightened, Elizabeth would have laughed in her face. But not even Morwenna was that good an actress to make her complexion pale and her pupils dilate.

"All right." Elizabeth made her hands relax on the reins so Grisette didn't shy and possibly hurt Morwenna or knock her rider to the ground. "I'll do what I can with Grandpapa."

"And save your precious reputation. Lily-white Elys can't be caught kissing the hired help." Her smile displaying a cynical twist to it, Morwenna spun and plowed away, her gown with its extra fullness flying around her in the breeze.

Her black gown, as though she were in mourning. Or perhaps that was all she could find large enough.

Gritting her teeth over the way she'd been manipulated into doing her cousin's bidding—far from the first time in their lives—Elizabeth wheeled Grisette around to find Rowan Curnow still waiting. He'd dismounted and was walking his gelding in a circle to keep him from standing too long, an action showing consideration for the well-being of his mount. She could believe he was a kind and considerate man, except he manipulated her, took advantage of her desire for moments of freedom—for what purpose? Surely not simply to spend time with her. No one simply wanted to be with her without some ulterior motive.

Since when had she ceased taking life into her own hands and managing matters for herself instead of letting others control her?

The answer left her hollow—since her attempts ended in disaster. She intended to stop Romsford's interest in her by kissing a stranger at a ball. She ended up with her parents all but announcing her engagement to the marquess. She escaped from London, only to spend hours alone in the night with a man who was beneath her touch even if she weren't a great heiress. And before that? Yes, she made herself as unapproachable as she could because she wanted to return to Bastion Point, and Rowan Curnow had given her the sobriquet of the ice-blue ice maiden.

Which she wished she were around him.

Watching him from the corner of her eye, she paused long enough to finger comb her hair and twist it into a plait. Rowan didn't mount straightaway. He retrieved what was left of her hat and brought it to her.

"I think it's done for." His beautiful blue eyes sparkled with laughter.

Elizabeth frowned at the once pretty but useless chapeau and couldn't stop a smile of her own. "I am afraid you're right. I think it only good for the rubbish bin."

"I shall oblige you." He tucked the crumpled hat into his coat pocket. "Are you ready to go home now?"

She nodded, and they trotted around a field newly planted, then cut through the parkland to reach the stable unseen from the house. In the stable yard, Elizabeth dismounted without assistance, then stood with her hands clasped before her. She should simply walk to the house, change her dress, and go find Grandpapa, if she could do so without Senara intercepting her. Yet Rowan Curnow had spent hours with her, making possible riding more than at a sedate pace. Simply turning her back on him seemed rude. She would even thank a groom, and he was higher in rank than a groom. But she could not go on meeting him. Not now. Not when she could still feel his lips on hers and her spontaneous response.

She loosened her fingers from the others and held out her hand. "Thank you for your service, Mr. Curnow, but we can no longer ride together."

"I understand."

Did he now? She wanted to kick herself for the annoyance over his easy acceptance of her dismissal.

"Accompanying you has been my pleasure, Miss Trelawny." For the briefest moment, his gaze dropped to her lips. For a moment, she feared he would try to kiss her hand. Even gloved, she didn't want that kind of contact. But he merely clasped her fingers for another instant and released her, bowed, and strode away without looking back.

Elizabeth nodded to the stable hands, who had emerged to take the horses, thought about saying something about them being bribed, and decided against it. If Curnow wanted to waste his money such, then it was his concern. And who could blame the hands for wanting a little extra money?

She entered the house through a side door and raced up to her bedchamber. Feeling a breeze flowing beneath the portal, she feared opening it in the event she found evidence of another intruder. Instead, she found Miss Pross leaning over the sill above the garden.

"The roses are beginning to bloom." She drew back into the room. "Where have you been all this time?"

"Riding."

"Without a hat? Take off that habit and sit."

"I lost my hat." Behind a Chinese screen, Elizabeth exchanged her habit for a dressing gown, then seated herself at the dressing table. "Is everyone awake and breakfasted?"

"Lady Trelawny has gone off to visit the village. Some of the children are ill." Miss Pross began to work a comb through Elizabeth's hair. "Nothing serious, but they need nourishing broths and jellies."

"And toys, if I know Grandmama."

"She does spoil them."

"She's very kind. I should have been here to go with her. It could be my duty one day." Elizabeth looked at herself in the mirror, trying to work out why Rowan Curnow would want to kiss her. Noting only her ice-blue eyes, she dropped her lids. "And Miss Penvenan and Sir Petrok?"

"Miss Penvenan is practicing Spillikins in the rose sitting room, and Sir Petrok is in his study. Shall I have your breakfast brought up, or will you go down?"

"No breakfast."

The notion of what she must ask Grandpapa sent nausea to her middle. Or perhaps the sight of her own pale eyes reminded her of Rowan Curnow's words, his touch, his kiss . . . and her wholly inappropriate attraction to him. But when he had spoken of Paine and the American War for Independence, he had grown so intense, so quietly enthusiastic about his subject, not at all trying to simplify what he said because she was female, her heart turned to moldable wax. That kiss threatened to melt her altogether.

A very dangerous man.

"I shall see if I can speak with my grandfather. Perhaps that pale blue muslin with the velvet spencer. Today is sunny, but cool."

"And this old stone house is always cold." Miss Pross wrapped her woolen shawl more securely around her shoulders.

Elizabeth donned the short jacket of blue velvet over her thin muslin gown and glanced at the mirror again. No, the deep blue didn't help to darken the color of her eyes, alas.

She'd always liked the color of her eyes. It was a family trait passed down from the ancestress who had saved Bastion Point after the English Civil War nearly destroyed it. Now, however, since Rowan's words regarding her frosty demeanor, the light blue hue of her eyes repulsed her. She didn't want to be an ice maiden.

Except with him. Icy was preferable to the way being near him warmed her clear to her marrow.

"What do you plan to do today, Miss Pross?" Elizabeth asked as she opened her bedchamber door.

Miss Pross glanced toward her own room. "If you don't need me, I intend to help plant the kitchen garden. It's time some of the herbs got into the ground."

"Enjoy yourself."

Miss Pross would. She often complained how she missed her home in Dorset, where she'd had a lovely herb garden. But her brother had died and the house had gone to a distant cousin by the laws of inheritance, and Miss Pross, with little money, needed employment. She welcomed the role of Elizabeth's governess, then, when the summons for Elizabeth to go to London came, her companion, confidante, and lady's maid.

Laws of inheritance didn't matter with Bastion Point. There was no entail. Grandpapa could give it to whomever he pleased, and Elizabeth intended to please him.

Except speaking up for Morwenna wouldn't do so. Less would him learning how she'd let the hired man kiss her in a meadow.

At the bottom of the staircase, she paused in the great hall to take several deep breaths. She must not be flushed when she entered Grandpapa's study.

"Miss Tre—"

Elizabeth waved the footman to silence. The clatter of the colorful sticks used in Spillikins rattled from the cozy sitting room at the back of the hall, and she didn't want Senara to know quite yet that she'd returned.

Silent on her kid slippers, she crossed to Grandpapa's study at the front of the hall and tapped on the door.

"Come in, Elizabeth," he called.

She entered and closed the door behind her. "How did you know it was I?"

"The servants scratch, your grandmother is away, and Senara doesn't dare come in here."

"Is that how you survived as a pirate for seven years?"

He gave her an exaggerated scowl. "I was no pirate, whatever the Royal Navy tried to claim. Now come in and sit and stop being impertinent."

Smiling, Elizabeth crossed the room, kissed his cheek, then settled herself in a chair facing his desk.

Most people called into the study were accused of a crime, from pilfering a cup of flour, to stealing jewelry, to suspicion of something worse in the event that person needed to be referred from the justice of the peace to the circuit judge during the assizes. Most of those persons were anxious, even terrified.

Elizabeth relaxed, inhaling the aroma of Grandpapa's pipe smoke lingering in the chamber, the beeswax and lemon used on his furniture to make it glow, and a hint of Grandmama's lilac scent from all the hours she spent reading or working on her embroidery at Grandpapa's side.

Grandpapa removed his pipe from a corner of his desk and

began to fill it. "To what do I owe this honor? You wish to talk to me, or you wish to escape Miss Penvenan?"

"The former, of course. We have scarcely spoken since I arrived."

"And a little to escape Senara." He clamped the stem between his teeth, removed a candle from the holder on his desk, and held the flame to the bowl of his pipe. "You don't mind my pipe after all those city ways of yours, do you, child?"

"No, sir." She edged her chair a little to one side so the smoke streamed past her instead of to her. "If you must indulge in such a vice, who am I to stop you?"

"You sound like your grandmother." Sighing, he tamped the burning tobacco into a bowl of sand. "I know I should stop, but it's a long-standing vice and not easy to give up. Rather like your impertinence."

Elizabeth laughed, suddenly happier than she'd been in too long ago to recall when. "It is so good to be home."

"I expect it is, though you should have come a more conventional way."

"And have Romsford abduct me off to Guernsey or someplace where I wouldn't so easily be able to stop him from claiming me to be his wife?"

"Yes, well . . ." Grandpapa cleared his throat. "I've written to your parents that the offered marriage contract is null and void, as I've changed your inheritance so that the wording of the contract is incorrect as to your assets."

"You changed—" Elizabeth's heart skipped a beat. "To . . . what?"

"I've given you the deed to houses in Truro, Tavistock, Plymouth, and London. They bring in rents of around thirty-five thousand a year."

"But that's ten thousand more than my dowry."

"Which I've removed. It seemed the most expedient way to null the marriage contract."

"Except he might keep trying." Elizabeth gripped her hands together in her lap. "I am certain he wanted my dowry. What else would cause him to pursue me so vigorously?"

"Other than the fact that you're beautiful and intelligent and a Trelawny? He wants a pure young lady for his wife."

Elizabeth ducked her head. "You're right on the last three of those, sir."

"I am right on all of those, child."

She shook her head. "I am too tall. My shoulders and hips are too broad and bony. And my eyes . . ." She covered her eyes with her hands. A shudder too close to a sob for comfort raced through her.

A *whoosh* sounded above her. Elizabeth jumped and uncovered her eyes in time to see the bowl of sand sail past her left shoulder and crash against the hearth.

"You broke your ash bowl."

"You set me in a humor to break many more things than proposed marriage contracts to unworthy men and this old pipe of mine." He tossed the stem onto the cold hearth. "When did my elder granddaughter grow to dislike her looks and think that is all that matters?"

"I do not think that is all that matters. The money matters as well. But it apparently was not enough to counteract my preference for philosophy and poetry over playing cards and being taller than and a better rider than most of the gentlemen in London who do not need my dowry. And those issues were obviously the things those who did need the money were overlooking to get it."

"I never should have let them take you away." He shoved back his chair and stalked to the window. "I saw no one here in

Cornwall worthy of you except for Conan, and he was still too young to take a wife. But I should have known my son and daughter-in-law would be more interested in making connections than your happiness. Their ambition knows no bounds, for which I blame myself. I once thought money and the right connections were all that mattered in life, and here I pay the consequences in my grandchildren." He turned back toward the desk and sorrow etched the lines in his face more deeply. "Is that the real reason you risked damaging your reputation by kissing a stranger at a ball?"

And worse, one in a meadow.

Elizabeth nodded. "I did not wish to go on the shelf never being kissed."

Grandpapa emitted a guffaw. "I hope you chose well."

Only if he approved of an upper-level servant, which he had made clear he did not. If anyone in Cornwall was not worthy of her, it was Rowan Curnow.

"I did not know his identity, since it was a masquerade. I only knew, as I said, that he was taller than I and not married or fat or smelly."

Grandpapa laughed so hard he drew out a handkerchief to mop his eyes. "I've missed you, child. But don't think I approve of you kissing strange men. Kissing men at all, mind you. Not until you're betrothed to one."

"So never." She suppressed a sigh.

"Now, Elizabeth." He sobered and leaned back in his chair, his arms crossed over the front of his plain blue waistcoat. "One day you'll fall in love with the right man. I'm so sorry about Conan for too many reasons to list, but we did have hopes for you there if no one in London took your fancy."

"I'd not have agreed to a marriage with Conan. We were friends, but perhaps too much like brother and sister for the right kind of affection between us."

"Your grandmother and I were friends for many years before we started courting. We still are friends after more than fifty years of marriage."

"You're fortunate."

"We are blessed. The Lord has seen fit to allow us to leave our past in the past and make us new creatures in Christ even at our age."

Elizabeth squirmed on her chair. Nothing clever or appropriate came to mind, so she said nothing.

"You look dubious." Grandpapa's eyes softened. "Have you forgotten your Bible readings?"

"I've not forgotten, sir, just . . ." She took a deep breath and plunged. "I think God wound us up and set us in motion like automatons, then let us go."

"Ah, Elizabeth." Now he looked sad. "Even your earthly father cares more about you than that. Why would you think God would care less than your earthly father?"

"Because he is not on earth."

"Yes, he is. He is in the hearts of those who invite him in, and he's right here waiting for the rest to do the same."

"So we can be puppets in his celestial fair?"

Grandpapa sighed and reached his hands toward her across the desk—big, once strong hands now growing gnarled with rheumatism, but still gentle and generous. "My sweet and beautiful granddaughter, that kind of manipulation is human flaw, and I am more guilty of it than most."

"As with Drake and Morwenna?"

"Drake and Morwenna needed stronger measures than their fathers were willing to put upon them when they were more of an age for it to do them good. They are willful and spoiled, and giving in to their desires does them no good."

"But Morwenna needs us." Elizabeth seized the chance to

change the subject away from God. "I saw her while I was out riding this morning. She's . . . frightened. She wants to come here for her protection."

Grandpapa's lips thinned, and his dark eyes snapped.

"Does God not teach you to show mercy, if he has been so merciful as to forgive your past?" Bold and possibly disrespectful enough to produce negative consequences, but she'd made a promise.

Grandpapa rose again and stalked to the fireplace where he jabbed at his broken pipe with the poker. "I'm still learning the line between mercy and discipline. If I give in to her, we may never learn the name of the father and she'll be condemned in the eyes of the world, if not God's, provided she repents of her misbehavior. I don't want that for her—condemnation in the eyes of the world. It's an uncomfortable way to live, and the child will suffer too."

"But what if she truly is in danger?"

He shot her a raised eyebrow glance over his shoulder. "Do you truly believe she is?"

"I don't know, but she thinks she is."

"Afraid of what?"

"I've no idea."

"And she won't say, will she?"

"No, but she looked scared."

Grandpapa nodded. "Her future is precarious. She's got the cottage and she'll be taken care of, but impending motherhood without a husband is an uncomfortable position to be in."

"It would not be so much so if she had her family behind her." Elizabeth spoke from her heart in this.

Grandpapa's lips thinned again and his eyes narrowed. Elizabeth braced herself for a verbal lashing regarding minding her own concerns.

Instead, he crossed to rest his hand on her shoulder. "My sweet granddaughter, we have offered to send her away. She wants to stay. We are seeing she's well taken care of. Other than that, we can do little. I'd rather she weren't in the house with my unmarried granddaughter, and now Senara is here, it would be even worse. We have your reputation to think about as well. When we know who the man is, we will arrange matters from there."

"And what if he is married?"

"Elizabeth." Grandpapa's silver-shot eyebrows shot to his hairline. "What has London done to you that you would think of such a thing?"

"I may be innocent, but I am not naïve."

"Alas. Well, we will cross that bridge if we must come to it."

"You will arrange a marriage for her anyway."

Grandpapa inclined his head in assent. "But we would rather she wed the child's father. And that is all we will discuss of Morwenna."

"But—"

"Enough. Your grandmother no doubt has arrived home by now and you have a tedious day of entertaining Senara. But you get a reprieve this afternoon."

"Not more guests." Elizabeth nearly wailed the objection.

Grandpapa smiled. "No, child. Lord Penvenan has requested permission to take you driving."

CHAPTER 12

ROWAN STOOD IN HIS BEDCHAMBER AT PENMARA THAT afternoon and watched the diminutive figure once again leaning on the gate between Penvenan and Trelawny land as though waiting for someone. Elizabeth's cousin, Morwenna, the black sheep of the Trelawny family. Even in her condition, she was a stunning female with those huge eyes and full lips. She looked like the sort who kept men at heel by the score. Perhaps Conan had been her latest victim and that was why he wanted her to be protected as well as Senara and Elizabeth, why he did not want to marry Elizabeth. But Conan had given no indication of that.

"You have got to be the one to go with Elizabeth," Conan had pleaded the night before he died when it had become apparent that they would have to separate to save both Elizabeth and Miss Pross with Romsford close behind them. "If I spend hours with her at night, Drake will make sure their grandparents find out, and they'll try to have me wed to her before the next day is out, if they can arrange it, which Sir Petrok Trelawny always can."

"What would be wrong with being wed to Elizabeth?" Rowan had asked what, to him, was a logical question.

"Nothing, except she'll never leave Cornwall once she returns, and there's too little here to hold me."

"Your land? Your people?"

"Will be better off if I sell it to someone with money. If I can break the entail, I have buyers."

"And what will they do to me if they find out?" Rowan wouldn't complain of Conan's predicted fate.

Conan had given him a sympathetic glance. "Nothing. They will scold her and most likely send you back to Charleston to keep it all quiet, but they would never want you to marry. She's destined for better things."

So he had gone with Elizabeth so Conan didn't have to. Rowan owed it to his friend, for, without Conan, Rowan never would have been in London. He never would have encountered Elizabeth at Hookham's or that ball. He'd never have been at that ball to flirt with her from behind their masks, let himself be swept into that bower, let himself be kissed.

So he encouraged her. Not gentlemanly of him. Kissing her in the meadow wasn't gentlemanly. Neither of them had protested at either incident beyond her accusing him of trying to ruin her.

He wasn't. He couldn't win her that way. How he would win her when she treated him as perhaps half a step riser higher than her stable hands, he hadn't yet worked out. How he would win her when his own employer—a man now carrying the right to call himself a baron, even if the property needed money like a sponge needed water—had decided to court her. Penvenan was far from a poor man, and Elizabeth was too rich for Rowan in his present occupation.

In competition with his own employer. Rowan felt sick to his stomach and worse in his soul, as though God had broken a promise. But it had only been wishfulness on his part and nothing the Lord ordained for him.

On the contrary, matters progressed as though the Lord had wholly opposite plans for him. Penvenan was off at that very moment to take Elizabeth for a drive in an open carriage. The vehicle rolled down the drive, newly acquired from somewhere in Truro, along with the team of grays pulling it. No effort or expense was too great to impress Miss Trelawny. Despite the difference in age, it was a good match by anyone's standards.

Whereas no one would wish to be matched with Miss Morwenna Trelawny, regardless of her beauty. But Conan thought she and Elizabeth and his sister were in danger, and had asked Rowan to help him protect them.

"Why?" The question had been natural for Rowan to ask. "Surely the smuggling gang has no interest in the ladies."

"I can tell you for certain tomorrow. I won't make accusations without some kind of proof."

But Conan hadn't lived through that night.

Because he had given Rowan the opportunity to rescue Elizabeth from Romsford, Rowan vowed to find out what Conan had refused to reveal without proof. Yet the more obstacles that stood in his way, the less Rowan believed his actions were what the Lord wanted from him.

"Face up to it, Curnow," Rowan said aloud. "The only time you were certain you were in the Lord's will it ended in disaster for you."

But not for a total of eighty former slaves living in freedom in Canada and the Northwest Territory.

Until he knew for certain what he was supposed to accomplish there in Cornwall, even if it meant never winning Elizabeth's heart for his own, he would keep the ladies safe.

He left the upper floor and ran down steps with carpet so worn the warp and weft had separated, creating a hazard to the unwary. He should recommend having it ripped up. Whatever the treads looked like beneath, they couldn't be worse than the runner.

Penmara, unlike Bastion Point, boasted no footmen lurking in the hall to open the door or run errands. Rowan departed without anyone noticing him and sprinted across what had once been lawn to arrive at the Bastion Point gate. Morwenna was walking away, head bowed, hands clasped over her belly, as though she were praying. She glanced up at his approach, his footfalls crunching through last year's brush, and paused.

"Mr. Curnow, is it not?" Though her speech held more West Country than did Elizabeth's, her tone held the same edge of haughtiness.

He smiled at that. "Miss Trelawny?"

"I prefer Morwenna. The Trelawnys have rejected me."

"That doesn't feel right."

"You called Elizabeth by her Christian name." She grinned. "You must have risked freezing your lips off kissing her."

Nothing about that kiss, short as it had been, had been cold, but Rowan wasn't about to claim that.

Morwenna shrugged. "I understand. You may not be a gentleman by Trelawny standards, but you're enough of one not to talk about kissing a lady."

Rowan still said nothing, letting her clear her heart of whatever bitterness toward her cousin she could before he tried to talk to her.

She said no more, simply peered up at him through eyelashes so long and thick they looked like they couldn't be real. "If you came chasing after me because you think I'm easy goods—"

"Never, Miss Morwenna." His ears burned. "I've a message for you."

"From Elizabeth?" She leaned forward and grabbed his arm. "Please tell me Grandpapa said I can come back to Bastion Point."

"I'm afraid not. That is, I don't know about that. I haven't spoken with Miss Trelawny since I took her home this morning."

"Then what do you want?" Her little hand squeezed his forearm with surprising strength. "Why are you talking to me, Rowan Curnow?"

"You looked frightened this morning, and Conan asked me to look out for you and your cousin and his sister."

She swallowed and pressed the back of her hand to her lips. "Why?"

"He knew something was likely to happen to him."

"I know." She nodded, and tears scattered from her big eyes. "He wanted out of the smuggling gang, and they threatened him if he tried. But why us females? No one should—that is, no one goes anywhere, Elizabeth hasn't been here, and I—" She shrugged and dabbed at her eyes with her fingertips.

Rowan handed her his handkerchief. "I don't know. I can understand the smugglers threatening him, but not ladies. And we were discussing breaking the entail so he could sell, not the smugglers."

"Which makes his death more senseless." She took his handkerchief. Instead of applying it to her eyes, she wrung the linen between her hands. "Without three male heirs, the entail must stand."

"And we could find no other male heirs for all the weeks we spent with those dusty records in London."

Too many weeks when they could have been taking other actions.

He covered her hands with his to stop their restless twisting of the handkerchief. "But Conan feared someone with reason, and you're frightened too."

"I wasn't. I've been friends with too many of the men in these parts to fear them even if they are part of the gang."

"You don't know which are with the smugglers and which are not?"

"We all try not to. It's dangerous to know."

"But they all knew Conan and Drake."

She looked at him as though he were stupid. "Of course. They use Penmara cellars and caves and Trelawny caves to hide their goods. And Drake and Conan . . . Well, they never could hide their breeding."

"And you can't identify these . . . er . . . friends of yours?"

She looked away, then back to meet his gaze with eyes so dark yet clear even a man teetering on the edge of giving his heart to another could drown in their depths. "Nothing more than friends." Her cheeks bloomed with color, and she looked down. "Friends with most, anyway. But none of them have ever scared me until today. This morning." She began toying with a stray curl over her left ear.

His body tensing, Rowan waited.

She started to speak, but the sound of voices drifting over the gate drew their attention to Bastion Point land. Three people approached, a man and two ladies.

Rowan's lips twitched. Apparently Penvenan hadn't been able to get away in the carriage with Elizabeth without Miss Penvenan attaching herself to the outing.

"I'm afraid we're going to have company soon, Miss Morwenna. You'd best talk fast."

"Sometime last night, someone put a dead bird and . . . and its broken egg on the windowsill of my bedchamber."

"A dead bird?" He kept his tone neutral with effort.

"With a broken egg." Suddenly Morwenna clutched at his lapels with both hands and pressed herself against him. "Their being there couldn't have been an accident. And it's someone who knows us. The dogs didn't bark."

"Conan's dogs?"

"Yes. They came to me in the woods one day. He'd been keeping them away from the house after the last one vanished. Another warning, and now I get a dead bird and . . . and—I don't know what to do."

She should take her hands off him and back away before Elizabeth saw this *tête-à-tête* and leaped to incorrect conclusions.

"That is revolting." Miss Penvenan's voice rang across the ten yards or so between them.

Too late.

"Have you no decency, Morwenna?" Elizabeth's low tones held more dignity but just as much disgust.

Despite her words directed at her cousin, the look she cast Rowan should have frozen off his nose.

"Of course she has no decency," Miss Penvenan declared. "I mean, she's—"

"Rowan." Penvenan's voice was sharp, authoritative, as he opened the gate. "What are you doing with this lady?"

"Lady." Miss Penvenan snorted.

"Keeping a promise." Rowan willed Morwenna to release him.

She merely smiled over her shoulder at her cousin and neighbor. "What do either of you ladies care what I do with Mr. Curnow? You think him beneath you."

Elizabeth's ice-maiden mask slipped into place, and she turned away. "I'd like to return home, my lord. Come along, Senara. We have been out nearly an hour, and after my ride this morning, I am quite fatigued and ready for a cup of tea."

"And perhaps a biscuit or two." Senara turned with Elizabeth, slipping her arm through her friend's.

Penvenan glared at Rowan. "I'll talk to you later."

"Yes, sir." Rowan watched Elizabeth glide away, each step

sending the bottom flounce of her gown swirling out for a hint of silk-clad ankle.

His heart ached. His face must have given something away, for Morwenna released his coat and patted his cheek.

"She'll never have you, you know, even if she did let you kiss her. She's not going to risk you going after her inheritance."

Rowan crossed his arms over his chest. "I don't care about her inheritance."

"Twenty-five thousand pounds for her dowry."

She may as well have given him twenty-five thousand blows, so crushed did his heart suddenly feel. "As well as her inheriting Bastion Point," she said. "She'll want a marquess at the least for that kind of blunt."

"She already rejected a marquess." He turned away. "Tell me if anything else untoward occurs. I'll look after your safety as best I can without knowing where an enemy lies. But I'd rather you not play your games at my expense." He started to walk away.

"No, wait." She stumbled after him, tripping on an exposed root and grabbing his arm. "Please, I'm sorry. I shouldn't have done that. Call it habit. I've always been known to . . . to—"

"Try to make her jealous?" He removed his arm from her hold. "It still works. Now, if you'll excuse me . . ."

"Who can blame me? She's everything except for looks— parents who don't squander their money, our grandparents' love and respect, years in London."

"I think she's beautiful. And those years in London weren't kind to her."

"Oh my." Morwenna's eyes widened. "It isn't just her money you want, is it?"

He didn't respond to that. "So, Miss Morwenna, was that all a hoax about the dead bird and egg?"

"No." She began to twist her hands together where her waist

should be. "That is completely true, and I think it's a warning or a threat like Conan received."

He cast his annoyance with her aside and gave her his full attention. "A warning of what, do you think?"

"A dead mother bird and her chick." To emphasize her words, she smoothed her hand over her belly.

He started to ask why, but realized he already knew.

CHAPTER 13

"Disgraceful." Senara tossed her head, endangering the black plumes on her hat. "I know she's your cousin, Elizabeth, but her behavior is the outside of enough."

"I'll not discuss Morwenna's behavior." Elizabeth injected her tone with all the ice she could manage, then turned to Lord Penvenan. "I hope you were not offended by my commenting that the walk has wearied me. I do thank you for escorting us. I haven't been able to walk like this in years."

"You never attended house parties?" He looked at her askance.

She shrugged. "We spent whole summers in the country. My mother's family has a home in Surrey, and my father inherited lands from his great uncle in Worcestershire. Neither county has the sea air."

"Neither county is Cornwall." Senara spoke with pride.

Elizabeth smiled at her. "Precisely. And in house parties, one must meander with the other guests."

Not that they hadn't been meandering that afternoon. When Senara would not allow them to leave in the carriage only large enough for two passengers, against all sense of good manners, Elizabeth had suggested a walk through the parkland and countryside instead. In truth, she rather welcomed Senara's company. What Grandpapa was thinking in accepting Penvenan's offer to take Elizabeth driving she could not think.

When she asked Grandpapa, he merely smiled and exited his study to greet Grandmama as though she'd been on a month-long journey.

"Not another man twice my age to court me," she'd wanted to call after him.

She would have, save for the butler and two footmen also in the great hall.

Yet why Senara wished for their company when she'd previously been so rude to the new owner of Penmara, Elizabeth intended to ask her as soon as he departed.

Departed to ring a peal over his hired man's head for his outrageous behavior with Morwenna. Yes, Morwenna was a horrid flirt, but Rowan Curnow hadn't in the least looked as though he wanted out of her clutches—literally.

Despite the frost of her demeanor, Elizabeth burned inside. Mortification over the fact that she'd let him kiss her was only the beginning. The core of her blazed with humiliation—produced outrage that he would even talk to Morwenna, let alone be so . . . close to her, as though they were old friends—or more.

They couldn't be. He hadn't been in Cornwall a month.

"I am quite certain the exercise is good for me too." Senara was prattling, as she'd prattled throughout the walk. "I've always been so busy taking care of Penmara, I got out too rarely, especially after you left, Elizabeth. And you never came back."

"My parents kept me too busy," Elizabeth murmured.

"I expect your suitors kept you too busy." Penvenan smiled at her.

She managed not to grimace. "My parents dislike Cornwall. It is too remote for them."

"The remoteness is what is so beautiful about it," Senara declared.

Penvenan nodded. "I agree with Miss Penvenan."

So the conversation went all the way back to Bastion Point. And so it had gone for the hour they had been walking. Elizabeth wondered what they would do if she simply started to scream at the top of her lungs and run for the isolation of her bedchamber and a locked door.

Move the lock to the outside, no doubt.

She managed to maintain her composure all the way to the house, where she turned to Penvenan and asked if he wished to come in for a cup of tea.

He glanced at Senara and shook his head. "I think I'll get back to Penmara." He bowed to both of them. "Thank you for a lovely walk, ladies. Perhaps we shall have that drive another day."

"Indeed we shall." Elizabeth turned to the front door a footman held open for her and entered the chilly dimness of the great hall.

"At least," Senara said the instant the door closed behind them, regardless of the servants present, "he didn't call Penmara home."

"I doubt he thinks of it as home." Elizabeth took Senara's elbow and steered her into the blue sitting room where the Spillikins sticks played across a game table like a splintered rainbow. "He has only been there for three weeks."

Senara dropped onto a chair and began to gather up the sticks. "It is my home, not his. It will never be his home."

"Senara, if you dislike his presence so, why did you insist on coming with us? It was rather rude of you."

"Did you want to go driving with him alone?"

Elizabeth huffed out a laugh. "No."

"He is so very old, I thought you would prefer my company. Though he does still have all his hair and teeth."

"He is very kind and—" She broke off before reminding Senara that Penvenan now had a title. "Thank you for being so thoughtful. I've just rid myself of one middle-aged suitor. I do not wish for another."

"Is there a young suitor you pine for?" Senara bent her head over the colorful sticks, concentrating on gathering the shorter or fatter ones to stand upright in her hands. "Does anyone hold your heart?"

"No one." Elizabeth stared out of the window through which the afternoon sun blazed in an effort to blot out a face with proud, chiseled bones and eyes the color of an evening sea. She would not, not, not think of his lips. He did not hold her heart, not even one string that kept it tethered firmly in her own control.

"Good," Senara was saying. "I want you to stay here at Bastion Point. I've been so lonely without you."

Elizabeth's conscience pricked her. She'd scarcely thought of Senara over the past six years other than the occasional letter. She thought of the grandparents and brother and returning to the rolling hills, the curve of beach, and the pounding sea. She even thought of Conan and going sailing with him in the early morning. She did not think about doing anything with Senara. Their friendship stemmed more from the familiarity of a lifetime than any shared interest.

"Will you play Spillikins with me?" Senara asked.

"Do you not want some tea?" Elizabeth poised halfway between game table and bellpull.

"No tea. I just agreed with you so we could come in." Senara grinned. "I knew he would never come in with us."

"You minx." Pushing back her amusement, Elizabeth seated herself at the table and studied the array of sticks before her. "I've not played in years. Should I pick one color?"

"You should choose the thinnest ones on the bottom. Those are likely to disturb fewer top sticks than the fat ones, do you not think?"

Elizabeth drew a long and thin blue stick from the bottom of the pile. Half a dozen other sticks collapsed in the gap her draw had created. With a sigh, she laid it on the pile.

Crowing, Senara took her turn, drawing out two fat green sticks, one triangular red stick, and a thin yellow one before the upper layer collapsed with a clatter.

"I've three and you have none, and now it is your turn again."

Elizabeth drew out a fat orange stick this time—and the mound collapsed. She shook her head. "I never win at this game."

"I get too much practice." Senara proceeded to increase her winnings.

By the time Grandmama entered the room a half hour later, Elizabeth had collected five sticks and Senara fifteen. The game was nearly over.

Grandmama wore amethyst satin and shimmering stones in the same color. An ermine-trimmed cloak in deep green graced her shoulders.

Elizabeth sprang to her feet. "Grandmama, you look stunning. Are you and Grandpapa dining out this evening?"

"We are. I think we forgot to tell you girls. Just a little dinner party at the Polkinghorns'. Nothing elaborate and all old ones like us, so we won't be late. Tomorrow is Sunday, after all."

An entire evening to entertain Senara on her own.

Elizabeth wished an ague would send her to her bed.

Instead, Senara went to hers early. They were in the middle of dinner served in the breakfast parlor instead of the dining room when Senara suddenly leaped to her feet, her hand at her throat, and fled up the steps.

"Is something wrong with the roast?" the footman serving them asked.

"I thought it quite fine." Elizabeth glanced at Senara's plate where a slice of roast beef lay in its own succulent juices and surrounded with peas. "She did not even touch hers."

Gathering up her skirt, she raced up the steps after Senara. She found Senara in her bedchamber in the middle of the bed with the coverlet wrapped around her like a cloak. Her teeth chattered, and her face had grown alarmingly pale.

"Do I need to send for the apothecary?" Elizabeth laid her wrist against Senara's brow.

It was cold and clammy, not burning with fever.

"I'll get a fire laid in here immediately and send a maid in to help you into your nightgown." Elizabeth opened the door to call to the footman in the hall since none of the upstairs rooms sported bellpulls. "Please send in a maid and hot tea." She glanced back at Senara. "Or would you prefer beef tea? More nourish—"

"No. No. No." Senara covered her face with her hands and began to rock back and forth. "Just tea. Weak tea."

Elizabeth conveyed this wish to the footman, then crossed the room to draw the blinds and light half a dozen candles. By the time she finished, a maid had arrived with tea and another with wood for the fire. Through it all, Senara never moved nor spoke, save for shaking hard enough to make the bed ropes creak beneath the mattress. Elizabeth's questions as to Senara's wish for care went unanswered. When she did nod in response to whether or not she'd rather don a nightdress than keep on her gown and then slid off the bed, Elizabeth departed to send a groom for Mr. Cardew, the apothecary.

She should return to her friend's side. She knew she should, but she entered the blue sitting room to await the apothecary. A book lay open on the settee. She picked it up to discover it was a collection of sermons by George Whitefield, some preacher from several decades earlier. A pencil mark marred the margin, drawing her eye to one paragraph.

> I see your hearts affected, I see your eyes weep. (And indeed, who can refrain weeping at the relation of such a story?) But, behold, I show you a mystery, hid under the sacrifice of Abraham's only son, which, unless your hearts are hardened, must cause you to weep tears of love, and that plentifully too. I'd willingly hope you even prevent me here, and are ready to say, "It is the love of God, in giving Jesus Christ to die for our sins." Yes, that is it. And yet perhaps you find your hearts, at the mentioning of this, not so much affected. Let this convince you, that we are all fallen creatures, and that we do not love God or Christ as we ought to do: for, if you admire Abraham offering up his Isaac, how much more ought you to extol, magnify and adore the love of God, who so loved the world, as to give his only begotten Son Christ Jesus our Lord, "that whosoever believeth on Him should not perish, but have everlasting life"? May we not well cry out, Now know we, O Lord, that thou hast loved us, since thou hast not withheld thy Son, thine only Son from us!

"Heh." She slammed the book shut and dropped it back onto the settee.

She no longer accepted that God loved her. Once upon a time as a child, she believed with her whole heart. That stopped—when? Yes, when the grandparents allowed her parents to take her away to London against her protests. They, apparently, like her parents, had viewed her as a pawn to advance the family through an advantageous marriage. Perhaps Grandpapa had only extricated her from a marriage with Romsford because he saw no advantage to the alliance. And now, to be good enough for Bastion Point, she must find some elusive treasure without a clue where one might be hidden.

God the Father seemed the same—only wanting her to follow him for his devices.

She was generally a good person, yet she'd done little other than some charity work to make her worthy. In truth, she was a worry to her parents over her spinsterhood, had been trouble to Grandpapa over Romsford and the marriage contract, and wasn't doing a terribly good job of entertaining and comforting Senara for Grandmama or Senara's sakes. She simply was not love worthy. She would never sacrifice as Abraham had been willing to sacrifice. She couldn't imagine loving a person that much, let alone a God who was nowhere near her.

She scowled at the book. Who was Whitefield that he expected a few words to convince people of the truth as he believed it to be?

A rap of the knocker prevented her from picking up the book again to find out. Expecting Mr. Cardew, she entered the great hall in time to see a footman usher in the plump little man who, beyond his leather medical bag, dressed more like a hunting squire than a medical practitioner, in his top boots and leather breeches. He was competent at his work, though, and had more than once patched up Drake, Conan, or her when they got themselves into scrapes—scrapes, gashes, and, with Drake, broken limbs.

He grinned at her and shook her hand. "How's that arm doing, young lady?"

"Hardly a scar." Elizabeth smiled down at the man, who barely reached her shoulder.

He'd sewn up a cut she received while learning to fence. "So what's wrong with Miss Penvenan?" Cardew glanced around as though expecting her to appear out of one of the rooms.

"A chill, I think. We were eating dinner, and she commenced shaking." Elizabeth started for the steps. "She's in her chamber. She's staying with us, you know."

"Of course I know. This is Cornwall." Cardew guffawed. "Everyone knows everything unless they're threatened to keep a secret."

Like the identities of the smugglers.

"Nasty business that, with Lord Penvenan." Cardew seemed to have had similar thoughts to Elizabeth's. "Can't think why a body would end his lordship's life like that."

"Nor can I." Elizabeth shuddered.

She preceded Mr. Cardew up the steps and down the corridors leading to Senara's bedchamber. A tap on the door brought the maid, who looked pale and shaken herself.

"Is she worse?" Elizabeth rushed into the chamber.

Senara no longer trembled with cold, but lay on her side, her knees drawn to her chest, the bedclothes tucked up around her ears and a fire roaring on the hearth.

"She l-l-looks dead," the maid whispered.

"Nonsense." Cardew hastened to Senara's side and set two fingers against her neck. "Pulse is good and strong. Miss Penvenan, can you hear me?"

Senara nodded.

"Good. Are you still cold?"

She nodded again.

"Hmm." He touched her brow. "No fever. Did you eat too many sweets again?"

Senara shook her head.

"She didn't," Elizabeth confirmed. "She didn't want any today."

Cardew tapped his chin. "Now that is worrisome. Is your belly hurting, Miss Penvenan?"

Senara shook her head, then croaked, "All of me hurts."

"Hmm. Well now." Cardew looked down her throat and into her eyes and touched her pulse some more. After a few minutes, he drew a green bottle from his bag and sent the maid for a glass of water. "A teaspoon of laudanum in a glass of water will help her sleep. If she isn't better in the morning, give her a few drops of this every four hours." He drew another bottle from his bag, this one amber in color. "That should set her right as rain."

He measured out a dose of the laudanum and helped Senara sit up enough to aid drinking the medicine, then gave the bottles into Elizabeth's care. She raised her brows in question at this action, but he gestured to the door and left the room.

"Elizabeth, I believe Miss Senara's troubles are more blue devils than an illness." Cardew paced away from the bedroom door. "She appears to have nothing wrong with her—no fever, no redness of the throat, and so on. But she's not herself, and with the recent death of her brother, I think her mind and heart are overset."

"But she has done so well."

A little too well, except for her anger with Lord Penvenan, which also seemed to have dissipated.

Cardew shook his nearly bald head. "We don't know why these things happen, but sometimes a body doesn't feel the impact of a death for weeks, and then—poof." He swept his hand out, nearly knocking a globe from a wall sconce. "Something can happen and the loved one left alive goes into a decline."

Elizabeth hugged her arms over her chest, feeling cold herself. "What should we do for her other than the medicine? Should I stay with her? Read to her? Something?"

"Let her rest and make sure she eats nourishing food, not those sweets she loves too well. Nothing too heavy. Chicken and fish and white soup." He paused at the top of the steps. "But just let her sleep tonight. Perhaps leave a maid in the room with her in the event she needs anything."

"And why did you give her medicine to me?" Elizabeth still clutched the bottles.

"Precaution."

Not liking the implication of his words, Elizabeth bade the little man good night, continued to her chamber to tuck the bottles in the chest with her chemises, and then hunted down Miss Pross to see if she was interested in playing a game of chess or Map of Europe. She preferred the former, since she didn't know another female willing to play the strategy game and be as good at it as she was. Miss Pross was usually better, and Elizabeth welcomed the challenge. Despite her concern for Senara, who slept soundly under the influence of the drug, the time sailed past until the grandparents returned from their dinner party.

Elizabeth rose from the table. "We will have to finish tomorrow."

Miss Pross also rose. "Monday, child. Tomorrow is Sunday."

"Of course." Elizabeth's nostrils pinched at the prospect of yet another tedious day keeping company with Senara, who stayed home due to the depth of her mourning, while the others attended the church in the village. It was an advantage of London—few people cared about the day of the week if they wished to have a party on that date.

Miss Pross departed, and the grandparents entered. Both looked tired, with shadows beneath their eyes, but their smiles and greetings for Elizabeth held warmth that assured her their love was genuine and near. But, of course, she had never given them much trouble.

"Has Senara gone to her bed?" Grandmama asked.

"No, she's . . . not well." Elizabeth told them of Senara's attack and the apothecary's visit.

Grandpapa sighed, looking even wearier. "I've seen this after battle. A man is all right for days, and then one day he starts blubbering like a babe."

"The poor child. We will go in and pray for her before we turn in." Grandmama seated herself on the settee. "Now I'd like a cup of chamomile tea. Will either of you join me?"

Grandpapa grimaced. "I'll take China tea."

Elizabeth gave the order and returned to her seat at the game table. She needed to again attempt to persuade Grandpapa to relent with Morwenna. She had seemed genuinely frightened. Then again, that disgusting display with Rowan earlier disinclined Elizabeth to give her cousin any favors. Still, Elizabeth didn't quite approve of exiling Morwenna. They had been friends once and—

"So you will do that, will you not, my dear?" Grandmama asked.

Elizabeth jumped and glanced up. "I beg your pardon?"

"You do beautiful needlework on ribbon. Will you work on a few yards we can give as prizes for the games involving the village girls?"

"Well, yes, of course. I'll need to go into Truro for supplies, though." Elizabeth squirmed. "Um, what games?"

Grandpapa raised his brows. "Have you not been paying attention, child?"

"No, sir, I was thinking about . . ." She hesitated.

"You haven't forgotten the midsummer fete, have you?" Grandmama asked.

"Yes, I had." Elizabeth smiled. "Or rather I wasn't thinking it was so soon."

Grandmama nodded. "Four weeks off. We decided not to cancel it despite Conan's death. He'd understand, we believe."

The annual event raised money to help the families of

out-of-work miners, too many of them now, and most from the Penmara mines.

"Conan's father's mismanagement is one reason so many miners are out of work," Grandpapa grumbled.

"Now, Petrok." Grandmama clucked her tongue. "Be nice. He was terribly young when he inherited, and his trustees were greedy, dishonest men."

Grandpapa turned back to Elizabeth. "So what has you wool-gathering, my dear? Senara? I know having her here is a burden, but we can scarcely send her home."

"Senara isn't much of a burden. And the apothecary believes she will be all right in time. She needs rest and fewer sweets and kindness." Elizabeth stared at the chessboard, plotting her next move. "I was thinking of Morwenna."

Grandpapa's face closed. "My mind is made up there. I will hear no more about it."

Elizabeth opened her mouth to argue, then clamped her teeth onto her lower lip.

"Elizabeth, I see you've been reading this." Grandmama spoke a little too loudly as she picked up the book of sermons.

"Only a little. I was—" Elizabeth caught her breath.

Where the book had been open facedown on the sofa, it was now closed with a bit of paper protruding from the top.

"It was rather interesting." Elizabeth crossed to Grandmama. "May I take it with me?"

Grandmama's eyes sparkled. "Of course."

Elizabeth looked past Grandmama so as not to meet her eyes and give away her guilt at the fib. A fib that held consequences, as now she must read the sermons because Grandmama, no doubt, would quiz her on their contents. Served her right. They thought her righteous and pure, and here she was deceiving them.

Deceiving them for what? She held no doubt in her mind

where the note came from—and from whom the note came. What baffled her was why. He knew she didn't want to see him again.

Another stab of her conscience smote her over deceiving herself on that head. She didn't in the least not wish to see him again. She told herself it was only to tell him how disgusting his display with her cousin had been.

Too restless to sit now, she carried the book to the door. "If you will excuse me, I think I'll go to my bed after all. Here is your tea." She opened the door to the footman, then slipped past him and raced to her bedchamber. Once inside, she lit a candle and tore open the note without trying to break the wax first.

Elys, please, I need to speak with you. Tomorrow. Cove. Low tide. R

The *R* was an ornate copperplate initial in comparison with the scrawl of the rest of the note. And he had spelled her Cornish name correctly. No one, not even Drake, spelled her Cornish name correctly, forever using an *iz* instead of *ys*.

Such a silly thing should never touch a lady's heart, never soften even the tiniest corner, but that carefully lettered name pummeled her with the memory of how softly he spoke it, and how softly he had kissed her—

She ripped the note in two. "You have nothing to say to me, Rowan Curnow." She ripped the pieces again.

She would not, would not, would not meet him the next day or any day. Would not give her heart to anyone with reason to want more than her person. She didn't need to make any kind of an alliance now that she would inherit property and especially once she found the treasure worth more than Bastion Point. She tossed the pieces of the note into the cold fireplace. But in the middle of the night, unable to sleep, she rose, lit a candle, and retrieved the fragments of paper to tuck them deep in a drawer of violet-scented gloves.

CHAPTER 14

ELIZABETH COULDN'T HAVE GONE TO MEET ROWAN EVEN
if she had allowed herself to do so. The vicar and his wife and
Lord Penvenan came back to Bastion Point after church services
Elizabeth did not attend in order to watch over a drowsy Senara.
After dinner—a cold collation so the servants could have the
afternoon off to visit families—Elizabeth sat at one end of the
Chinese drawing room with Mrs. Kitto and Grandmama while
the men sat at the far end of the chamber, a room large enough
to seat twenty without being crowded. Senara, though saying she
felt better, had elected to stay in her bedchamber, and Miss Pross
was keeping her company with a game of Map of Europe and
reading to her from the latest Gothic novel.

"So why didn't you marry in London?" Mrs. Kitto asked.
"You're such a pretty girl."

"I'm a full head taller than most men. I think it set them off."
Because she thought she sounded harsh, she added, "And I'm
particular."

"You need a nice Cornishman." Mrs. Kitto smiled, turning
her sweet, elderly lady's face into a map of wrinkles that showed
she had smiled a great deal during her life.

Of course she had. The vicar adored her. Much to her embarrassment, Elizabeth had once caught them holding hands during
an alfresco meal on the village green.

"It's a good thing," Mrs. Kitto continued, "that you have an eligible gentleman so close at hand." She cast a glance to the other end of the chamber.

Elizabeth gripped her hands together in her lap. "He seems quite fine."

"He has expressed his wish to court Elizabeth," Grandmama announced. "It would make us happy to see her settled as we grow older, and her parents show little interest in her returning to them."

"For which I am thankful." Elizabeth pressed her hands flat against the sofa cushions.

She rose. "Would you care for more tea, Grandmama, Mrs. Kitto?"

"That would be lovely." Grandmama nodded. "And go ask the gentlemen if they wish for some."

Elizabeth nodded, then crossed the red-and-gold carpet to the cluster of chairs on which the gentlemen rested.

"I need to purchase some riding stock," Lord Penvenan was saying. "We can't continue to borrow from your stables, Sir Petrok. The way Curnow spends his days in the saddle inspecting the estate and overseeing the builders, I fear we will overuse our privilege."

"Not at all. They spend most of their days eating their heads off— Ah, Elizabeth, what is it?" Grandpapa rose.

The other gentlemen followed.

"Grandmama sent me to ask if you'd like more tea."

They agreed they would, and Elizabeth headed for the door to make the request of the footman stationed outside in the corridor. Behind her, Mr. Kitto was telling Penvenan about a horse fair in Redruth.

"You might find something suitable for your needs. What are you seeking?"

Elizabeth's hand shook on the door handle. She so wished to return to the men and discuss the merits of horse conformation. It was far more interesting than Grandmama and Mrs. Kitto's endless talk of fete preparations, receipts for the meat pies they would serve, how many lemons they must require for the day's supply of lemonade . . .

"Curnow is my resident expert on the livestock," Penvenan answered the vicar. "He spends most of his time on the horse farm in Virginia these days."

No wonder he rode so well.

Elizabeth shook her head to clear it of an image of Rowan on horseback and gave the order for more tea. Back on the sofa with the older ladies, she asked Grandmama when they could go to Truro.

"Tuesday, weather permitting."

❧

The weather was not permitting on Tuesday. Rain fell so hard during the night and into the morning, even Elizabeth didn't want to step outside the house. She curled up on the rug before the blue salon fire and worked on embroidering the hem of a gown she thought too dull while Grandmama read in the melodious voice Morwenna had inherited. Elizabeth's voice, to her ears, was too clear, too sharp—like icicles.

Because she was an ice maiden.

She certainly felt a little cold inside—cold and hard and a bit calculating. She was going to allow a man to court her simply to make the grandparents happy. She wanted to make them happy in the event the treasure eluded her.

Stormy days like this, while the winds roared, the rain lashed, and the sea pounded the base of the cliff, the house stood like a fortress against the onslaught of an enemy with her tucked up safe and warm inside. Safety, solidity, warmth that would eventually melt the hard core of ice inside her.

Stormy days were also an excellent time to explore the house for clues, if not the treasure outright. With Senara keeping to her room, Elizabeth began with the library in search of books on family history. She was perched atop a stool to reach the uppermost shelf and row of dusty volumes containing the Trelawny family chronicles when Grandpapa entered.

"What are you doing up there with those old books?" His dark eyes twinkled up at her. "I read you the parts suitable for a young lady."

"You want me to find a treasure." She jumped off the stool with the first volume of the family chronicle. "I thought those journals might carry a hint of what it is."

"Oh, my dear." Grandpapa's eyes shadowed. "If only our ancestors had found this treasure and I'd found it as a young man . . ."

She stared at him. "What do you mean?"

"Treasures in life that are worth more than dowries and property and the amount of money deposited in The Funds." He squeezed her hand. "Perhaps you should read those journals. In reading about their lives, perhaps you can work out what was missing. I think you already knew at one time in your life. But no time for reading now. Your grandmama wishes for you to join her in the garden parlor."

Journal in hand, Elizabeth started down the corridor leading to the cozy parlor overlooking the garden. Above her, a series of thuds sounded, rather like men in boots were moving furniture. Then a high-pitched scream threatened to shatter the windows and more thumps resounded through the main staircase—loud, rhythmic thumps. More screams.

Elizabeth dropped the ancient book on the floor and raced

for the front hall. That wasn't furniture plummeting down the steps. It was a person. A female, one who could shriek like a banshee. A maid or—

"Senara!" Elizabeth reached the bottom of the steps in time to catch her before her head hit the stone floor of the entry hall but not in time to stop herself from falling under the impact of Senara's weight.

The two of them landed in a heap at the feet of the butler and half a dozen footmen. Elizabeth lay winded, with Senara's head butted into her middle. Senara was whimpering and twitching like a puppy in its sleep.

"Miss Trelawny, Miss Penvenan." Unflappable as ever, the butler crouched beside them. "Are you all right?"

Absurd question. Of course they weren't all right or they wouldn't be lying there like a heap of old rags.

She managed to gasp out, "I think so."

"I'm not." Senara began to wail.

"Where are you hurt?" Elizabeth levered herself to a sitting position and addressed the servants. "Send for the apothecary. Fetch Grandmama." She turned to Senara. "Do you think anything is broken?"

"I don't know. I don't know." Senara's voice rose. "Everything hurts."

"Of course it does." Elizabeth patted Senara's hand. "You just fell down the steps."

"Fell?" Senara glared up at Elizabeth. "I was pushed."

"Nonsense. Who would push you?"

No one had been close to the steps. The upstairs footman had been called to the other end of the corridor and hadn't been close enough to be positive no one was there. "But I don't think 'twas so. There weren't nobody at my end of the hall either. Quiet as a tomb it were."

Senara continued to insist she was pushed until the apothecary arrived, assured everyone Senara hadn't suffered anything time wouldn't heal, and fell asleep under his latest tincture.

Elizabeth and Grandmama returned to the garden parlor and their needlework. "Do you think she was pushed?" Elizabeth asked.

"No." Grandmama shook her head. "She most likely fell and didn't want to admit it."

"It's very odd."

But then, Senara was odd. Her behavior had been odd all their lives, full of histrionics and tantrums. But claiming an assault when she had merely been clumsy was another matter.

Seated before the fire, her head bent over snarled threads, Elizabeth tried to think why anyone would want to push Senara. She might be annoying, but she was harmless.

"Why would she invent the notion of someone pushing her?" Elizabeth mused aloud. "But the idea of someone pushing her is just as absurd. Perhaps someone dripped rainwater onto the step and she slipped and struck her back on the railing. And speaking of rain, do you think it will keep any callers away, or should I change my gown?"

"No need." Grandmama studied a length of creamy ribbon from her workbasket. "I doubt anyone will come in this deluge."

❦

But in the middle of the afternoon, Penvenan arrived with Rowan Curnow. Rain poured from their hat brims and off the capes of their greatcoats. She had seen the former day before. Elizabeth hadn't seen the latter since Saturday, and her heart stuttered to see him looking so well.

"Gentlemen, do give your coats to the footman and come sit

by the fire." Grandmama invited them into the parlor. "I'll order hot coffee and pastries."

With a flounce, Senara snatched up the novel Miss Pross had been reading and retreated to a corner to peruse on her own. Miss Pross followed with the knitting.

Both men looked at Elizabeth where she stood on the hearth rug, her hands full of snarled thread.

"We are intruding on a lovely domestic scene." Penvenan strode forward to take her hand.

Elizabeth dropped the thread to take the fingers in their cold leather glove. "It's a productive way to while away the rain."

Rowan sauntered forward and retrieved the dropped threads. "No *tabula rosa*?"

Elizabeth's lips twitched at the reference to John Locke's philosophy on education and the blank mind of the child. When he straightened and his blue gaze touched her eyes, then her lips, her mind became a *tabula rosa*.

"Your silk, Miss Trelawny." He lifted her hand and laid the floss onto her palm. He had taken the time to remove his gloves, and his hands were warm.

She closed her fingers around the tangled threads and felt the edge of yet another note tucked amongst them. "Thank you." She managed the proper response, though she wanted to shove the note down his throat and cry, "Stop this. I will not meet you."

"Do make yourselves comfortable, gentlemen," Grandmama was saying. "Mr. Curnow, feel free to pull that chair closer to the fire."

"Thank you, ma'am, but I am off to talk with Sir Petrok about a mine matter." He bowed to Grandmama, nodded to the two ladies in the corner, and departed.

All too conscious of the note in her hand, Elizabeth started to draw the extra chair forward. Penvenan waved her back. "If you were more comfortable on the hearth rug, return to your work. You looked charming there."

Silk threads scattered across her skirt and her hair hung in a tail down her back, but she accepted the compliment and returned to her position on the hearth rug. "You needn't have come out in the rain, my lord." Perhaps not the most gracious way to begin a dialogue.

"I'd had enough of account books that don't add up." He lowered his voice. "My cousin was not the best at keeping an accounting of expenses and income."

"My brother was quite good at his arithmetic," Senara called from the corner. "He simply refused to put on paper where much of his income came from."

If only his secretary would stop putting things on paper, Elizabeth thought.

"Another difficulty. But estate business is dull. Tell me, Miss Trelawny, what is your favorite country activity besides riding?"

"Swimming. Fishing. Playing royal tennis or cricket." She may as well be honest straight off.

Penvenan cleared his throat. "Not picnicking or being rowed on a lake?"

"We live on the sea. Rowing isn't practical. Sailing is fine, but only if I can handle the tiller."

Grandmama cleared her throat, warning Elizabeth she was going too far, even if she spoke the truth.

"At least I did when I was here as a girl. I didn't enjoy vigorous activity in London."

Unless she managed to sneak out of the house for an early morning gallop in the park, as she had sneaked out of the house to gallop with Rowan.

If the note was another invitation to ride, she might find it difficult to resist.

"Maybe we can go sailing when the weather is fine," Penvenan suggested. "I haven't played royal tennis for many years. Would you be willing to teach me?" He smiled, and her heart softened a little.

He had a nice smile, rather gentle, and his eyes held a wistfulness. Perhaps he was lonely.

"I can try," she agreed. By her agreement to meet with Lord Penvenan the next day, she did not agree to the note's request to meet Rowan.

❧

The next day, as sunny and clear as the previous day had been dark and gloomy, but with the road too muddy for travel, she donned a gown that came only to the middle of her calves, with a pair of Drake's pantaloons beneath, and took Penvenan onto the court Grandpapa had built a decade earlier. They never played a game. Elizabeth spent a quarter hour teaching him how to serve, then another quarter hour showing him how to hold the racket. When he didn't manage to strike a single ball she lobbed to him, she suggested they go inside for lemonade.

Rowan, no doubt, could play. Or perhaps not. Workingmen didn't have time to learn games requiring special courts. If he were to court her, they would have just as little in common ground as did she and Penvenan, perhaps less.

❧

But how she and Rowan could have less in common than herself and his lordship Elizabeth didn't know. Penvenan was twice her age.

When they attended a dinner party at the Pascoes' estate

the following Friday evening, he gathered in the library with the older men, while Elizabeth found herself in her usual abandoned position against the wall. The other young people danced.

Senara, not dancing due to her mourning, sat beside Elizabeth, frowning at the frolic. "All these girls act like Morwenna always did."

"They are shocking flirts."

One young woman clung to a youth's lapels as Morwenna had clung to Rowan's. Elizabeth shifted on her spindly chair and switched her gaze to the left, then right of the too-friendly couple.

"A pity your beau has neglected you," Senara said. "Not very good of him, is it?"

Elizabeth said nothing.

"You don't seem distressed over it, though," Senara continued. "Do you not care for him?"

"I like him well enough."

"Well enough to marry?"

"It's early yet, but it might be worth it. If I can't inherit without marrying Lord Penvenan, since that seems to be what the grandparents think I need, then I expect I'll do so."

"You cannot inherit with him. He'll get it all." Senara curled her short upper lip.

"That is the rub of it, isn't it?"

"But you'll do anything to make your grandparents happy."

"I expect they want the alliance with Penmara land. I was supposed to marry Conan, apparently."

Senara pressed her lips together and said nothing.

Elizabeth made her way to Grandmama, pleaded a headache, and asked if they could leave. She tried to think of a way to ask the grandparents how she could face a future of being seated with the women who were already grandmothers while her husband talked about interesting things with the older men. But she could say nothing in front of Senara, and when Penvenan called to take her driving the next day, the grandparents looked so happy, she couldn't disappoint them.

She always hated disappointing them. All her life they had sheltered her, except when they sent her to London. The grandparents had given her a happy childhood, and now they had kept her from her parents' machinations with Romsford.

Yet was not propelling her into Penvenan's arms little different from her parents' attempts to force her into those of the marquess? The price she paid to have her grandparents' love and approval. That was the difference with her parents—the grandparents loved her when she was obedient. Even when she had done everything they asked, her parents merely asked for more.

Heart too frozen to ache, Elizabeth sat straight backed and stony faced in the pew on Sunday, her first service to attend since returning to Cornwall. She kept her gaze fixed on the vicar, on the cross, on the window over the Penvenan pew, its stained-glass dull with the mist behind. She looked anywhere so as not to look at that pew's occupants. Rowan still wanted to talk to her, his attempts to catch her eye said, and the smile Penvenan bestowed on her reflected a gleam in his dark eyes, rather self-satisfied.

Because he had gotten into the habit of taking her arm anytime he saw her, a proprietary hold, Elizabeth slipped outside too quickly for him to have gotten away from those who wished to pay homage to the new lord of Penmara, and headed up the quiet, mist-shrouded lane from the village to Bastion Point. Despite her efforts to escape, however, footfalls hastened up behind her. Apparently his lordship had caught up with her.

A hand touched her arm. "Elys."

She jumped. "Rowan. I mean, Mr. Curnow, what are you doing chasing after me?"

"I need to talk to you about Morwenna." He tucked his arm

through hers, and instant warmth seeped through her. "Or simply talk to you."

"If you wish to carry on with my cousin in her current condition, it is none of my concern." She drew away, and the chill of the day bled through her veins. "Perhaps Grandpapa will approve and turn over her dowry in exchange for a wedding."

"I have no interest in your cousin other than her safety."

"Ha."

"Please, Elys, she needs your help."

"What she needs is morals." She increased her pace to reach the safety of Bastion Point all the sooner.

He kept up with her without effort. "And you are so righteous selling yourself for a title and more land?"

She staggered as though he'd struck her. Her soft leather shoe slid over loose pebbles wet with the fog, and she dropped to one knee. "How. Dare. You."

"I dare because it's true. And it's a waste." He grasped her hands and lifted her to her feet. "Are you all right?"

Her knee throbbed. Her heart felt as though it would explode out of her chest. She couldn't speak for a lump forming in her throat.

Behind her, voices drifted through the mist.

"Penvenan is coming. We don't have much time. Have you talked to your grandfather?"

Elizabeth swallowed. "I have. He cannot risk her ruining my reputation with her presence." She wrenched her hands free and stepped back.

This time her foot met empty space.

"The ditch." Rowan caught her upper arms. "You need a keeper. Don't you think before you—"

"Rowan, let her go." Penvenan's shout rang through the air. Her grandparents and Senara were close behind.

Rowan drew her closer to him, onto solid ground. "Take better care of yourself."

"By staying away from you."

And from a sudden impulse to throw herself against his chest and cling to him, feel the tenderness of his hands on her face, his lips on hers, a moment of feeling cherished.

"Rowan." Penvenan plunged out of the fog and slammed a fist into Rowan's shoulder, shoving him back. "I told you to get away from her."

A white line formed around Rowan's lips, and lightning flashed through his blue eyes. He clenched his fists.

Elizabeth gasped. Surely he wouldn't strike Penvenan, though she wouldn't blame him. Penvenan had struck him an unnecessary blow.

Rowan turned away. "I beg your pardon, Miss Trelawny." And he walked away, vanishing into the misty shadows beneath the trees. Cowardice or respect. Or simply no desire to lose his position?

"Are you all right, my dear?" Penvenan's arm slid around her waist.

"I slipped and he caught me is all," Elizabeth offered as an explanation.

"Your dress is torn."

She glanced down. So it was, and her knee throbbed beneath a warm trickle of blood. "Clumsy of me," she muttered.

"Let me help you home." He kept his arm around her so firmly she couldn't break away without another fiasco. She welcomed it, though, as she hobbled the rest of the way to Bastion Point. But where Rowan's merest touch left her aching for more, Penvenan's near embrace left nothing in its wake. Not an auspicious way to feel about the man courting her. More than an inauspicious way to feel about the man he employed.

With the excuse of changing her gown and tending to her scrape, she abandoned his lordship to the grandparents and went to her chamber for Miss Pross's nursing.

Senara followed. "I thought they were going to resort to fisticuffs over you." She perched on the edge of the bed and bounced. "Would you have enjoyed that, having two men fighting over you?"

"Certainly not. The entire incident was unnecessary."

Senara's eyes gleamed. "And was it unnecessary to have his lordship's arm around you all that way?"

Elizabeth winced as Miss Pross picked gravel from her knee. "No, but neither was making a scene to get him to take it away."

"He certainly looked happy about it," Senara said.

"I'm not, and think I should send him packing for such familiarity."

Miss Pross and Senara stared at her.

"Truly?" Senara's eyes, dark and thick-lashed like Elizabeth's cousin's, widened. "But will that not make your grandparents unhappy?"

"Yes." Elizabeth sighed. "So I likely won't."

Not yet. Not until she found a truly good reason to convince the grandparents he wasn't suitable. That momentary flash of temper wasn't enough. They would claim he had been provoked.

He had been—more than he knew.

Her knee bandaged, Elizabeth stepped behind the dressing screen to don a fresh gown. "Senara, will you go down and tell the grandparents and his lordship I'll be along straightaway?"

"Of course." Senara departed.

Miss Pross began to unhook the soiled dress. "What's troubling you, child?"

"Noth—" Elizabeth took a deep breath. "I don't think I can

continue the courtship, not even to please the grandparents. But what if I tell them so and they send me back to London?"

"My dear, you are old enough to go where you will. It might not be proper, but if you're unhappy with the gentleman, you shouldn't keep making a pretense."

"I don't want to go anywhere else. This is the only place I've ever been happy." She faced her companion turned lady's maid. "I want that again."

"You won't find it in stone and mortar."

"Yes, yes, I know. I hear the sermons. I'll only be happy when I turn my life over to the Lord. Sounds rather like turning my inheritance over to a husband. And that won't please me. But then, without the husband, I may not get the inheritance."

Unless she found a way to persuade the grandparents she had found a treasure in life that transcended being a man's chattel.

"Enough talk. I'd best get downstairs."

Yet when she wore a fresh gown and Miss Pross had made repairs to her coiffeur, Elizabeth didn't go downstairs to the parlor, where the drapes would be drawn against the cold and damp and everyone would have their chairs close around the fire. She needed what Bastion Point had always given her—fresh air and freedom, room to take a deep breath and feel the sea air on her face.

She slipped through a side door and into the garden. The fog lay so thickly over the ground she doubted anyone could see her from the house. Water dripped from tree branches and trellises in a rhythmic *plop, plop, plop*. Her kid slippers made no sound on the gravel path. When she opened the garden door to the cliff, even the sea sounded distant, its roar muted beneath the blanket of water. But she tasted salt spray on her lips and the tang of the water in her nostrils. The cold dampness awakened something deep inside her, a stirring need to run and shout and dive into the flattened waves.

For a moment, she paused at the head of the path. It would be treacherously wet. No matter, she had traversed it in the dark. She could traverse it in the fog.

She took two steps onto the path. Stones clattered away from her feet. She hugged the wall of rock from which the path had been carved and continued with care. One step. Two. Three.

Something crunched behind her like another footfall.

She paused. "Is anyone there?"

No one responded. The roar of the sea lured her on. One step. Two—

Something struck her right shoulder, throwing her forward. She screamed and flailed at the wall, scrabbling for a handhold. Her left hand met smooth, wet rock. Her right grasped empty air. Loose, damp stones slid from beneath her thin soles, and she began to fall, sliding faster and faster, rolling and tumbling and plunging over the edge of the path toward the sea.

CHAPTER 15

ROWAN HEARD THE SCREAM. IT TRAVELED THROUGH the fog like current through an electricity machine. On his way to see Morwenna when no one could see him do so through the fog, he halted and turned his head toward the cry.

The sea. The scream had come from the direction of the sea, the cliffs, Bastion Point.

He started to run. Tendrils of mist wrapped around him like vaporous vines thick and blinding. He waved the water from his face, trying to see through the gloom.

The sea. A female's cry had come from the sea. A female who loved the sea enough to walk the cliffs in the fog.

"Elizabeth."

He prayed for another scream to guide him. He heard nothing but the muted rumble of the surf warning him to slow his pace so he didn't miss the path and topple over the edge.

The edge, a sixty-foot drop to sand at low tide and pounding surf at high. Which would this be? He calculated. High, or nearly so. Incoming waves to pound a body against the rocky cliff, if someone had lost her footing and fallen. Other alternatives were as bad—or worse. Lawless men operated in darkness and in fog. He'd heard of wreckers luring ships onto the rocks to have their cargos picked clean and passengers and crew murdered.

He paused altogether and peered through the fog in search

of lights where none should shine. Briny mist stung his eyes, and another cry, as faint and weak as that of a distant gull, teased his ears.

He commenced running again, heedless of the proximity of the cliff. The Bastion Point garden wall loomed up before him as welcome as a beacon. He could find the cliff path from there, winding and steep, treacherous on a fine day, deadly now.

No, not deadly, merely hazardous to a body who knew the way. One body, one lady, knew the way well.

He descended the path as swiftly as he dared. Halfway down, he began to call her name.

No one responded. Below him, the sea rumbled and splashed with the incoming tide. It surged up the path, retreated, swelled higher.

Rowan paused at the edge of the surf, peering through the fog. "Elizabeth, are you there?"

Broken, helpless, weighed down by petticoats and gown.

He plunged into freezing water that swelled to mid-thigh. "Elys? Are you—"

A flash of white caught the corner of his eye. He turned, pressing against the cliff to keep his balance in the heaving sea. Another flash of white, a hand, an arm ghostly pale against the water.

He dove for it, caught the hand, caught a fistful of long hair, dragged her forward, lifted her face from the surf.

She spluttered and choked and emitted a high, thin shriek. Her arm resisted his hold. The other hand came up. Her hand, wet and slippery in a kid glove, wrenched from his grasp.

He held on to her hair. "Stop struggling. I've got you."

Grasping the frill around the neck of her dress with one hand and holding her head up with the other, he dragged her toward the path, digging his heels into the sand to keep his footing against the waves buffeting his legs. In seconds, his hands and feet went numb from the cold. In moments that felt like an hour, he reached the path and lifted her above the waterline.

"Stay there." He rested one hand in the center of her back. "I've got you."

She lay coughing and choking and scrabbling at the stony ground. Her hair tumbled around her like seaweed. Her dress clung to her body and legs in sodden folds that revealed far too much smooth, white skin. Both shoes and one stocking were completely gone. The more she struggled, the more she revealed— such as a livid mark through the torn shoulder of her gown and a growing bruise on her thigh.

He averted his eyes and laid his cheek against hers. "Calm yourself. If you keep struggling, you'll come right back into the water, and I need to let go of you long enough to get out myself. Understand?"

She nodded, coughed up a quantity of water, then dropped her face onto her hands still clad in once elegant kid gloves. Shudders ran through her in waves, but whether she wept or merely shook from cold wasn't obvious.

What mattered at the moment was her lying still enough for him to release her and haul himself onto the path. For a few minutes, he sat with his back to the cliff and his legs still buffeted by water. He couldn't move for the numbness in his limbs, but if he didn't, they would catch a chill or lose consciousness and slip back into the water.

"Must. Get. Up." He rolled to his hands and knees. With the aid of handholds in the rock, he hauled himself to his feet. "Can you walk, Elys?"

"I think . . ." She too rose on hands and knees, but swayed so alarmingly, he grasped her around the waist and lifted her himself.

"I'll carry you."

"You cannot. I—" She bent and coughed up more water, and this time the sound she made afterward was definitely a sob.

"It's all right." He held her against him, her back against his chest, his arms around her waist. "You picked a stupid time to go swimming, but you're not the first person to do so."

This time the snort she made was definitely an attempt at a laugh.

"Good girl." He freed one hand to smooth her hair away from her face and over her shoulders, exposing the tear in her gown and the beginnings of a bruise.

"You banged yourself up good when you fell. Do you think anything's broken?"

She shook her head. "Just . . . hurts."

"These stones are going to hurt worse. I am going to carry you."

"No, you cannot. I can walk."

"If you insist. Let's get to a fire."

He kept his hands on her waist, supporting her as she took her first step. With each footfall up the path, she winced, possibly from that bruise he mustn't think about having seen, possibly from the stones beneath her bare feet. Likely from both. When they reached the top of the cliff, he didn't ask any more questions; he picked her up and cradled her in his arms.

"You cannot. I'm even heavier from the water."

She was, and his boots felt like anchors on his feet, but he couldn't bear for her to feel more pain.

"It's not far to the house." Though he could scarcely see it through the fog. "I'll be happier with you safely away from the cliff."

"Me too." She wrapped one arm around his neck and laid her head on his shoulder. "So tired."

"It's the cold. We'll get you warm soon." He held her as close as he could, though his body held little heat to warm her. "Whatever possessed you to go walking on the cliff in a fog?"

"I needed to think." She tugged at his hair. "You were out in it too."

"And a good thing for you I was, and was wise enough to not risk falling off the edge of the world."

She turned her face away from him, then took a deep breath that rattled just a little but pressed her against him in a way sure to warm him in a manner he didn't need or want under the circumstances. "Rowan." She coughed and clung to his lapel with her other hand. "Rowan, I didn't fall. I was pushed."

He staggered, nearly dropped her. "How do you know?"

A stupid question if ever he heard one.

The look of disgust she flashed him said as much. "Something struck my shoulder."

"The right one."

"Yes, how do you— Oh, my gown is torn there."

"You have a bruise forming. But it could have been a falling rock."

"And struck my right shoulder and not my left or my head?"

"Right. Not likely." Now his insides felt as though someone had replaced them with an anchor. He stopped walking. "What happened? Tell me everything you remember."

"I can't now. They'll miss me. But you should know that Senara fell down the stairs a few days ago and says she was pushed too."

"Will you talk to me at some point for the sake of your beautiful skin?"

Of which he'd seen far too much that day for his comfort.

"Perhaps . . . Perhaps now I should. I didn't think—"

"When?" he asked.

"We go to Truro a week from tomorrow. Grandpapa has a meeting with his solicitors and I'll be shopping. I'll arrange something and let you know if you can manage to be there."

"I'll be there. With Miss Penvenan claiming she was pushed down the steps, and now this with you . . . Yes, I must talk to you." He brushed his lips across her brow, then carried her up the front steps of the house.

The front door opened before they reached it. "Miss Trelawny? Whatever happened?"

The butler's exclamation brought a half dozen people crowding into the entryway where Rowan stood holding Elizabeth, both of them dripping half the Irish Sea onto the rug.

"What's happened to my granddaughter?" Sir Petrok demanded.

"What are you doing with Miss Trelawny?" Penvenan nearly bellowed.

Lady Trelawny, Senara, and Miss Pross swarmed around them exclaiming, touching Elizabeth's face, issuing orders of a practical nature. In moments, two footmen were bearing Elizabeth upstairs, Miss Pross bustling ahead and the other ladies trailing behind, Lady Trelawny still issuing orders, the last one directed for him. "Petrok, take that young man into the parlor and get him dried off."

Sir Petrok motioned for Rowan to precede him into a parlor with a blazing, crackling fire, but Rowan hesitated. "I'll ruin anything I go near, sir."

"I think you should return to Penmara," Penvenan said. "Immediately."

"I'd like an explanation of why he and my granddaughter look like they've been swimming." Sir Petrok's eyes were hard. "We'll get you a blanket. Teague?"

The butler spoke to a footman, who hastened down a corridor

behind the staircase. In moments, the servant reappeared with an armful of blankets. "And if Mr. Curnow will remove his boots, no harm will come to the furnishings or carpet," the butler said.

Rowan leaned against the front door to remove the ruined footwear. As he swathed himself in the warmth of the blankets and headed into the parlor, two maids with mops and buckets appeared to clean up the floor.

So much for servants having Sunday afternoon off. Only, apparently, when the "family" didn't need them.

"Were you meeting her in secret?" Penvenan attacked the moment the door closed. "How did you lure her onto the cliff, and why—"

"Enough, sir." Rowan crouched before the fire, not sure he would ever feel warm again, and tried to be firm yet respectful to a man he knew he was supposed to show respect to but whom he found difficult to serve, let alone honor. "I don't know why she was on the cliff. I was out walking—"

"In the mist?" Sir Petrok asked.

"Yes, sir. I have many concerns with the new moon in a few days' time."

"Don't we all." Sir Petrok nodded. "Continue."

"I heard a scream. You know how sound travels in a fog. So I went to investigate and found Miss Trelawny in the water."

"So you saved her life." Sir Petrok sank onto a chair and picked up a teacup. His hand shook, and he set it down. "How can I thank you?"

"No thanks are necessary, sir. I was honored to be of service."

Penvenan opened his mouth, then snapped it shut and cast Rowan a glare.

Rowan didn't care. She had agreed to talk to him, and he'd gotten to hold her.

"Maybe," he said, "while the ladies aren't present, we should talk about what we will do if the smugglers decide to operate during this new moon."

"I doubt they will," Sir Petrok said. "After last month, they'll want to lie low. Nonetheless, we'll have riding officers spread out along the cliff and beaches and a few tucked inside the caves. If anyone tries to land cargo, they'll get an unwelcome surprise."

Rowan fixed his gaze on Penvenan. "Even so, sir, we should keep the ladies close to home."

And he would guard Morwenna himself, regardless of the consequences.

❧

On the twenty-third of May, the day after the new moon, he faced those consequences in the form of Penvenan pacing back and forth across the stable yard, a white line around his lips and a vein pulsing at one temple. He turned on Rowan the instant he came within earshot. "Where have you been all night?"

"Playing guard dog." Rowan kept his tone calm, neutral.

"I don't believe you were merely guarding." Penvenan smacked his riding crop against his gloved palm.

Rowan gave the implement a narrow-eyed glare. "Do you intend to use that on me, sir?"

"Maybe if I had a dozen years ago, you'd have turned out better."

Rowan's face froze to mask the pain of those words. Some men would be proud of how he had turned out. Austell Penvenan thought Rowan lacked in every aspect because he chose conscience over an unjust law.

He managed a stiff smile now. "I admire your forbearance, sir, though your tongue-lashings have stung quite enough."

"If you've been with a female, I will take this crop to you—or a horse whip." He smacked the crop against the leather again for emphasis.

Rowan sighed. "Do you not yet believe that the biblical principles by which I live my life keep me from that kind of behavior? I would no more spend the night with a female not my wife than I would steal from your strongbox, and you've trusted me with a key to that for four years." He turned toward the house. "Now may I go get some breakfast, then rest for an hour or two? I have been keeping watch over Miss Morwenna Trelawny."

As her dogs were no good if they didn't bark at people they knew.

Which was no help. They might know everyone in the parish.

"Why are you watching over her?" Penvenan took a step toward him.

Rowan shrugged as though his night's vigil meant little instead of the significance he had worked out after Elizabeth told him she'd been pushed off the cliff path. "I made a promise to Conan, and the smugglers might have taken out revenge on her with their night's work interrupted."

"Huh. She was likely involved with them up to her pretty eyes."

"An interesting theory I hadn't considered." Even more likely now that he added his other suppositions to it.

He started for the house. "I'll see that the repairs on the roof are well underway today, sir. Are you riding with Miss Trelawny today?"

"On my own. Miss Trelawny is laid up from that tumble she took, silly chit."

Rowan halted but kept his face turned away. "Is she injured badly?"

"She has a mild chill and enough bruises to make her stiff. Why she had to go walking on the cliff . . ." He sighed, and even that held affection.

Rowan's desire for breakfast vanished. "Walking on the cliff alone was a foolish thing to do. I expect . . ."

She was running away from the confines of her life.

"Enjoy your ride, sir, and have a care." He faced Penvenan. "Do you wish for me to come with you?"

"I do not need a minder. But thank you."

"That dead bird was not a very subtle warning. They want Penmara empty."

Penvenan shrugged off the idea. "Will you be going to that horse fair?"

"It's next week."

"Good. I don't like to continue borrowing mounts from the Trelawnys." With a nod, Penvenan headed in the opposite direction.

Rowan returned to the house head down, hands clasped behind his back. He and Penvenan had parted on what, for them, were cordial terms. Maybe Penvenan had been angry because he was worried about Rowan's welfare. He did upon occasion consider that Rowan got himself into dangerous situations. If only Penvenan would admit that he'd gotten himself into one as well. Unfortunately, he was too much enjoying his new role as lord of the manor—and Elizabeth's approved suitor—to heed any warnings.

Rowan eschewed breakfast as well as a rest, and climbed onto the roof to slam nails through shingles and into roof beams himself.

CHAPTER 16

A WEEK'S CONFINEMENT IN HER BEDCHAMBER WAS surely enough to drive anyone to madness. By Friday, she had taken to asking everyone to leave her chamber so she didn't have to play one more game or listen to another sermon or novel read to her. She read the first volume of the family chronicle, but learned nothing of treasure other than the pirate gold accumulated by her ancestress. That, Elizabeth now knew, was not what Grandpapa meant. That realization left her frustrated and hollow, restless and yearning for air.

By Sunday, though walking down steps proved painful, she looked forward to services for something new in her narrow existence. But during breakfast, Senara slipped into another episode of chills and shivering, not surprising after her recent ordeal. She asked Elizabeth to stay home with her. Elizabeth acquiesced, though she had been looking forward to the short walk to the village and seeing people.

"Miss Pross will stay with you," Grandmama said. "Elizabeth needs to go with us."

"Bu-but Miss Pros-ss is a s-servant," Senara protested between chattering teeth.

Grandmama proved adamant and Senara too unwell to object without getting from bed and going to church.

"I don't like these spells." Grandmama's brow furrowed as

she and Elizabeth descended to the front hall. "She has always been a robust girl."

Elizabeth inspected the angle of her hat in a mirror over the hall table. "The apothecary believed it is an upset of her mind because of losing her brother so awfully. It's been little more than a month now, not time enough to heal from that kind of a loss. Add the accident to that, and it's surprising she hasn't gotten completely crazed. Is this too flirtatious an angle for church?"

A feather curved over the brim and kissed her cheek.

"I think it charming." Grandmama narrowed her eyes and smiled. "Wanting to look your best for a certain gentleman?"

Elizabeth turned from the mirror. "I doubt any gentleman cares about the angle of my hat when he can see the weight of my purse."

"Elizabeth, you know that isn't true." Grandpapa entered the hall and they headed for the village, servants trailing behind. "Granted, you have had a considerable number of fortune hunters sniffing around you, but Penvenan is not the same as the Romsfords of the world."

"My parents declare Romsford was never interested in my dowry." Elizabeth tucked her hand into the crook of his elbow. "Do you know differently?"

"He has a sizable fortune, yes, but he wants land in Cornwall. I gather he thought you would help him gain that."

"However do you know that, Petrok?" Grandmama asked from his other side.

"He's been asking about available land in Truro these past weeks."

Elizabeth skidded to a halt. "He's still there?"

"Yes, oddly enough."

The idea of going to Truro no longer pleased Elizabeth. Yet she must see Rowan. He believed her when she said someone had pushed her. The instant she told him she'd been pushed, his sea-blue eyes had brightened like someone drawing a curtain back from a sunny window. He knew something he wanted to tell her. He—

He had kissed her brow.

She shouldn't see him. She was being courted by another man, the man who employed him. And she wouldn't do so if she didn't need to know why someone had pushed her off the cliff path.

Not that she hadn't tried to tell Grandpapa. He had smiled and shaken his head. "Your death would gain no one anything." He patted her hand. "You just rest and think twice about walking on the path in the mist next time."

She needed to go to town. But the thought of coming face-to-face with the marquess chilled her. If he wanted land in Cornwall, and she stood to inherit . . .

No need to worry. Grandpapa would keep her safe. The grandparents and the men from Penmara would protect her. The latter stood on the porch of the church side by side, but not looking at one another. They both smiled and bowed to the Trelawny party, and Lord Penvenan offered Elizabeth his arm.

"So good to see you up and about, my dear. Feeling well enough to go to Truro tomorrow?"

"I think I'll go mad if I do not." She met Rowan's gaze past Penvenan's shoulder.

He inclined his head, then moved before them to open the door to the Trelawny pew. As she passed him to slip inside, he released the door, and it jostled her arm, knocking her Bible out of her hand.

"I beg your pardon." He bent and retrieved the book, then returned it to her. "No harm done."

"Clumsy of you, Rowan." Penvenan glared at him.

Rowan smiled and crossed to the Penmara pew.

"I apologize for my . . . *employé*," Penvenan said to Elizabeth. "Shall I accompany you home from service?"

"If you like." Elizabeth nodded to him, then slipped into the pew. Beneath the wall surrounding the seat, she opened her Bible and looked at the pages where a folded scrap of paper created a bulge that hadn't been there earlier.

The Red Lion. One of the clock. Urgent. Go nowhere alone.

No Elys, no ornate *R*, just those cryptic words scrawled with a graphite pencil.

How he expected her to meet him at a public inn on a Monday afternoon she knew not, yet she would manage somehow. That he took her claim of being pushed seriously left her shaken and cold, as though she were about to start shivering like Senara.

She grasped her Bible as though it were what held her steady and in place. Not quite the "holding on to the Word of God" she had heard some religious people advocate, yet it helped to have something solid to wrap her fingers around, the leather of the cover supple in her hands, warming through her gloves. She never let go of the Bible throughout the service, through liturgy and prayers, singing of Psalms, and the sermon.

"In the eighth chapter of the book of Romans," Mr. Kitto spoke from the pulpit in his clear yet gentle voice, "we are told that God commends his love for us, for while we were yet sinners Christ died for us. And earlier, in the fifth chapter, we are reminded that nothing can separate us from the love of God. Yes, my children, I believe that God loves us, each and every one of us, without reservation and without prompting from us . . ."

Elizabeth shifted to avoid placing weight on her still-tender left leg. She wanted to walk, run, ride like the wind, anything to blow away the restlessness creeping through her.

"God loves us unconditionally," Kitto was saying.

Not likely. She had nothing to offer him. As a child she thought she did, and she knew God loved children. As a young woman she felt as though she trod the ballrooms and assembly rooms with less direction than someone blindfolded in an old mine, and she stopped believing in the security of a God who loved her regardless of what she had to offer. He wanted her life, after all. Since she was unwilling to give it to him, then God wanted nothing to do with her, as her parents wanted nothing to do with her now that she had refused to do their bidding. And now her grandparents wanted her to consider an alliance with Penvenan. More acceptable than Romsford, but disregarding her wishes. *I can't accept you, Lord, for I do not understand unconditional love.*

The service ended with Elizabeth none the wiser, no less restless, no less in need of seeking something to fill the hollowness invading her heart. With a smile that felt false on her lips, she greeted Lord Penvenan and allowed him to walk her back to Bastion Point.

He stayed for the cold dinner. The Kittos joined them. Miss Pross descended to say Senara was sleeping, but seemed to be having disturbed dreams.

"She whimpers in her sleep like a puppy." Miss Pross's little rosebud of a mouth pursed, and she shook her head. "And she's been off sweets for weeks. I believe she's gotten thinner."

"We should find her a husband when her mourning is passed," Mrs. Kitto declared. "She needs a home and a family of her own."

Elizabeth refrained from asking who in Cornwall would

marry Senara Penvenan with no dowry, unless her cousin would provide one for her.

Bold as doing so was, Elizabeth asked Lord Penvenan about a dowry for Senara on the way to Truro the next day. With the Trelawny carriage full, he had taken her up in his chaise, so they could talk without fear of Senara overhearing.

"That is one matter of business I intend to take care of today with the solicitors. She cannot return to Penmara until I wed." He shot Elizabeth a sidelong glance she chose to ignore. "Yet I cannot expect your grandparents to take care of her until then either. Now, what do you plan to do with your day in the city?"

"Truro," she said with more than a little asperity, "is not a city. It is a provincial town that offers little more than a few inns and shops and the stamping of tin for sale."

"Pardon me?" Penvenan laughed at her. "I forget you have spent much of your life in London. Then what do you do in a town with so little to offer?"

What would he do if she told him she intended to make an assignation with his secretary? Most likely send Rowan packing back to Penmara. At present, he rode behind the carriages like one of the outriders. Somehow, in three hours, she must meet him.

The rendezvous appeared impossible. The carriages set the ladies down amidst the shops and drove off for the men to conduct their business. With Senara trailing behind complaining about how all she could wear was borrowed blacks for the next five months, Elizabeth, Grandmama, and Miss Pross chose ribbons and silk thread for embroidering, linen with a little inexpensive lace for maid's caps, and some spangles Elizabeth wanted to sew onto the gown she still found excessively dull even with the embroidery she had added to the hem.

She paused at the window of one shop that, quite daringly, displayed bathing costumes. Hers was at the house in Brighton awaiting a summer excursion to the seaside town, and she hadn't been able to bring it west with her. "May I buy a new one, Grandmama? I do so miss sea bathing."

"You are too old to cavort about half dressed." Grandmama grasped her arm and dragged Elizabeth away as though she were a child begging for sweets.

Perhaps she could swim in the costume she had worn for tennis.

"I'd think you had enough of being in the sea after your fall last week," Senara said. "Isn't it frightfully cold?"

"Not when one is dressed enough to move one's arms and legs." Elizabeth cast a long glance at the display.

Senara giggled. "Don't you mean undressed enough?"

"Girls." Grandmama's tone scolded as though they were schoolgirls. "We shall stop into the dressmaker's and then go on to have some refreshment."

Elizabeth glanced at a clock placed in the window of a jeweler's shop and saw her opportunity to get away. "May we stop first? I fear my leg is growing a bit stiff."

It was nothing painful enough for her to require a rest at once, but enough that she didn't really fib.

And it worked. Grandmama stopped and frowned at her, her eyes gentle and kind. "I should have thought of that. We'll go back to the inn first. It's right around the corner."

They entered the private parlor, and tea and cakes soon followed. Although she dropped two large lumps of sugar in her tea, Senara only ate two cakes and an almond macaroon. Elizabeth took no sugar and only managed to nibble at a seed cake. For no good reason, a congregation of plovers seemed to have taken up residence in her middle. The closer to one the clock grew, the more the wading birds seemed to splash about and cause more of a disturbance.

She didn't like being deceitful, though now that she sat, it felt so much better than standing about or walking the cobbled streets, so perhaps she was not being too terribly deceitful . . .

"I'd rather stay here than go on to the dressmaker's," she blurted out in a rush.

Three pairs of eyes turned startled glances on her.

Her cheeks grew warm. "I didn't realize my leg would feel so much better sitting still."

"But I need your advice at the dressmaker's," Senara protested.

"Miss Pross and Grandmama can advise you better than I."

Absolute truth. Elizabeth knew nothing of appropriate mourning dress. Providing Senara with a few gowns made for her had been a generous gesture from Penvenan.

"I'm afraid I grow disagreeable at dressmaker shops, and if I'm forced to stand about, I'll be worse." Elizabeth smiled to soften her claim.

"You never grow disagreeable, Miss Trelawny." Miss Pross patted her hand. "But you do look a bit pinched around the eyes. Perhaps this excursion was too much too soon."

"Perhaps it was." Grandmama tapped a forefinger on her chin. "I suppose you may stay here safely if you remain in this room. But will you not grow bored?"

"There are some books here I can read. I'm never bored if I can read a book."

And if Rowan arrived.

At two minutes of one, the other ladies departed. Elizabeth

chose a book on fishing called *The Compleat Angler* and settled to wait for only a few minutes.

A few minutes became ten, then twenty. At the half hour mark, she ventured as far as the top step to see if perhaps Rowan had expected her to wait for him in the open like some shopgirl.

Rowan was nowhere in sight, but his employer was. Right outside the entrance of the inn, Austell Lord Penvenan stood in earnest conversation with the Marquess of Romsford.

CHAPTER 17

ROWAN LEANED AGAINST THE PANELED WALL OF THE inn, arms crossed over his chest, lips flattened against his teeth— teeth he gritted hard enough to grind them down to nubs if Penvenan's conversation continued much longer. More than a half hour had passed since Rowan was supposed to meet Elizabeth. He'd seen her poised at the top of the steps, then whisk out of sight again. He wanted to go after her, but if he did, Penvenan would see him. Romsford would see him. They would end their dialogue, which was a little too enlightening for Rowan.

"Why Cornwall?" Penvenan was asking Romsford. "It's not a particularly hospitable county. Wouldn't Kent or Dorset be more comfortable?"

"Those mines on Penmara land are lucrative." Romsford rubbed his hands together. "If you have no intention of reopening them, then sell them to me so I can."

"I'll open them." Penvenan smiled. "If I get an infusion of guineas to do so. And I should have that infusion before the summer is out."

Romsford snorted. "If you think she'll wed you, you need to think again. She's too cold to be any man's wife. You'd be better off courting the younger one, even if she is used goods."

The men laughed together like comrades, which they could

only be if they had met on Penvenan's previous journeys into Truro. If they had, Penvenan had mentioned none of it to Rowan. But there they were, now striding toward the taproom discussing land and ladies as though both were equal in their ability to bring wealth to a man.

Rowan wanted a bath.

Even if he never persuaded Elizabeth to care for him, for yet one more reason he must stop her from getting entangled with Penvenan. He had collected a whole list of reasons. It should be enough to persuade her.

In the hope he still had a few minutes in which he could talk to her, he left his corner and took the steps two at a time. Without bothering to knock, he opened the door to the first room. It was empty, dark, and cold. Two more doors proved to be locked. But the fourth opened onto a parlor warmed on this sunny but chilly day, to a fire on the hearth and a lady in pale blue standing before it.

She spun on her heel at the opening of the door, then planted her hands on her hips, set her lips into a hard, thin line, and stared at him from beneath lowered lashes.

"Good afternoon, Elys." Rowan closed the door. "Thank you for waiting."

"I had little choice so as not to reveal my presence to Lord Romsford and Lord Penvenan." She had taken on that clipped, London tone.

"I had little choice but to be late."

"I know." For a heartbeat, her shoulders sagged; then she straightened them again and jutted her chin. "What were they about in a comfortable coze like that?"

"The Penmara mines. Romsford wants to buy them."

Elizabeth's eyes widened. "What would he do with those mines? They haven't been productive in a decade or more."

"He says they only want for some investment."

"And he couldn't settle for a coal mine in Durham?" Her jaw worked as though she ground her teeth. "Is that his excuse for still being in Truro?"

"I can't be certain, but it seems so. Penvenan can't sell the mines, you know, because of the entail. But he needs funds to reopen the mines."

Elizabeth's lip curled. "I thought he was wealthy. Is he just another fortune hunter?"

"He's wealthy enough not to be a fortune hunter." Rowan gripped the back of a chair until his knuckles whitened. "But if he wants to be lord of the manor, he needs to rebuild that manor, and that takes a great deal of the ready. Opening mines as well . . ."

Let her draw her own conclusions. He wouldn't tell tales out of school.

Elizabeth's face gave away nothing of possible conclusions as to why Penvenan courted her. Face impassive, she leaned just a little forward. "Why can he not break the entail?"

"One needs three male heirs in direct line to inherit to break an entail. Conan was trying to do that when he invited Penvenan to come to England and help him search for another male heir."

"Does the entail break with only one male heir left?"

"Without three heirs to agree to break the entail it can't be broken until the last one dies."

"And you haven't yet found another one?"

"Not in London, but we're still hunting through the records at Penmara."

"I think I don't like this." Elizabeth walked to a chair as though she intended to sit, but hesitated. "We cannot talk here now. There isn't time. Someone is likely to return, and they mustn't find you here. Are you staying in town with Lord Penvenan?"

"I intended to, as I'm heading to a horse fair near Redruth tomorrow."

"Oh, a horse fair." Her eyes lit "I wish . . ." She turned her back on him. "Can you make an excuse to return to Penmara? I'd rather ride back than make poor old Miss Pross ride on the box with the coachman."

"I'd prefer not to stay here. But can you ride for two hours? Your injuries . . ."

That bruise on her thigh must still pain her some. Remembering it pained him some.

He cleared his mind of the image and swallowed. "I'll find his lordship and tell him I'm returning with your party. I expect he'll understand me preferring to spend the night at Penmara as opposed to here at the inn."

"Thank you." She kept her back to him, but between a coil of shining brown hair and the stiff collar of her spencer, her neck grew fiery pink. "We'll have some refreshment here, then leave around four of the clock. You, um, may join us."

"I will see what my . . . lord says." He bowed, though she couldn't see him, and departed.

He found Penvenan in a chophouse eating roast beef and potatoes with Lord Romsford. A decanter of wine rested on the table between them, and they appeared altogether convivial. They appeared so convivial Rowan stood on the establishment's threshold for several moments gritting his teeth some more and praying.

Lord, I want to serve you, but not with this man. And I want to honor this man you've directed me to serve, but I cannot.

Yet if he dishonored Austell Penvenan, did he not dishonor God's commands?

He took a deep breath and strode through the room to the two older men, paused at the table, and inclined his head, awaiting to be acknowledged.

"What is it, Rowan?" Penvenan's tone held the impatience he had shown Rowan for most of his life.

"I'm returning to Penmara, sir."

Romsford glared at him from his one good eye. "Do I not know you?"

Rowan's hands curled into fists, and he tucked them behind his back. "Yes, sir, I believe you might remember me."

"Of course." Romsford's upper lip curled. "You played fast and loose with my betrothed."

Penvenan scowled at this reference to Elizabeth.

Rowan gave the marquess a steady look. "Begging your pardon, sir, but I have never played fast and loose with any female. It would dishonor them, myself, and, above all, the Lord." Rowan bowed. "Now, if you will excuse me, I have an invitation to accept."

He strode away at the same measured pace at which he had arrived, every second expecting Penvenan to call him back and order him to stay in town or worse—head to Plymouth and the first ship crossing the Atlantic. But the command didn't come, and when he turned to shoulder open the door, the older men had resumed their conversation as though he hadn't interrupted. Snatches drifted through the smoky air, and Rowan paused to listen.

"If you want to do business with me, Romsford," Penvenan was saying, "you will forget you tried to betroth yourself to Miss Trelawny. She's mine."

"Title and lands not enough?" Romsford laughed as though Penvenan had made a great joke. "Don't think I've given up there—the Trelawny heiress, that is. I'd come to think of her as—Your man is still here."

Penvenan shot a glare in Rowan's direction that warned him to leave. *Dismissed like the servant he thinks of you now.* His heart hurt. He had believed he served the Lord then, yet should the aftereffects be so painful if he was right?

Two things salved his wounded spirit—Elizabeth was neither man's and never would be. And he had another chance to see Elizabeth—alone. Rowan climbed the steps to the private parlor and knocked on the door. Voices beyond it halted, then the door opened and Elizabeth herself answered it.

"Thank you for coming, Mr. Curnow."

"Who invited him?" Miss Penvenan demanded.

Elizabeth smiled. "I did. He's going to ride back to Bastion Point with me so Miss Pross can ride in the carriage."

Relief crossed the spinster's face. Senara Penvenan glared, and the grandparents gave Elizabeth identical narrow-eyed looks.

"Come in, Mr. Curnow." Elizabeth stepped back. "We were just having some refreshment. Tea? Or should I send for coffee?"

"Why are you treating him like he's your equal?" Miss Penvenan thrust out her lower lip. "He's a servant and an American."

"He saved my life, Senara. It's the least I can do for him." Elizabeth winked at him. "And send for coffee."

"That alone shows how foreign he is—coffee instead of tea." Miss Penvenan sneered at him.

Rowan smiled and bowed. With Elizabeth being so gracious to him, he could take any number of insults from Senara.

And Elizabeth had learned her graciousness from her grandmother. Lady Trelawny invited him to sit, and Sir Petrok commenced a dialogue about what kind of horses Penvenan should seek at the fair, what to avoid, warnings about seller tricks. Elizabeth joined in, and between the hot coffee and hotter pasties, a Cornish delight worth taking back to America, Rowan's heart lifted.

In another half an hour, after a short verbal tussle between

Elizabeth and her grandparents, Rowan rode beside Elizabeth, him on his own mount, her on the mount of an outrider now perched on the carriage box beside the coachman. The carriage and several more outriders thundered ahead, and a groom followed a discreet distance behind. Other travelers leaving the town edged around the cavalcade—farmers with livestock, several small children in a two-wheeled cart, with older children walking behind and a man guiding the horse. Men of business rode, and a girl with a flock of geese darted back and forth to keep her honking charges from biting passersby or getting themselves crushed under feet or wheels.

Between the tumult and proximity of others, neither Rowan nor Elizabeth spoke for the first quarter of an hour. Gradually, the road out of Truro sorted into lanes leading to villages or up and over the spine of Cornwall to the southern coast. The carriage drew ahead, and the Bastion Point groom Henry, likely with a newly acquired half a crown burning a hole in the pocket of his breeches, fell farther behind.

Elizabeth glanced back. "Bribery again?"

"I prefer to call it a fee for service."

"Why?"

"Because it's more polite."

Elizabeth shook her head. "No, why the discretion? We were merely discussing entails and how Penvenan cannot break the one on Penmara because there aren't three male heirs."

"Not legitimate ones."

Elizabeth arched her brows toward the brim of her hat. "You know of illegitimate Penvenans?"

"Possibly." He drummed his fingers on the pummel and frowned at the rutted track that called itself a road. "I should have worked this out sooner, but when she kept refusing to say anything, it made no sense to me. But after your fall . . ."

Elizabeth was staring at him as though he'd lost his reason.

He grinned. "I'm rambling because this is difficult to even speculate over, let alone tell you."

"Would you like to write it down?" Elizabeth's eyes twinkled beneath the shadow of her hat brim. "I believe I have a pencil and paper in my reticule."

Rowan avoided her eyes and concentrated on her hat ribbons, icy blue satin tied in a bow beneath her left ear, the knot resting on the soft skin he would rather enjoy having the privilege of kissing.

He wrenched his gaze away from her altogether. "I think Conan was the father of Miss Morwenna's baby."

"What. Did. You. Say?" She reined in and turned sideways to face him. "Morwenna and . . . Conan in . . . um . . . ?" Her color heightened.

Henry nudged his horse closer, his face registering concern.

"We have an audience," Rowan murmured.

Elizabeth inclined her head and snapped her reins to get her gelding going again. "How did you fix on such a notion?"

"Why else would anyone threaten her but if she were connected to Penmara in some way?" Rowan waved Henry back and edged his mount closer to Elizabeth's. "Conan wanted away from the smugglers. If he was trying to stop them from using his beach, and if even one of them suspected more than friendship . . . If Conan and Morwenna were closer than they should be, and the gang somehow knew that, they might be inclined to threaten her and the baby."

Elizabeth shook her head once, then again. "But he's dead now. Why would the threats continue?"

"To warn the other Penvenans not to interfere with them using their beach and caves. Senara is tucked behind the Bastion Point walls, and Austell Penvenan knows to watch his back."

Rowan took a deep breath. "Which is where you come in."

Her head snapped back, and she stared at him with wide eyes and pupils huge and dark. "Lord Penvenan courting me makes me someone they can use to threaten him. He leaves them alone, or I get . . . hurt."

"It's the only idea I've come up with so far as to why anyone would wish to harm you." He made his voice as gentle as he could. "Especially now that he's been threatened as well."

"He's been threatened? You never told me."

"When did I have the opportunity?"

"You haven't, but he should have."

"He refuses to take matters seriously."

"He should." Moisture glazed her eyes, and she blinked, then turned away. "I know I don't want to. I've never had an enemy in Cornwall. But I know I was pushed, whatever Lord Penvenan and Grandpapa insist, and we mustn't forget that Romsford's here now, and he wants Penmara's mines. Could he not threaten me and Morwenna as a way to . . . to compel his lordship to lease him the mines?"

"That seems rather diabolical, especially for a peer of the realm."

Her rather elegantly long, slim nose wrinkled. "Many peers have been diabolical. And remember, I ran away from marriage to him because the rumors of how his other wives died are not all smoke and gossip."

"Is it the only reason you ran from him?" Rowan gave her a half smile.

She smiled back. "There is other talk, substantiated talk, that his morals are less than stellar. I may not be the most faithful of Christians, but if only half of what I've heard of his activities is true, I want nothing to do with him."

"Which is why we were all more than willing to help you

elude him." He started to reach out a hand to touch her, caught a glimpse of Henry from the corner of his eye, and dropped the hand to the reins. "I still want to keep you safe, Elys. I'd like to wrap you and Miss Morwenna up in cotton and bundle you off someplace safe."

"I expect you'd like your own little harem." Her tone held sarcasm; her head tilted away from him.

"I would like to see you ladies safe." His own speech grew precise, clipped, and he had to force his hands to relax on the reins so the horse didn't rear. "I would like you away from Penmara until we discover who killed Conan Lord Penvenan and why these threats are coming. I would like to give you the security you seek. I would like to—"

"But you're not in a position to do so, are you, Mr. Curnow?"

The sharpness of her tone sliced through his speech. The razor-edge of her words sliced through his heart.

"There are just no clues." He breathed deeply to keep his frustration at bay, at least in his voice. "And no one in the village talks to me about anything but work."

"Of course not. You're an outsider."

"Not to put too fine a point on it," he muttered.

For the next quarter mile, silence like a rapier hovered between them. Words blazed through Rowan's head, burned on his tongue, that he wasn't quite as much of an outsider as she assumed. *Tell her, tell her, tell her the truth.*

But if he was right about Conan's death, about Conan's fears for Morwenna, about the threat to Morwenna and Penvenan, or the assault on Elizabeth, revealing more about his purpose in Cornwall could get a number of people killed, including himself.

CHAPTER 18

ELIZABETH HAD NEVER SEEN A MAN SHRINK IN SIZE. OF course he could not truly do so, yet at the utterance of her pointing out how he didn't belong in Cornwall, Rowan Curnow appeared to grow shorter, narrower in the shoulders, paler.

Her stomach shrank, drawing her head down and her shoulders in. "I am sorry, Rowan. That was an inexcusable thing for me to say after all you've done for me. I'm unforgivably high in the instep."

"And sharp of tongue." His shoulders straightened, and he pressed one hand to his chest. "Stabbed right through the heart."

"You mock me."

"And you disparage me."

"Disparage. That is a rather big word."

"For a mere *employé*?" He tugged at his forelock like a stable hand. "I know lots of big words, Miss Trelawny. I learned them in college."

She startled. "You went to college?"

"Providence Rhode Island. Brown University class of 1807."

"I thought you were jesting about that."

"I know you did, but I wasn't." He turned his face away, but not before she caught the hurt in his beautiful eyes.

She dropped her gaze to a patch of white hair between her mount's ears. The rocks and gorse and clusters of mine buildings they passed suddenly grew blurry. She blinked. She shouldn't care that she'd hurt him. He'd come chasing her.

And she'd encouraged him, the first man to dance with her twice in one night, by all but forcing him into a bower and kissing him like some kind of wanton chit from the opera chorus because she didn't want to be a spinster who had never been kissed and because she wanted to ruin her reputation and because she . . .

She was a self-centered prig.

"Why would a man from South Carolina go all the way north to Rhode Island to school?"

"You know where the states are located?" His eyebrows arched comically high with surprise.

"I've looked at maps of America. It seems so . . . vast."

"It is, and full of wild forests and mountains that are so beautiful." He glanced around them at a countryside that was also wild and beautiful, but in a stark, rugged way marred with mine buildings, too many of which crumbled from abandonment and neglect. "I didn't want to leave South Carolina, but Penvenan thought it wise I vacate the state for a while to spare my neck."

She glared at him. "You want me to ask you why, so I'll not."

"And I didn't tell you, but I will." He looked back at Henry, still a discreet dozen yards behind. "My mother died when I was fifteen and left me to Penvenan to raise on his plantation. He has a lot of slaves. I don't like it. I don't care that he inherited most of them and freeing them is nigh on impossible with the laws as they are. I don't see him doing anything to change the law or get around it, so I decided to take matters into my own hands."

Elizabeth fought down her revulsion at this barbaric practice. Most plantation owners in the Caribbean islands held by England owned them too. She didn't think Grandpapa's plantation did, but wasn't certain of that. She would ask. If so, she'd write to Drake to free them—if that was possible, if Drake had actually gone to the plantation and not off on some misadventure instead. Months would pass before a letter could reach her.

"How did you free them?" she asked Rowan.

He smiled at her as though she'd given him a precious gift. "What makes you think I did?"

She just kept looking at him.

"I only managed to get a few away and on their way to Canada and freedom. Penvenan's overseer got suspicious, so I turned to another man's plantation." He bowed his head.

"And . . ." Elizabeth prompted. "Surely freeing men in captivity is nothing of which you should be ashamed."

He shook his head. "It isn't, except this man was having financial difficulties and intended to sell those slaves to pay his debts. Because I helped them escape, he lost everything he owned."

"Oh no. What happened to him?"

"He sent his family to the West Indies to his wife's family there, but on the way, his two sons were taken up by the British Navy."

"But they were Americans, were they not?"

"I don't think they tried very hard to stop their impressments." Rowan's face hardened. "And the man vowed he would kill the man who helped his slaves escape when he found out who it was."

"So Lord Penvenan knew it was you."

"He suspected it was I. He'd learned that I was the one who took his slaves and thrashed me good, for all I was already a head taller than he."

"But he knew it most likely wouldn't stop you." She didn't even try to keep the admiration from her tone.

His smile, quick and spontaneous, blazed a hole through the

barrier she tried to hold up against him. "He knew, and he sent me north. I did well at the university. I wanted to go into the ministry, but Penvenan scuttled that notion."

"Why? Surely that would have been an honorable profession."

"He wasn't about to have me preaching against slavery and stirring up antislavery sentiment. So he said I owed him for my education, for saving my worthless hide, and for putting up with my insolence. So here I am in Cornwall making a fool of myself over a beautiful ice maiden."

Or perhaps not so icy a maiden.

The words slid through her mind unbidden, unwanted, like a stiletto between the ribs. Perhaps he wasn't making a fool of himself where she was concerned because every word he spoke lured her like a magpie to a brand-new penny.

And she was as foolish as that magpie who didn't realize the object of attraction was as useless to him as Rowan Curnow was to her. He was a copper penny to her golden guinea. Blended, the penny would lower the value of the guinea. How many times had Mama said, "A lady is raised or lowered to the level of her husband"?

As though she were nothing more than a seesaw tilting up and down at someone else's whim instead of her own desires.

Too little in her life had been of her own desires since her parents dragged her away from Bastion Point. Going after the whole inheritance was the only chance she saw for gaining something by her own volition. She would not, she could not, allow a man with a fine physique and a distracting mouth, a voice like warm caramel, and words that fascinated, turn her away from her purpose. Bastion Point was where her future lay, not with Rowan Curnow and his uncertain future going hither and yon at another man's whim.

Yet she couldn't hold back her smile upon looking his way,

nor from offering him words of encouragement. "I think if you still want to become a minister, you're capable of accomplishing that goal."

"Thank you." The Bastion Point gates rose into view over the next hill, and he slowed his mount from a trot to a walk. "Maybe one day, but right now I need to be right where I am."

"If you would rather be elsewhere," she reposted with some asperity, "do not hang about on my behalf. I find it uncomfortable enough having Romsford lurking around Truro and trying to purchase land in Cornwall."

"Be assured it won't be Penmara." Rowan tugged the bell rope to summon the gatekeeper.

Once the gates parted and the three of them rode through, conversation grew impossible. The trees of the parkland formed a tunnel of quiet where voices carried farther away than Henry rode.

No more conversation with the man seemed like the best course of action for her. At the same time, the idea of not seeing him again left her with a hollow in the center of her person, the kind of aching loneliness she'd never before felt when at home in Cornwall or browsing a bookshop in town, the kind of emptiness she experienced in the middle of balls in London.

The frozen mask she'd learned how to adopt during those balls now firmly in place, she dismounted without assistance, tossed her reins to a groom, and headed for the house, heedless of whether or not the lad had caught them. The gelding would go nowhere but to his stall for his dinner. Elizabeth didn't want her dinner; she wanted a long walk on the beach.

But walks on the beach might not be safe.

At the line of trees planted to separate the stable yard from the east lawn, Elizabeth heard footfalls behind her and whirled, words of rebuke blazing on her tongue. "You, with your reckless suppositions and accusations, have made me a prisoner here. I cannot walk or ride on the beach without fearing another accident. I cannot walk or ride into the village without fearing some kind of accident. I came back to Cornwall for freedom, and all I find is chaos."

"It isn't of my making, Miss Trelawny." Rowan tucked her hand into the crook of his arm.

She curled her fingers into the hard muscle beneath the soft wool sleeve.

They reached the front steps, and out of sight of viewers in the house or stable for the moment, Rowan faced her and took both her hands in his. "Elys, be careful, whether or not you choose to believe me. If you wish to go riding or walking, come with me."

Her hands shook with the effort not to curl her fingers around his. "Will you not be too occupied watching over Morwenna?"

"I'd prefer you persuade your grandparents to let her come back to live here. She's too alone in that house of hers."

"I think the grandparents are unmovable, and I'd rather not tease them into being angry with me."

"And of course Miss Morwenna's exile from Bastion Point prevents her from hopes of inheriting it."

Elizabeth flinched away from him and crossed her arms over her chest. "They might send me back to London."

"I doubt that."

"They sent me once before."

"Then be as cautious as your conscience will let you." He touched his forefinger to her chin. For a heart-stopping moment, she feared he intended to kiss her right then and there. She tensed with anticipation.

Instead, he met and held her gaze. "Come with me to the fair tomorrow."

"You think I can get away for an entire day?"

"I think you can if you wish to."

Yes, she most likely could with Miss Pross's loyal compliance. A desire to be left alone for a day expressed, a locked bedchamber door to keep Senara out, and judicious timing as to when she left and returned to the house. It wouldn't be the first time she had effected such an escape. Sadly, it was likely to be the last, a foolish, downright stupid, glorious bid for the freedom she'd missed in London and scarcely regained in Cornwall.

"I'll go."

His smile alone was worth the risk. "Around the point at sunrise." He strode away.

She should stay home like the good and obedient granddaughter she pretended to be, that she wished she were content to be. Yet at that moment, with his voice in her ears and his touch warming her skin, she couldn't care. She would go with him the next day, make arrangements with Miss Pross and slip away to a few hours of freedom.

On the other hand, how much freedom lay in the deception of pretending she was staying in her room when she was miles away? She didn't like doing it. The notion pricked her conscience.

Her limited activity since returning home hammered at her soul. The grandparents had changed, grown more strict in what they expected from their grandchildren—obedience or risk exile. They hadn't quite ordered her to allow Penvenan to court her with an eye to him offering her marriage, but they had made clear to her that was what they wanted. A settled and secure future nearby lay in that direction. Surely they meant the best for her in that.

She wanted to please them and ensure she kept their approval. She wanted to keep their love and gain the security of possessing Bastion Point. She wanted to be courted by someone who cared about her, who loved her. Perhaps that had been the attraction Penvenan held—she thought him wealthy enough that he courted her for feelings only. He was wealthy, but like Romsford, he wanted more. That more included what she brought, not necessarily her.

Surely the grandparents knew. Yet she feared they were no different from her parents.

On her way upstairs, she paused on the landing and leaned against the wall, her fingertips to her temples. A moan escaped her lips.

The grandparents had never seemed infallible to her. Yet they had exiled Drake. They had banished Morwenna unless she complied with their wishes. Now they nudged Elizabeth into a courtship she was doubtful she wanted. That Penvenan was a slave owner must not matter to them, for surely they knew.

Can you truly guide me, Lord? I am rather in need.

And if she only turned to the Lord when in need, was she any different from those whom she criticized for only caring about a body's rank or wealth and ability to advance their cause?

I feel so lost and empty.

How much more lost and empty must Morwenna feel, alone save for a paid maid-companion and a fatherless child on its way? Or perhaps not fatherless, but orphaned.

The notion of Conan being the father didn't seem possible. Conan had always treated Morwenna like a younger sister, a comrade in their games, nothing like what produced children. But six years could make a great deal of difference. On the other hand, Conan had seemed inclined to marry Elizabeth, according to Drake and the grandparents. He had, however, let Rowan be the one to get her away from Romsford rather than doing so himself. Conan had been anxious to get back to Penmara—

To look out for Morwenna? Only one way to learn—Elizabeth must call on Morwenna and ask her for the truth and why she refused to tell. Before she could do that, however, she was going to the horse fair with Rowan Curnow regardless of the consequences.

CHAPTER 19

THE LAST TIME ELIZABETH DESCENDED THE SECRET STAIR-case, she'd entered the caves to bid her brother good-bye, perhaps even farewell. The last time she saw her brother, she'd believed he had sent Rowan Curnow to help her, which would have meant Drake found him acceptable company for his sister. It would have meant so if Drake had ever heard of him. Rowan had deceived her through letting her draw false conclusions, then lying about knowing Drake, yet she descended the steps so she could meet him on the Penmara beach to minimize anyone seeing them.

More than likely, she'd regret her action later, especially if the grandparents learned that she had left Bastion Point land with Rowan Curnow. They would never understand her break for freedom while she worked out whether or not to allow Lord Penvenan to court her.

After another tedious night of drawing and watercoloring an embroidery pattern with Miss Pross while Grandmama read sermons and Senara netted a reticule, Elizabeth decided she'd shrivel and dry like a potted plant left too long in a dark room without water. At least that was her excuse for her actions—a poor excuse at best. Knowing it was didn't stop her.

The sight of the cave, a surprisingly, comfortably appointed room of rock lined with paneling to lend it warmth, gave her pause. A book still lay open on the table, as though Drake had been reading it when dragged away or told to leave. It was a Bible open to a passage in the book of Judges, where Jael killed Sisera.

"What an odd passage to be reading." Shaking her head, she unbolted the door and pushed it open to the dark, damp, and winding path to the edge of the water even at low tide.

Rowan awaited her around the headland. He held two horses Elizabeth didn't recognize. At sight of her, his eyes widened, and he laughed. "Where did you find those clothes?"

"I had them in the things Mama sent me from London." Her cheeks warmed as she smoothed the skirt. Gathered to lacings around her waist, it barely fell to her ankles in folds of plain, dark blue. Her stockings were plain white lisle, her shoes little more than clogs, and her bodice, white with red and gold embroidery, laced down the front from a neckline too low for modesty. She filled it in with a blue silk kerchief and had wound another kerchief, this one in red, around the band of her plain straw hat in such a way she could draw it down as a half veil if the need arose. A heavily fringed red shawl completed the ensemble.

"You look like a pirate wench." Rowan's gaze dropped to her lips. "Another masquerade?"

"In my first season. I spent the entire evening seated behind an orange tree in a giant pot."

"I did find a lot of fools among the London males."

She forced herself away from the warmth in his eyes. "We had best be going." She approached the smaller of the two horses, a gelding at least three hands taller than Grisette. "This is a nice lad." She stroked the horse's strawberry roan nose. "Whose are they?"

"They belong to the Pascoes." He rounded the gelding. "I decided not to impose on your grandfather today so I wouldn't have to explain why I needed two mounts. Shall I help you up?"

"How many horses are we going to look for today?"

"Just two riding horses and a pair of carriage horses for Penmara, and a mare or two for me."

"You? Can you—" She realized how impertinent was the question she'd nearly asked, and joined him at the gelding's left side so she could mount.

When she hooked her knee over the saddle horn, her right shoe flew off. Rowan retrieved it, knocked out the sand that had collected inside the brogue, and handed it up to her. She took it, then realized she couldn't slip it on without upsetting her balance atop her mount.

"I think . . ." Her throat felt suddenly dry. "I fear I cannot put it on myself."

He removed the shoe from her suddenly nerveless fingers and cupped her foot in the palm of his hand. His thumb caressed her instep and her toes curled. A quiver raced through her, a frisson of pleasure or warning of danger.

"You have remarkably small feet for a lady as tall as you are." He slid on her shoe and stepped away from her. "Have a care not to lose one of those again." He mounted his own horse and headed up the beach without another word, without looking at her.

Shaken, she followed, though instinct shouted at her to turn back, ride home to Bastion Point as fast as she could. Back to refuge. Back to safety.

Back to a day of callers and more embroidering.

She followed Rowan until they had passed Penmara and headed onto a little-used lane through abandoned mines and hovels where some out-of-work miners still lived. Smoke trickled from one or two of the houses, dingy laundry flapped on lines, and rusting mine equipment lay like broken skeletons near the shafts.

Elizabeth turned her face away from the ugliness. "I can't

help but think opening these mines at nearly any cost would do a world of good. Think of all the people who will have work."

"If there truly is copper in them still."

"Everyone says there is still copper down there, but there was a cave-in about ten years ago that left the mine flooded, and the Penvenans had no money to buy an engine strong enough to pump it clear."

"Penvenan would like to make a profit." Rowan grimaced at the surroundings. "It's ugly, isn't it?"

"Do you expect poverty to be pretty?"

He gave her a glance of surprise. "I didn't think Miss Elizabeth Trelawny of Bastion Point thought about poverty at all."

"Of course not. I only think about gowns and jewels and houses. I've no care for the beggars I saw every day in London."

"You wouldn't be unusual if you didn't."

"Sadly, no." She tucked a stray wisp of hair back into the plait down her back. "But Trelawnys have always taken care of whomever we can."

Rowan said something that sounded like, "You'll feed us, but not love us."

Her heart rolled over. He knew so little about her. And yet he knew all about her anyone could know. He even knew her longing to lose the inhibitions of society. But he didn't understand her need for the security of things that could not be ripped away from her, like living in a house she could not be sent from in a moment and the love of those around her.

"Why," she demanded out of frustration, "would you want me to love you when doing so would make me a fool?"

He flashed her a grin and laughed. "Maybe not following your heart makes you a fool."

"You presume a great deal, sir."

"Do I? Then what are you doing with me today?"

She stared between the gelding's ears and smoothed the silky red mane. "Following the part of my heart that says I've been immured long enough." She said nothing until they left the abandoned mines behind. "I came back to Cornwall to escape too many hours in drawing rooms, interminable dinner parties, and sedate rides in an open carriage."

"And I came to England to find Penvenan heirs. Seems neither of us got what we came for." He edged his mount closer to hers and reached across the space between to clasp one of her hands on the reins. "But we got so much more. The Lord has a way of working that way."

She shot him a look intended to be scornful. She feared it came out more inquisitive.

"The Lord will show you the way to go if you ask." Rowan seemed to be answering a question she hadn't intended to ask.

She shook her head. "He has never paid me any mind."

"Jesus died for you too. That's a lot of attention to start with. He knows the number of hairs on your head."

"And likely made them straight instead of curly, and me tall and big-boned instead of petite-like—" Her throat closed for no good reason, and she turned her gaze to the rolling hills, green beneath the brightening sunlight.

"Miss Morwenna?" Rowan's voice was so soft, so gentle, Elizabeth's eyes burned. "To deny her beauty would be dishonest. But saying so doesn't deny yours."

"No, it is simply dishonest."

"Fishing for a compliment, miss?" His eyes glinted like a sun-washed sea.

She smiled. "It sounds that way, but I meant no such thing. I was pointing out how absurd that claim is."

"It's not absurd; it's to show you how much the Lord cares about you."

"I know. I am sorry for teasing you. I simply cannot . . . accept . . . that belief."

"Have you asked him to help you accept it?"

"That seems silly."

"That's because it's so easy. I'm afraid following is a bit more difficult. Right now I'm having a rather difficult time accepting some of the things I have to do as being in God's will, but I can't find another direction either."

"What sort of things?" She leaped at the chance to turn the subject away from herself.

He didn't respond. Around them, the lane joined the main road where other travelers passed in wagons and on horseback. Few people used carriages in Cornwall. The highways were little more than rutted tracks for the most part. Noting one or two farmers she recognized, Elizabeth released the sheer veil on her hat to hide her face from their view.

It also hid any telltale expressions from Rowan's view, giving her time to think about what he said, speculate over what he was doing that was giving him doubts. She pondered what might happen if she asked God to help her accept his love and caring about the path of her life. He might tell her to take actions she didn't want to, like obey her parents and marry Romsford if he asked her again, or please her grandparents and wed Penvenan. Perhaps worse, at least worse than marrying Penvenan, God might ask her to champion Morwenna's cause regardless of the consequences, cease her bursts of rebellion, or even give up Bastion Point so Morwenna or Drake could have it.

Her stomach rolled at that idea. Suddenly, she grew aware that this horse didn't have Grisette's smooth gait. Each pace jarred her until her insides felt shaken, until they grew heavy like churned butter.

"Did you choose this horse from the Pascoe stables?" she asked Rowan.

"No, ma'am. I wouldn't choose something so clumsy."

"And that one is worse?"

"This one is a fine choice, but isn't trained to a sidesaddle."

"Ah, to be able to ride astride, as I did as a girl."

"It would be safer the way you like to race."

"I expect it would, but I suppose I must give up racing."

A verse of Scripture ran through her head, though she didn't know she'd memorized much of the Bible. "Where in the Bible is the verse that says, 'When I was a child, I spake as a child, I understood as a child, I thought as a child: but when I became a man, I put away childish things'?"

Rowan arched a brow. "The thirteenth chapter of First Corinthians. Why?"

"It just ran through my head. Seems someone quoted it to me enough I remembered it."

And that was what she must now do. After today, she must forget about sneaking away to horse fairs, racing down the beach, her desire to swim . . . Rowan Curnow.

But today she could enjoy herself.

Outside of town, a field held makeshift paddocks filled with horses and foals, with the stallions in open stalls of their own. Roaming through these displays, pie men, costermongers, and flower girls hawked their wares. Two men indulged in a juggling competition on one side, and on the other, two men drew a crowd as they wrestled. Music from fiddles and flutes flowed over the scene like warm custard on a pudding.

Elizabeth's body began to hum like a plucked cello string. She reined in and slid to the ground, suddenly too restless to remain in the saddle and sit still while the horse did the work. "What do we do with these?"

"Pay someone well to make certain they don't get sold." He scanned the throng, then dismounted and led the way around paddocks and vendors to an empty enclosure at one side, where a grizzled man leaned against a rail chewing on a straw. "Will Blamey." Rowan held out his hand.

"Rowan Curnow." The older man shook the proffered hand. "See you got yerself a pretty filly already."

Elizabeth blushed.

Rowan winked. "Always more fun to have company." He turned the horses over to Will Blamey, then grasped Elizabeth's hand and headed for one of the pie men. "Hungry?"

"Ladies don't admit to hunger."

"I expect they don't. But today"—he spun her to face him—"you're going to forget you're a lady."

And so she did. She wore no gloves, so his hand was warm and strong around hers, the calluses abrasive in a way that kept that cello string vibrating. She ate meat pies with her fingers and swallowed them down with lemonade. She drew Rowan to the wrestling competition and explained that Cornishmen were usually no-holds-barred in the sport.

"It looks vicious," he admitted.

"It can be, but I don't know of anyone ever being so much as maimed." She slid a look from the corner of her eye. "Want to try?"

So much time passed before he shook his head, she pushed him toward the ring with her hand in the middle of his back. "Go ahead. You're surely big enough to hold your own."

The muscle she felt through his shirt and coat spoke of his strength. No wonder he could lift her into the saddle.

A violin added its clear notes to the concerto in her blood, with only one tiny string plucking out a warning—a warning she chose to ignore for the time being, but should have heeded.

Instead of joining the raucous men around the wrestling matches, he stepped closer to her so her arm encircled his waist.

With his arm around her shoulders, he turned her toward the horses. "I'm here to buy a brood mare for one thing. See any you like?"

"Depends on what you want."

He told her, and they began to look. He kept his arm around her. She considered shrugging it off and removing her arm from around him, then realized the intimacy was part of her disguise. No one would suspect Miss Elizabeth Trelawny of strolling through a fair with a man's arm around her. She would never do so in society gatherings.

She knew no one in society whose arm she'd want around her, not even the man she considered marrying.

The man she had considered marrying.

They continued through the equines, talked with owners and brokers, and examined teeth and feet, gaits and coats. In the end, they purchased five horses and made arrangements for their delivery to Penmara. They ate sausages slathered in mustard and returned to their search. Every time their activities required they separate, they returned to the half embrace, their strides long and swinging in unison, their flow of conversation growing more and more sporadic. By the time the sun had begun its descent on the far side of its zenith, Elizabeth could barely get out, "We must be going."

"I know." Rowan faced her, standing too close—close enough for his breath to fan her lips.

He bent his head. For a heart-stopping moment, she thought he intended to kiss her right there in front of a hundred Cornishmen and women. Her own lips parted.

He brushed her lips with the pad of his thumb, then grasped her hand. "Just one country dance?"

They joined the motley throng forming two lines for the dance. Several fiddles, a drum, and a Spanish guitar joined together to swoop out the lively tune. Hands clapped. Feet stamped, skirts swirled high enough to display beribboned garters holding up cheap stockings.

Clumsy in her crude shoes, Elizabeth moved like an automaton the first time down the line. Then a farmer with hands like hams and a reek of the stables upon him picked her up by the waist and whirled her around. Her shoes disappeared beneath the dancers' feet. She shrieked. She laughed. She remembered dancing at fairs and village fetes as a girl, and forgot she was Miss Elizabeth Trelawny of Bastion Point. She was a serving girl, a pirate wench, a gypsy maid on a day's celebration of life.

She lost sight of Rowan in the ever-changing figures of the dance, then he was there again hooking his elbow through hers to swirl in a dizzying circle, and vanished again as the movement sent her spinning into the hands of the next man along the line. Her healing leg began to ache. Her feet hurt from the stones and trampled grass, and she suspected she smelled as ripe as her companions. But she didn't want those moments of abandon to end.

Until Rowan clasped her hands again and led her down the center of the two lines, away from the dancers, and behind the shelter of a sweetmeats cart. She was still laughing when he kissed her.

The kiss was neither the timid contact from the ball, nor his bold yet gentle embrace in the meadow. He kissed her with his lips firm on hers, his tongue tangling with hers sweet and savory, gentle and exhilarating. She wrapped her arms around his neck and buried her fingers in his hair. He held her close, sheltering her from the world to which she did not wish to return. Her wants, her desires, the longings of her heart begged for more than brick and mortar, coffers filled with gold, and commands she must behave in a way that pleased everyone except herself.

"I love you." He spoke the words with his lips still on hers. "Come away with me. We can marry on Guernsey on our way to America."

America. Of course he intended to return to his homeland.

Slowly, she lowered her arms and stepped out of the circle of his embrace. Thickness invaded her throat, and she avoided his eyes for fear she would drown in their sea-blue depths. "I cannot marry you and go to America. The grandparents . . . Morwenna . . . England . . ."

As much as family demands might impede her and brick and mortar confine her, they were all she knew.

She swallowed against a rising tide of tears. "And I don't know if I love you enough to be poor with you. And since you are poor . . ." She turned away.

"I likely want you for your inheritance as much as does my . . . employer. I forgot you think that's all anyone wants from you. If I could convince you otherwise . . ." His chest rose and fell in a silent sigh, and he curved his hand around her arm. "I'd better get you home before dark."

As she paced beside him in silence, she made a decision she expected to regret. Although she knew she could never have a relationship with Rowan Curnow, at the risk of displeasing her family, she could no longer consider marrying Lord Penvenan.

CHAPTER 20

SHE TOLD THE GRANDPARENTS OVER BREAKFAST THAT she could not wed Lord Penvenan. "Provided he asks, of course."

"That is your decision to make, my dear," Grandpapa responded without a hitch. "We won't foist a husband on you whom you don't want."

"Though we would rather you were wed. Even wealthy ladies have a difficult time alone in the world."

"It's precisely because I am a wealthy woman I cannot wed him." She propped her elbows on the table against all training and rested her chin in her hands. "He's just one more fortune hunter."

The grandparents stared at her.

"Austell Penvenan is a very wealthy man," Grandpapa spoke at last. "He's been quite forthcoming about that."

"And has he been forthcoming about being a slave owner?" Elizabeth shot back.

Grandmama sighed. Grandpapa reached for his pipe.

"Remove your elbows from the table, Elizabeth," Grandmama admonished.

"We knew about the slaves." Grandpapa began to fill his pipe. "It is one reason Penvenan wishes to marry money. He would like to free his bondsmen, but to do so, he must have money to send them out of South Carolina and resettle them somewhere more hospitable to freed slaves."

"But Ro—Mr. Curnow said—" Elizabeth clasped her hands on her lap. "Mr. Curnow mentioned none of this. You'd think the man's secretary would know of those kinds of plans. Wouldn't he be needed to make these arrangements?"

"Perhaps," Grandmama said, "Mr. Curnow didn't want you to know."

Grandpapa made a wordless exclamation and spilled tobacco fragments across his plate. "Why would he conceal a thing like that?"

I love you.

Had he withheld the entire truth to keep her from favoring his master over him? Elizabeth's hands clenched. Doing so was dishonorable.

She sounded a little belligerent, and she needed to know the truth from someone. "Does he not need my money to open the mines and make more for himself since he cannot sell Penmara land?"

"He can lease out the mines," Grandpapa said. "I believe he intends to do that."

"So he doesn't need my money for the mines?"

"Elizabeth." Grandmama reached across the small breakfast table. "You need not concern yourself as to whether or not Lord Penvenan would only offer you marriage for the sake of your inheritance. I believe he would offer for you were you poor."

Elizabeth snorted. "No one, Grandmama, wants a plain girl without money."

The grandparents exchanged a look, then Grandmama asked, "Who has broken your heart, child, and convinced you that you are unattractive beyond your inheritance?"

"No one." Elizabeth stared past Grandmama to the sun-drenched lawn carefully coaxed to grow all the way to the top of the cliff. "Everyone."

We can marry on Guernsey.

She wanted to lay her head on the table and weep for the fear inside that would not allow her to believe in the selflessness of any kind of love, whether God's or that of an *employé*.

"We never should have let your parents take you to London." Grandpapa dumped tobacco back into its pouch and tucked his pipe into his pocket. "You never thought things like that of yourself before."

"Conan never would have made you feel that way." Grandmama dabbed at her eyes. "And as we said, we don't wish to make you feel as though you are required to wed Lord Penvenan. On the other hand, we'd like to see you settled and secure, as we're growing no younger."

"I'll be settled and secure with my own fortune." Elizabeth pushed back her chair and rose. "Please excuse me. I need . . . air."

She needed to call on her cousin. Slipping out of the house without telling anyone other than Miss Pross—close-lipped, loyal Miss Pross—of her destination two days in a row was risky. This time, however, she wouldn't be gone for long. Not like the day before. Not like those glorious hours of laughter and country fare and dancing. And that kiss.

Her insides quivered like jelly at the memory. She paused in the passageway to the garden exit and pressed the back of her hand to her lips. Rowan claimed to love her, yet he had withheld important information about his competition . . .

No, no competition there. Regardless of whether or not she would ever accept that Rowan Curnow loved her, she doubted she could ever accept a marriage from Austell Lord Penvenan. To do so would be unfair to him and herself.

Even if she never quite believed he loved her, after a night of tossing and turning on her bed, of leaning out the window to stare at the sun rising over the sea, of trembling in every limb at the mere mention of his name, she feared she was in love with Rowan Curnow.

⚜

Of course she was there. Rowan knew if he dared pay a call on Miss Morwenna Trelawny that Miss Elizabeth Trelawny would find him there. He no sooner raised the brass knocker, a pointless exercise with the dogs barking inside, than a crunch of a footfall on the path drew his attention. He turned, and there she stood, not two yards behind him. For a heartbeat, their eyes met, then her cheeks grew pink. She dropped her gaze to the graveled path and folded her arms across her waist.

Rowan smiled at her. "What a pleasant surprise to see you."

He hadn't expected to see her for days, or maybe never after she barely spoke to him on the way home the night before. Yet there she stood so close, awkward, embarrassed at the encounter . . . and not backing down an inch.

As he knew she would not. She wouldn't be the woman he loved if she did.

She straightened her shoulders a bit and looked past him. "I cannot imagine why I am surprised to see you here, Mr. Curnow."

"You should be." He propped his shoulders against the door and crossed his arms over his chest. On the other side of the panel, someone clipped out a command, and the dogs fell silent. "I've never been here before. Not at the house, anyway."

"Indeed."

"But I haven't seen Miss Morwenna about, so came to be sure she's all right."

"Of course." She crossed her own arms over her chest.

Rowan grinned. "Would you rather I called on you?"

"I'd rather you remembered your place."

"And what place is that?" Though he maintained his casual stance, his tone held a sudden edge. "That place in your heart you won't let me into?"

Her nostrils flared. "You're Lord Penvenan's secretary, are you not, someone to whom you owe your livelihood and education? You would think you could be honest about him."

He gave her a blank look. "I don't know what you mean. I've never told you anything but the truth about Lord Penvenan."

"It is not what you told me that is at issue here; it is what you did not tell me that matters."

She was right there. He needed to apply any acting skills he possessed to continue pretending as though her accusation didn't hurt and now baffle him.

"What, pray tell," he asked in his strongest slow, southern drawl, "did I neglect to tell you?"

One would think he was a lawyer with the way he'd learned to twist words so he told the exact truth without denying removing inconvenient bits and pieces. Neglect, indeed. He hadn't told her many things, but not neglectfully. Those omissions had been quite deliberate.

"You didn't tell me Lord Penvenan wishes to wed me so he can use my fortune to free his slaves."

"He intends to do what?" Rowan shot upright so fast he nearly toppled forward off the stoop. "What are you talking about?"

"I think it grossly unsporting of you to try to spike his guns with me by stopping at telling me he owns slaves. I had—"

"I know nothing of him planning to free them."

"—begun to think perhaps you're an honest man—"

"More honest than most."

"But I suppose I should have known better when you let me believe my brother sent you."

"Indirectly he did. He sent Conan, who—"

"That is the late Lord Penvenan to you, regardless of—"

"Elizabeth, get off your high ropes and listen." He stepped off the stoop and closed the distance between them. "Lord Penvenan and I've discussed him courting you, and he has never confided in me that he wants your dowry in order to free his slaves now or ever. On the contrary, I heard him say he would use your dowry to restart the mines."

"As soon as we are wed, I presume."

"Where did you hear this faradiddle about freeing the slaves?"

"He told my grandfather, so I cannot believe he did not tell his secretary. I'd think he would have to, since would not a secretary carry out the practicalities of such an endeavor?"

"One would think so, but this is the first I've heard of it." He hesitated, considered for a moment, then added, "I don't see how he can en masse. He has to replace them with free workers, and free workers who will work the rice fields are not that easy to come by. Or did you think he could exchange Cornish miners for field hands in a shipload or two?"

"I did not think."

"You so rarely do before leaping to conclusions."

"I—" Her eyes widened, her lower lip puffed out, and she snatched it back between her teeth.

Rowan sighed. "And so do I. I didn't mean to hurt you."

"As if you could." She looked away. "What do I care that you cannot tell me the truth?"

What, indeed? She cared enough to make him absurdly happy.

Afraid he would say too much now, he turned his back on her and applied the knocker. This time the portal opened before Rowan released the brass ring.

"Do you expect me to jump up and run to the d— Mr.

Curnow and . . . Elizabeth?" Morwenna herself stood in the opening, pale and still pretty despite her unbalanced bulk.

Rowan bowed. "We have come to see how you're faring."

"We did not come together," Elizabeth added.

"You wouldn't lower yourself." Morwenna cast her cousin a narrow-eyed glare. "So to what do I owe this honor of a call from the big house?" Sarcasm dripped from her tone like water from a downspout.

From the corner of his eye, Rowan caught a flash of hurt in Elizabeth's expression. Then she smoothed her features into her indifferent mask like a beautiful maiden carved of ice.

"I believe we both came to be assured that you're all right," Rowan said, still watching Elizabeth. "May we come in?"

"By all means." Morwenna stepped back to allow them access.

Elizabeth swept past Rowan and paused just over the threshold. Her nostrils flared, then pinched, and she glanced around. "Where did you get the dogs?"

"Conan's dogs." Morwenna's face worked. "I found them wandering in the woods the day after . . . after—"

"I never heard of Conan having big dogs." Elizabeth moved farther into the entryway that was perhaps the size of a neckcloth. "Senara has not mentioned them once."

"She hates dogs. I expect she was the one who set them loose." Morwenna opened a door to the left of the entrance. "Oggy, Pastie, stay."

"Oggy and Pastie?" Elizabeth laughed. It was such a clear, bright, and unexpected sound, Rowan smiled.

"Ridiculous names, I know." A softness melted the hard, bitter lines around Morwenna's mouth, a mouth too young and pretty to show such unhappiness. "But he loved pasties, oggies, as they are here in Cornwall. And if two dogs don't look like pasties, it's these two."

They were some kind of deerhound, long and lean and elegant save for the water-matted coats. They rose, stretched, and ambled forward to sniff the newcomers.

Rowan watched Elizabeth, expecting her to shy away from large, wet tongues and shedding coats. But she held out her hands, one to each, and scratched the dogs behind their upright ears.

"Are you not big, beautiful boys?" she crooned to them in a gentle undertone. "Or are you a little girl, Pastie? I hope so. Oggy isn't a nice name for a girl, is it?"

Rowan exchanged a glance with Morwenna. She didn't look surprised.

"Elys has always liked dogs, and horses and cats too, I believe." Morwenna looked at Elizabeth with something akin to sadness. "We played with all the animals, even the sheep, when we were children here together."

"Were you friends then?" Rowan asked.

"As much as cousins can be. Our parents left us with the grandparents, so we were stranded here. Not that we cared. The four of us—Senara, too, sometimes—often played—" Her voice broke. She blinked hard several times, then turned away, rubbing her lower back. "Do you care if I sit?"

"Of course not." Rowan turned back to Elizabeth, who now knelt before the dogs, holding the massive front paw of one and allowing the other to prop his muzzle on her shoulder.

She glanced up, smiling. "Are they not dear?"

"I believe they are deerhounds." Rowan grinned too.

She wrinkled her nose in a way that made him want to kiss it. "That was a poor pun. Conan didn't have these dogs before. He'd a yappy little terrier who hated everyone except him."

"That was the one who disappeared," Morwenna said.

"I heard." Elizabeth stroked the female's neck, and the

male butted his head under her chin. "But I didn't hear how." She wrapped an arm around each dog despite the quantity of gray hair they left on her pelisse.

"Someone took it," Morwenna said. "His rooms were locked."

Elizabeth startled. "Why would anyone steal an old dog?"

"To remind him he might be the lord letting them use his beach and caves, but they—the smugglers—rule in these parts. And in the end—" Tears suddenly spilled down Morwenna's cheeks. She covered her face with her hands, and her shoulders shook, though no sound emerged.

Rowan took a step forward, realized going to her comfort was inappropriate for a mere secretary, and went to Elizabeth instead to help her to her feet. The dogs abandoned her to rush to Morwenna's side, laying their heads in her lap, nuzzling her arms.

Elizabeth took Rowan's proffered hands and allowed him to raise her to her feet. She didn't immediately let go, but stood staring at him with something like panic shadowing her eyes. "Morwenna never cries," she said barely above a whisper.

"Apparently she does." A glance over his shoulder showed him Morwenna wiping her eyes on the sleeves of her gown. "Miss Trelawny, can we do anything to help?"

"Can you bring Conan back to life? Or ensure I stay alive long enough to—" She laid her hands on her belly.

Elizabeth's cheeks bloomed roses, and her hands tightened on Rowan's. She held his gaze for a moment as though trying to say something to him she didn't speak aloud, then she released him and crossed the room to kneel before her cousin.

The dogs shouldered against her, and she wrapped an arm around each as though needing their comfort and strength.

Rowan strode up behind her, wishing she'd lean against him for strength instead of a couple of smelly canines. He held his hands behind his back so he didn't rest them on her shoulders or, even better, kneel beside her and take over support from the dogs.

Morwenna glanced from her cousin to Rowan, and back to Elizabeth. "Why are you on the floor, Elys? Or here at all?"

"Why are you still weeping for Conan?" Elizabeth released the dogs and spread her hands before her as though wanting to, but unable to bring herself to the point of reaching out to Morwenna. "I never knew the two of you were such particular friends, or that you even liked one another above half."

"No." Morwenna looked past Elizabeth, met Rowan's gaze for a moment, then stared at her hands crossed over her belly. Her hair fell into her face and stuck on her still damp cheeks. She looked so young, too young to be a mother, sad, and alone without anyone to brush back her hair for her or bring her a handkerchief. Rowan's heart ached for her and for Elizabeth, and a spark of rage against the older Trelawnys ignited inside him.

All the older Trelawnys deserved his wrath, the grandparents especially. They made claims of loving the Lord and wanting the best for their grandchildren, yet they showed no mercy to Drake or Morwenna. And they told Elizabeth some nonsense about Penvenan needing her dowry to free his slaves in order to manipulate her into marrying the new baron. Even if Penvenan had made up the bambury tale, the Trelawnys chose to impart the information to bend Elizabeth to their will. Under that kind of a regime, how could they expect their grandchildren to repent of their waywardness?

"You know the grandparents will likely lock you in your room if they learn you've been here," Morwenna was saying.

"Yes, most likely." Elizabeth didn't move.

And Rowan ground his teeth. Elizabeth would never accept unconditional love with her family for examples.

"But I need to talk to you." Elizabeth twisted her hands before her, then, at last, reached out and grasped her cousin's. "Morwenna, Mr. Curnow believes Conan is the father of your baby. Is he right?"

Morwenna paled, and the knuckles of her hands grew so white her grip must hurt Elizabeth. Neither of them moved. Morwenna didn't speak.

"Morwenna." Elizabeth's voice was so gentle, Rowan couldn't resist reaching out to her and resting his hand on her shoulder. It felt as stiff as a horsehair-filled cushion. He rested his other hand on her other shoulder and began to gently knead the taut muscles.

She never moved her attention from Morwenna. "Row—um, Mr. Curnow thinks that is why you're in danger."

Morwenna shot a glance at Rowan, then dropped her eyes to his hands. A faint smile touched her lips. "He has interesting notions, does your Mr. Curnow."

"He's not my—" Elizabeth released her cousin's hands and covered his. "Stop that."

Rowan stopped, but didn't move his hands. "Miss Morwenna, Conan asked me to watch over you and ensure your safety. Why would he do that if he didn't think you were in danger? Why would he warn you of danger if it were not true? And why would you be in danger unless you know more of his death than you've said to the authorities? But then, he didn't know he was going to die, so—"

"All right." Morwenna flung up her hands. "Yes, it's true. Conan is the father. So now that you know, Elizabeth, run home and tell the grandparents you know the truth behind my indecent condition." She smiled with a twist to her upper lip. "Of course, then you have to admit you came calling on me without a chaperone and with this mere secretary of Lord Penvenan's."

CHAPTER 21

Elizabeth's hands clutched Rowan's, then she snatched them away and scrambled to her feet.

One of the dogs whined and pushed closer to Morwenna.

Morwenna fixed Elizabeth with her dark eyes shining, and a smile curving her lush little mouth. "They won't be so quick to give you everything if they know how you carry on behind their backs."

"I do not . . . carry on." Elizabeth's heart raced as though she were running.

She had carried on behind their backs the day before, deceived them for a few hours of play—hours that would lose her everything if they learned the truth, especially that embrace, the proposal, the temptation . . .

"I do not carry on," she repeated. *Not like you. And with Conan.*

The truth confirmed sent a surge of pent-up energy through her, a desire to kick something.

"How could you?" She lashed out with words. "He is not— was not—lowborn like Sam Carn and the rest of your paramours, you trollop, you fusty—"

Gently, but firmly, Rowan laid his fingers across her lips. "Leave off the street cant, Elys."

Elizabeth shoved his hand away. "Street cant suits her. Did you think he would marry you?"

Morwenna looked away, her chin wobbling. "Yes."

"But he knew better than to ally himself—"

"I think that's enough, Elizabeth." That low, drawling voice cut across her taunt like a saber through an enemy.

She jerked back a step. "How dare you tell me when I've said enough?"

"Words once spoken can't be taken back. I don't want you to regret something you say."

Elizabeth's mouth went dry at the admonition from a man she thought she could manage like Morwenna managed men. He claimed he adored her. He wanted an alliance with her for something. He should let her get away with whatever she liked.

But of course he should not. And she did not want him to.

Her regard for him rose at the same time her regard for Conan plummeted.

"I never thought Conan would treat a lady, at least by birth, in such an immoral way." She barely got the words out as her throat clogged with unshed tears. "He was kind and decent."

"He was." Morwenna's tears fell freely. "And he intended to marry me."

"Then why did he not?" Elizabeth lashed out the question.

"Do you know how difficult and expensive a special license is?" Morwenna demanded.

Elizabeth's nostrils flared. "And you couldn't have the banns called?"

"No."

"Why not? He wanted to wed you in secret so he could keep from admitting he had taken the village—"

"I think," Rowan broke in again, "we should let Miss Morwenna explain herself without epithets."

Another rebuke. Elizabeth's ears burned. Her cheeks blazed. She pressed her hands to her face and discovered they shook.

He sounded like he didn't approve of her. He was looking at Morwenna with kindness, if not approval.

Knees suddenly weak, Elizabeth sank onto the nearest chair and fixed her gaze on her cousin. "Then tell me why no banns? You know the grandparents would have approved of the union."

"They would love an alliance between the two houses, though they wanted Conan to marry you." Morwenna wiped her eyes on her sleeve again.

Elizabeth reached into one of her pockets for a handkerchief, but Rowan got his out first.

Morwenna thanked him, wiped her eyes and nose, and continued.

"He feared for my safety. He feared if we did something as public as a reading of the banns in church, the gang would use me to keep him working with them." She clutched, released, and clutched the handkerchief. "He even feared all the Trelawnys might be in danger, like Drake and you and even your parents and mine, if they ever come home, and the grandparents. He's been afraid for Senara too, and wanted to sell Penmara, except for the entail, but was considering abandoning it and moving to America. It's not as though he's doing—" She gulped. "It's not as if he were doing the tenants any good, and the mines are all closed and . . ." She began to sob in raucous, hiccupping gasps.

The dogs crowded close to her. Rowan crouched before her and covered her restless hands with his. He murmured something Elizabeth couldn't hear over Morwenna's weeping. From the expression of compassion on his face, it was kind, soothing, even affectionate, as though he and Morwenna held a relationship about which Elizabeth knew nothing and no one intended to tell her. He appeared to care about Morwenna.

Elizabeth didn't begrudge Morwenna the comfort. Why

should she care if Lord Penvenan's secretary offered Morwenna some understanding in her bereavement?

Because he says he loves you.

She was a vain cat, she was, begrudging Morwenna comfort because Rowan Curnow was the one doing the consoling. A horrifying notion shot through Elizabeth. What if Rowan offered to give Morwenna as much respectability as she could have? The baby would be his by law. They might be wrong about Grandpapa. He might be happy to give him Morwenna's dowry, more than enough to set up a man for life.

Rowan didn't need to marry Elizabeth for her inheritance. He could have Morwenna for hers—Morwenna who was so pretty even in her condition. Perhaps even more so. She was even beautiful weeping. She was small and possessed glossy ringlets, big dark eyes, and pink roses in her cheeks. No one would ever give her the sobriquet of ice-blue ice maiden.

Pain shot through Elizabeth's heart, sharp enough she wished she could abandon her upbringing enough to howl like Morwenna. Elizabeth had allowed the less admirable side of her nature to break through her reserve because she thought what she said to Morwenna in front of Rowan Curnow didn't matter. So what if he thought her vicious to her cousin? Morwenna had been more than vicious to Elizabeth all their lives, taunting her about her height, her straight hair, her pale eyes. One point Elizabeth always won over Morwenna was in good behavior, even in her tongue in front of others. Yet she'd behaved badly in that area today, and too late, with the words or implied epithets flung at her cousin, realized everyone in the room mattered. Morwenna had been hurt enough by Conan and now both his and her families, and needed kindness, not criticism. And Rowan mattered because he was Rowan. Kind and generous, forthright and intelligent Rowan Curnow—

The man Elizabeth had fallen in love with, the man she might let love her, given another chance.

No, no, no, she could not.

It was too much of a risk to trade the security there in Cornwall for a man who could, apparently, switch affection from one cousin to the other in a day.

A tremor raced through her as though an earthquake shook the cottage. A breath labored into her lungs. She stared at Rowan crouching before Morwenna, holding her hands, soothing her with soft words, and shot to her feet. In a moment, she stood on the path before the house without truly remembering crossing the parlor to the entryway or opening the door. From the corner of her eye, she spotted the woman hired as companion and housekeeper and perhaps guard dog for Morwenna digging in the garden. She started to rise. Elizabeth waved her off, gathered up her skirt, and ran.

She ran as fast as her long legs would carry her. She ran as she hadn't run since she was a schoolgirl playing some chase game with Conan and Drake, Morwenna, and some of the village children. She ran toward the sea, not thinking she might strand herself on the beach regardless of potential danger.

But no matter how far and fast she ran, she couldn't outrun the soul-deep knowledge that her fears were realized and she had indeed lost her heart to the last man she should.

❧

The click of the front door latch drew Rowan's attention from the weeping lady before him. He glanced up. Elizabeth had gone. He should go after her. She shouldn't be walking around the countryside alone. Yet he couldn't leave Miss Morwenna in her state. Distress such as hers could bring on her travail. He'd seen it once with one of the women he was helping to freedom. As much as he wished to follow Elizabeth, he dared not leave Morwenna alone until she calmed.

"Miss Morwenna?" He spoke her name for perhaps the dozenth time. "You should tell your grandparents about you and Conan."

Morwenna shook her head. "I can't risk it. I can't risk anyone finding out. They might hurt my baby."

"But with Conan gone, why would they want to?"

"You don't know these men. They're dangerous to anyone who tries to leave them or betrays them. Conan is dead. Drake was nearly captured. It's how they survive despite the riding officers." A spasm shook Morwenna as though she were already in labor. "They would kill the baby and me as a warning to others that once they are involved, they can't leave. I've told you it wouldn't be the first time. And they must suspect about Conan and me already. Remember the bird and egg?"

"Then let me place a guard on this cottage. I should have done so sooner."

Morwenna shook her head, tears scattering like rain. "They'll know. And who around here can we trust? Anyone could be involved."

A sad fact along the Cornish coast. For all the time he'd spent in the village tavern, Rowan still didn't know the local men well enough to know who could and who could not be trusted. He could break Morwenna's confidence and tell Sir Petrok, but did even he know who was loyal and who was not?

"All right then. I'll tell the servants at Penmara to keep a lookout for your maid should she arrive with a message."

Morwenna wiped her eyes on a now-sodden handkerchief and gave him a long, scrutinizing look. "Why? Why are you doing this for me? Conan couldn't have been that good a friend. You didn't have time to know him well."

"He was kin to Penvenan." Rowan chose his words with care as he rose and crossed the room to examine some trinkets laid along the mantel. "And I owe Penvenan my life."

"And you're in love with my cousin." In the mirror over the hearth, he saw Morwenna smile.

He smiled back, the sheepish grin of the dreamer he should have ceased being years ago. "Guilty as charged."

He picked up a carved jade apple with leaves of some translucent green crystal. "Do you have a bolt-hole, somewhere to go if you truly feel threatened?"

"I'm a Trelawny. Of course I do."

"Where?"

"I'm not supposed to tell anyone." But she told him where to meet her on the beach.

He handed her the jade apple. "Send this to me if you feel the need to run there."

A door banged at the back of the house, and she closed her hands around the curiosity. "My chaperone. She won't be pleased to see us here alone."

"I'm only a servant. I don't matter." The words emerged with more bitterness than he intended, than he realized he felt. "But I'll be going." He headed for the partially open door.

"Mr. Curnow?" Morwenna called after him.

He waited.

"The reason I know Elizabeth will tell no one about what I told you all today is the very reason you should find someone else to love. Only one thing matters to Elizabeth now—inheriting Bastion Point."

"I know."

If only he could give his heart to someone else.

"She's a fool, of course," Morwenna continued. "I think you're worth a dozen fine houses."

"Thank you."

"A lot of ladies would care for you like you deserve."

Was she offering?

He glanced at her over his shoulder. Her tears had dried. Despite red and swollen lids and blotchy cheeks, she glowed with a beauty rich enough it belied the talk of her lack of morals and concern for others. And for a moment, he considered taking her up on her unspoken offer. An alliance with her would solve many difficulties for her and for himself.

But his heart, his soul, his body ached for Elizabeth. He felt nothing when he held Morwenna's hands. He felt far too much when he simply looked at Elizabeth, nay, simply thought about her. When he considered a life with Morwenna as his wife, his mind went cold. When he thought of Elizabeth as his wife, he longed to find her, hold her, seek a way to convince her no amount of wealth protected a heart absent of love.

"Send to Penmara if you need anything." He departed with her soft laughter rolling behind him.

He looked for Elizabeth along the lane leading back to Bastion Point. The only motion in the distance came from the trees. He'd lingered too long at Morwenna's side, trying to comfort her, and getting his heart battered with the truth in return.

He needed to let Elizabeth go.

But not to Penvenan. That was just too cruel.

Keeping an eye out for her, Rowan made short work of the mile between Morwenna's cottage and Penmara. Penmara lay in all its dilapidated glory against a backdrop of blue sky and bluer sea. With a new roof and a great deal of paint, replacement glass for cracked and broken windows, and new furniture, the manor would prove a fine house once more. And Austell Penvenan intended to make it a fine house again. It would raise his status even higher in the eyes of Charlestonians, who still honored nobility, despite having thrown over the king forty years earlier. As far as Rowan knew, Penvenan had no interest in freeing his slaves.

Rowan entered the house to find Penvenan. As expected, he sat behind a massive and scarred desk in the one truly livable room in the manor—the library. One more estate ledger lay open before him.

He glanced up at Rowan's entrance, then returned to tracing a column of figures on the page with the tip of the quill before dipping the other end in the pot of ink to write in another ledger.

"Why did you lie to the Trelawnys?" Rowan demanded.

Penvenan kept reading figures.

"You have no intention of freeing your slaves with or without Miss Trelawny's dowry," Rowan pressed.

At last Penvenan looked up and smiled. "But there, Rowan, you're incorrect. The lady believes every man who courts her is after her fortune, so I had to give her a reason why I didn't want it for myself."

"Even if it's not true?" Rowan pressed his fists against his thighs, his insides taut.

"But it is true." Penvenan's eyes went out of focus, distant, almost dreamy. "If I have to acquire land in Canada or the Northwest Territory to relocate all four hundred slaves and transport every man, woman, and child in Penmara to South Carolina to work the fields and tend the houses, I'll do so to have Elizabeth Trelawny as my wife."

Rowan stared at Penvenan, Morwenna's words shrieking through his head. *She'll never have you.* She wouldn't, not now that Penvenan was willing to give her his heart as well as his title.

The former would please Elizabeth, as she could believe him. The latter would please her family. And Rowan had too little ammunition with which to fight back unless he sacrificed his pride and told her the truth about himself and endangered the lives of too many people.

CHAPTER 22

ELIZABETH FED A FILAMENT OF YELLOW SILK THREAD through the eye of the needle and began to work the complex knots that formed the centers of the purple daisies decorating the cream satin ribbon. She needed to create ten yards of the stuff for prizes at Grandmama's charity fete, and had only produced three with but a week to go before the festivities.

Concentration on any task required she sit still, whether attending church, listening to Grandpapa's daily Bible readings and prayers, or even eating a meal. She wanted to ride, walk, dive into the cold, clear water of the sea, anything but perch upright on a chair in the garden parlor, with Grandmama reading sermons aloud or working on her own embroidery, Miss Pross stitching away at one project or another, and Senara reading as many novels as she could obtain, then starting over again when she'd finished all in the house.

Walking and riding required an escort. Swimming, according to the grandparents, was out of the question for a young lady Elizabeth's age. The escort she could have in Lord Penvenan. Despite having told her grandparents she would not marry him, they no doubt now thought she had changed her mind. He called every day. He took Elizabeth driving. It was more sitting, listening to him talk, his plans for Penmara and his "people" back in America. It required no action but that she look as pretty as possible, and smile, offer an occasional comment or insert the right question at the right time, and avoid any of his lordship's attempts to touch her.

He never asked to play tennis again. Occasionally they walked in the garden. More often than not, they sat in a parlor or drawing room, depending on how many people were present, and Elizabeth performed more of the social skills she'd learned at her mother's instruction and demonstration. And all the while she needed to steer him or anyone else clear of talk of a future between her and Penvenan.

She longed for those weeks of morning rides with Rowan Curnow. He, however, had been playing least in sight. At least he didn't come near Bastion Point. He arrived in church every Sunday. He bowed to her across the sanctuary. He never spoke and never responded to her attempts to catch his eye. Each time her heart tore a little more.

He did, however, visit Morwenna, Elizabeth learned from a snatch of conversation she overheard between Grandpapa and Penvenan.

"I don't think there's any significance in the calls on Miss Morwenna," Penvenan had said. "Rowan has an overly kind heart for outcasts and what he calls the downtrodden."

As had a masked stranger at a ball, asking her to dance twice and touching her heart for the first time.

"But it could be encouraged, if you like." Penvenan's voice droned on.

"It is something worth considering," Grandpapa had responded in a thoughtful tone.

"You could do worse for the girl than my . . . secretary."

Feeling as though she were about to burst into tears, Elizabeth had scurried on before she overheard anything else about an alliance between Rowan and Morwenna. Morwenna could do worse than Rowan Curnow. Elizabeth didn't blame him for calling on her cousin. Nor did she blame him for staying away from her. She'd treated him abysmally. Too late, she realized that even if he only wanted her fortune, she'd have him. Now, if he had held any regard for her, he had abandoned his attempts to woo her. Because of her arrogance, she'd frozen him out of her life and left him vulnerable for Morwenna's machinations.

"'The Lord Jesus Christ, my dear sisters,'" Grandmama read from a sermon by George Whitefield, "'doth choose you merely by his free grace; it is freely of his own mercy, that he brings you into the marriage covenant: you, who have so grievously offended him, yet, the Lord Jesus Christ hath chosen you; you did not, you would not have chosen him; but when once, my dear sisters, he hath chosen you, then, and not till then, you make choice of him for your Lord and Husband.'"

Jesus didn't want her for his bride. If he did love her, she'd rejected him so much he, like Rowan, had likely given up on her as eternally lost.

"'The Lord Jesus Christ when he first comes to you,'" Grandmama continued, "'finds you full of sin and pollution; you're deformed, defiled, enslaved, poor, miserable, and wretched, very despicable and loathsome, by reason of sin; and he maketh choice of you, not because of your holiness, nor of your beauty, nor of your being qualified for them; no, the Lord Jesus Christ puts these qualifications upon you, as may make you meet for his embrace; and you're drawn to make choice of the Lord Jesus Christ because he first chose you.'"

If only she could find room in her heart to believe the claim that Jesus made her fit for him, that he loved her for nothing more than her. No one ever had, not even the grandparents. They only seemed pleased with her because she still allowed Penvenan to court her. They no longer spoke of treasures beyond the price of Bastion Point and other material goods. They spoke of her security lying in making a good match just like Mama. If she ran off with Rowan, or anyone unworthy of a Trelawny, the grandparents would likely rob her of the only stability she'd ever known—the land, possessions, Bastion Point.

But how could she wed Austell Lord Penvenan when she loved his secretary, of all things?

The sermon was right. She was miserable and wretched. She couldn't continue to ply her needle on something as frivolous as purple daisies on a satin ribbon.

She tossed the embroidery into her workbasket and rose in one fluid motion. Senara dropped her book. Grandmama stopped reading in midword.

"Please excuse me. I need some air." Without a by-your-leave, Elizabeth swept from the room and all but ran to the nearest door. It led to the walkway leading directly to the stable. She might not be allowed to ride alone, but she could visit Grisette over the fence around her paddock. The mare came to her, nuzzling Elizabeth's hand in search of a treat.

"I am sorry, girl. I came in too much of a hurry to bring you something."

The mare snorted and trotted away, tail high.

"It looks as though even your horse wants something from you." Senara spoke from so close behind Elizabeth, she jumped.

"What are you doing here? You dislike horses."

"I dislike riding horses. They are beautiful to look at. Besides, you looked overset. I wanted to be sure you are all right."

"Thank you." Elizabeth faced her friend and leaned against the rail.

Senara had grown quieter over the past few weeks, especially since her accident. She rarely complained about Penvenan taking over Penmara. In fact, she'd complimented him on the improvements already taking place. She'd grown thinner too, and rarely wanted to play more than a round or two of Map of Europe or Spillikins. Coming out to the stable yard, spotlessly clean, yet still reeking of equines, to be sure Elizabeth was all right was another sign that life surrounded by people who were caring for her despite her bad behavior was having a positive effect.

Elizabeth gave her a warm smile. "I am simply weary of being inside on such lovely days as these. I could have stayed with my parents for all the exercise I am getting here."

"That will all change once you're wed." Senara did not smile. "At least I presume you're going to marry my cousin."

"It is a good match," Elizabeth hedged. If she told Senara outright she wouldn't marry him, Senara would tell the grandparents within the hour.

Even though the grandparents no longer spoke of treasure, Elizabeth continued to read the family chronicles in search of what they had not found. Perhaps she could trade that knowledge for marriage.

"At least he wants my fortune for something altruistic." If she said it enough, she might convince herself to accept a proposal.

Senara grimaced. "But he is so old. He'll be in his dotage before your children are out of petticoats. They cannot make you wed, you know. The Hardwick Marriage Act ensures that."

"It also said they could not force me to wed Romsford, but there are ways to persuade a female to wed against her will—place her in a compromising position, social ostracism, confinement..."

Confinement—what she was nearly suffering now.

She allowed her gaze to travel across the yard to where one of the grooms pretended to clean a trough while watching her the whole time. He was willing to take a bribe. What if she bribed him to take Grisette to the beach in the early morning? She could sneak down through the secret staircase and the caves.

This was a new quarter, and she'd spent next to nothing of her pin money, an allowance greatly increased by Grandpapa with little to spend it on.

"Your grandparents would do none of those things to you," Senara was saying. "They care too much about you."

"Hmm." Elizabeth caught the groom's eye. "Senara, just a moment, please. I need to give the grooms some instruction about Grisette's care."

She was despicable and loathsome for lying to Senara. Despicable and loathsome like the sermon said.

Shaking off the guilt, she crossed the cobbles to the groom. "Do you know when low tide is tomorrow?"

He ducked his head. "Five of the clock, Miss Trelawny."

"Excellent. I'll see you there. With this mare."

"But, miss—"

"A crown."

"Six shillings just for that?"

"It could cost you your position."

He shrugged. "I'll find another. Lord Penvenan'll be needing new grooms with the horses he just bought."

"Indeed. And I'll recommend you. Now see that Grisette is more thoroughly groomed in the future."

There, that instruction salved her conscience.

She returned to Senara. "Let us go into Grandmama's garden. I think I'd like a rose for my hair when Lord Penvenan comes to dinner tonight."

"A white one," Senara said. "It will make you look so maidenly, just what gentlemen like. And you can wear a white dress."

"I look awful in white."

"But it must be white. Heroines always wear white." Senara slipped her arm through Elizabeth's. "You know, it will be odd, you being mistress of my house."

"It will be odd being mistress of any house. But I don't think it will be Penmara."

"Of course it will. You know you'll give in to your grandparents and marry him. You want to please them more than yourself."

"Pleasing them does please me."

They walked toward Bastion Point, the house Elizabeth yearned to govern. She would expand the garden and build a gazebo set up high enough so one could sit inside on a summer's day and observe the sea over the wall. She would plant fruit trees, and she'd build a glasshouse so they could have lemons and strawberries all year around.

But that kind of control would only come upon the death of her grandmother, and that was unthinkable.

Everything in life came with a price, and some were too high to pay.

So she sent word to the stable to cancel her morning ride on the beach and greeted Penvenan with warmth that evening. The grandparents' smiles gave her some comfort. The gleam in Penvenan's eyes when he looked at her gave her more than a little pause. Perhaps he did care for her. Perhaps, if she let herself, she could forget Rowan.

So she considered until she caught sight of Rowan riding on the beach the next morning. Astride one of the horses he had chosen with her assistance, he raced along the sand like a centaur, one with his mount, both magnificently beautiful. She leaned over the sill to get a better view. Her heart felt as though it soared after him. *Wait, wait, wait for me.*

Too high a price to let him go for the sake of her lack of confidence, her lack of belief in her worth as more than a fount of guineas?

Since he made no attempt to see her, she suspected she had

already paid it. He had turned his attentions to Morwenna, proof Elizabeth was right about what he wanted from her.

Heart heavy, she prepared for a day of work on the fete. That morning Grandmama and Miss Pross, Senara and Elizabeth, along with other ladies in the neighborhood, planned to begin decorating the village hall while menservants built new booths for selling food and goods on the green. Lord Penvenan had promised to bring some of his repairmen, so she had best dress well. Grandmama expected it of her.

Despite their claims, Elizabeth had begun to suspect that the only treasure in life the grandparents thought she should find was a respectable husband. But surely they wanted more for her.

That thought in mind, she returned to the window. He no longer rode but stood beside his mount in conversation with someone just out of sight.

Gripping the window frame to keep herself from plunging headfirst onto the beach more than sixty feet below, Elizabeth leaned out farther in an attempt to glimpse his interlocutor. Her hand slipped on the frame. Her feet lost purchase on the floor. For a heart-stopping moment, she balanced on her middle, then managed to grab the casement and drag it shut. Then she sank to her knees, heart lurching, breath heaving, eyes burning.

Rowan Curnow was talking to Morwenna at the mouth of the cave tunnel.

He heard the window slam above him and glanced up. No telling who had watched him from above, but he could guess. His gaze snapped to the window near the garden corner of the house.

Morwenna laughed. "Do her good to see you not pining for

her. But I'd best be going before she comes down or sends someone to run me off."

"She won't. She hasn't told anyone about you and Conan yet."

Yet one more reason to love her—her understanding and discretion.

"Yet," Morwenna's lip curled, remembering what she'd told him about Elizabeth only wanting to inherit Bastion Point. "She might after all out of spite. Our Elizabeth isn't used to not getting her way."

Rowan started walking with Morwenna across Penmara's shoreline with its wider beach and gentler slope up to the house but rough surf, as though the cliff had caved into the sea many centuries earlier. "I'd say Miss Elizabeth rarely gets her way."

Morwenna snorted. "Elizabeth has everything."

"Except a belief in her ability to be loved without wealth."

"I expect that's partly my fault." Morwenna's shoulders slumped. "I teased her mercilessly, especially about her ice-blue eyes."

And he had called her the ice-blue ice maiden. How cruel of him. She was anything but icy to him in moments of abandon. Stolen, inappropriate moments of abandon.

"I'll see you safely home," he said with an abruptness verging on rudeness. "Don't come out here again."

"But the cave must be—"

"I'll see to the cave. Everything will be ready if necessary." He tucked his hand beneath her elbow to lend her support, but didn't say another word.

At the gate to her cottage, she turned and laid her hand on his arm. "I regret what I did to her, especially if it's costing you too. I regret . . ." She sighed. "I regret a lot of things. If I can ever help you . . ."

"The Lord will work it out if it's his will."

Leaving her safe inside her home, he returned to Penmara with a burden pressing upon him. He kept saying he was working in God's will, but didn't know how he could when he was uncertain what that will was.

He especially didn't know on days like this when his plans to continue supervising, and even helping with, the repairs on Penmara took him into the village with Penvenan. The villagers barely spoke to him. He was a foreigner. He was from Penmara. He was someone not to be trusted. The out-of-work miners were happy to take Penvenan silver in exchange for their work. They even accepted Rowan's wish to join in the hard, physical labor of nailing down shingles and replacing damp-ruined walls. But they spoke little in his presence. Conversations amongst themselves stopped whenever he approached.

That most of them no doubt belonged to the local smuggling gang, that at least one or two of them knew who had killed Conan and why, he also didn't doubt. But he had learned all too quickly that he would have to live in Cornwall for another decade before these men would accept him as a local man—if they ever did.

He wanted to leave Cornwall, run, if he was honest with himself, from seeing Elizabeth, run from Penvenan's control over his life, run from too much greed-induced pain of those around him.

And I accused Elizabeth of running away.

One often did see one's own faults reflected in others. They both ran from what the Lord wanted for them. Elizabeth wouldn't accept that God loved her and wanted her life. Rowan wouldn't accept that God apparently wanted something for his life other than what he himself wanted.

"Give me the strength to accept it, Lord." With the prayer on his lips, he entered the house to find Penvenan eating breakfast in the second room they had managed to restore—a parlor with a gate-leg table they used for meals.

"Come eat," Penvenan called to him. "We're going into the village to help with the fete preparations."

Rowan's heart leaped. More than likely Elizabeth would be there as well.

He filled a plate from the sideboard and seated himself across from Penvenan. "What are we expected to do?"

"Build booths for selling things. Assist the ladies any way we can."

Rowan's brows arched. "They don't have their servants do the labor?"

"Apparently not for this charity event. I'm no good at things like hammering nails, but you should be by now."

"Maybe you should have apprenticed me to a builder instead of sending me to the university." The edge of bitterness slipped out unbidden, unwanted, and all too true. "I might be better earning my living on my own if you had."

Penvenan leaned forward, the ends of his cravat dangling perilously close to the remains of egg on his plate, his eyes glittering and hard like obsidian. "You were never meant to work for your living. Your mother intended for you to be a gentleman. I did not fail her."

"If being a gentleman means living off the work of others who have no choice but to break their backs and health," Rowan said from a constricted throat, "then, yes, sir, I failed her. But it was fail her ambitions for me or fail the Lord's calling."

"What about honoring your mother and father?"

Rowan stared at congealed grease on his plate. "A matter I struggle with still."

"Like your infatuation for Miss Trelawny? Miss Elizabeth Trelawny?"

Rowan flinched. "One cannot control the heart. She is a fine and beautiful lady."

"She is not beautiful. Passably pretty, yes. But her cousin . . ." Penvenan smiled.

Rowan braced himself.

"Miss Morwenna Trelawny is a beauty even in her condition."

Rowan chose his words with care. "When did you meet Miss Morwenna?"

"I haven't, but I saw you with her this morning. Considering an alliance there? I expect Sir Petrok will be happy to accept you as a grandson-in-law and pay you well."

"I," Rowan enunciated through stiff lips, "have no intention of marrying for money. Now, if you will excuse me, I will gather together any materials we need to take into the village."

He walked out—or did he run away again?—and ordered a wagon to be filled with building materials. He was already dressed appropriately for hard labor in canvas trousers, boots, and a heavy linen shirt. Penvenan should change out of his fine coat and pantaloons, Hessian boots, and fancifully tied cravat, but Rowan doubted he would lift a finger to perform actual work. He hadn't done so in all his life. No doubt Penvenan would take the day to press his suit with Elizabeth.

Which he did. While he pounded nails into rough boards, Rowan saw them from across the green, Penvenan holding yards of bunting for Elizabeth to drape over completed booths. While he paused to draw splinters from his hand, Rowan caught a glimpse of Penvenan holding Elizabeth's hand as he talked to her. She stood ramrod straight with her cool mask in place, and Senara stood beside them, her pouting lower lip visible from a hundred feet away.

"I know how you feel, Miss Penvenan." Rowan yanked a particularly large splinter from the base of his thumb, then grabbed up an abandoned tankard to wash away the blood.

Instead of water, the tankard held ale. It stung and stank like a skunk. It also splashed onto his shirt.

Time to leave the village green. Maybe the time was coming for him to leave Cornwall altogether. But not until he found some answers or knew the ladies were safe.

He cast one last glance at Elizabeth and wished he hadn't. She was walking toward Bastion Point with her hand resting on Penvenan's forearm, and he covered her hand with the fingers of his other hand.

"You can kiss me with abandon, Miss Trelawny," Rowan murmured to the couple's retreating backs, "but you only let him court you in the daylight."

Lord, is it time to give up all hope in that direction?

Rowan received his answer that night when Penvenan returned from Penmara. His smile was bright, his footfalls light. "Congratulate me, Rowan. Sir Petrok has given me permission to make an offer to Miss Trelawny."

"I wish you well, sir." Rowan's face felt as stiff as Elizabeth's too often became.

He considered mentioning the danger to her connection with Penmara, but it was pointless since Penvenan didn't believe the truth of it. Like everyone else, he thought Elizabeth's fall from the cliff path had been an accident.

"When do you propose to . . . propose?" He managed a credible smile at his word play.

Penvenan's smile broadened. "On Midsummer's Eve, at the fete."

CHAPTER 23

GRANDMAMA FROWNED AT THE ARRAY OF DRESSES LAID upon Elizabeth's bed. "Whatever possessed your mother to purchase white for you?"

"It's fashionable this year." Elizabeth grimaced. "And she wanted me to look still young and innocent."

"You are still young and innocent and look it without our making you appear jaundiced." Grandmama turned to the dressing room. "What else do you have you haven't worn yet?"

Elizabeth hugged her arms over her middle and retreated a step from the fashion display. "What does it matter whether or not I have worn the gown? I've been here for two months. It's to be expected."

"Yes, but this is a special occasion." Grandmama began to hunt through Elizabeth's gowns.

Elizabeth retreated another step, then another until her back touched the mantelshelf. "Grandmama, this is a village fete, not a coronation ball."

"And so much more can happen today." Grandmama shot Elizabeth a wink.

Her morning chocolate turned into a whirlpool in her middle at the notion of what else could happen that day. She had read the signs as clearly as though they hung in painted splendor over a street of shops. Penvenan had walked her home from setting up for the fete. Penvenan had closeted himself with Grandpapa for an hour, then departed whistling. The grandparents had smiled a great deal ever since.

Last night Senara had suffered another one of her shivering attacks, and Elizabeth considered joining her in her own sickroom as a way to get out of going to the fete. Yet what was the use? The moment of reckoning would come eventually. The only way to avoid it would be to leave Cornwall. She might if she had anywhere to go.

We can get married on Guernsey . . . On their way to America, of course. Not a risk she was willing to take. And if she wouldn't give up anything for him, then she must not love him. Surely love would supersede apprehensions regarding his lack of fortune and true love for her. She was thinking with her head and not her heart.

Her head said marry Lord Penvenan.

She forced herself away from the mantel and into the dressing room. "I have an idea. If I wear this lilac sarcenet spencer over the white cambric, there won't be so much white around my face." She pulled the light silk garment off its hook, then reached up to a high shelf. "And here's a matching hat. Kid slippers or the morocco boots?"

In the end, she wore the boots. Though they were white and would get terribly dusty and grass stained, they were sturdier than the slippers, and she would be rushing about a great deal as one of the hostesses of the fete.

Since Miss Pross was tending to Senara, who preferred not to go into public for a celebration so close to her brother's death, Grandmama's maid arrived to help Elizabeth lace up stays and button the dress up the back. The gown's neckline was square and a little too low for the country, but the spencer buttoned from its bottom at the high waistline to the hollow of her throat.

The maid rolled Elizabeth's hair into a knot low on her neck and secured it with several pearl hairpins to match the pearls on her ears. A white chip straw hat with a lilac satin ribbon bow in front completed the ensemble, and Grandmama declared Elizabeth charming.

"You look like a summer day." Grandmama opened the window over the garden. "And the weather is perfect."

Elizabeth glanced out the other window, half expecting to see a horseman galloping along the beach, though the tide mostly covered the sand below the house, and he would be gone now if he had been there at all.

She expected to see him at the fete. No doubt Penvenan would have his secretary performing all the laborious tasks he had avoided himself. She had seen Rowan swinging a hammer with the grace and speed of someone who did so often, and she had seen him pulling splinters from his palm. She wanted to help him, ensure the wound was properly cleaned, simply hold his hand.

She paused on her way down the staircase and gripped the banister for support. What was she thinking that she should accept an offer from Austell Lord Penvenan? Not when she wanted to hold another man's hand. The very idea surely made her some kind of wanton.

She must be good. She must make the right choices. She was only lovable when she was obedient. Didn't even the Lord demand obedience?

Except, according to the vicar, the Lord loved her even when she was disobedient. If only the grandparents and parents were the same . . .

She shook her head and continued down to the entryway to meet the grandparents and most of the servants. She smiled as befitted the occasion. This was a day of revelry for the county.

Everyone who could attended the fete, eating pasties and drinking lemonade, buying and selling items they made over the winter months, and enjoying the music, the singing, the dancing to celebrate the arrival of summer's bounty, including the abundance of daylight just past the longest day of the year.

It felt like the longest day of Elizabeth's life before midafternoon. She never stopped moving from booth to booth, church hall to the center of the green and the games. Children's laughter rang out like bells over the lower pitch of singers. Although the sun blazed across a nearly cloudless sky, a steady breeze swept from the sea and across the land to keep the air pleasantly cool. Roasting meats, baking pastry, and lemons scented the air, but Elizabeth didn't have the opportunity to grow hungry. She judged who had made the best pies from last year's dried apples and whose needlework demonstrated the most skill. She awarded prizes to the young women who participated in the races, and she carried messages from Grandmama to Mr. Kitto, from Mr. Kitto to—

She came face-to-face with Rowan Curnow outside a roped-off circle where Mrs. Pascoe and her daughters read stories to a throng of children. He carried a box full of slates and chalk held before him like a shield. Elizabeth carried nothing but her fan and reticule, poor substitutes for a defense wall against the warmth in his deep blue eyes. Coolness on her neck reminded her she had unbuttoned the top two fastenings on her spencer. With Rowan not a yard from her, she wished she hadn't, but at the same time, she wanted a long swim in the chilly waters of the Irish Sea.

She opened her mouth to speak, but no words emerged. In no way could she say what she wanted to. *Why were you talking to my cousin? Why can't you stay here in Cornwall? How can I ever believe you love me?*

"You should call on your cousin, Miss Trelawny," Rowan said. "She's lonely and frightened."

Elizabeth took a half step closer. "Nothing's happened to her, has it?"

"She has the dogs to guard her, but as her time draws near, she grows—" He broke off, his gaze flashing past her shoulder. "Good day, Miss Trelawny." He passed her to go to the rear of the group of children and deposit the crate of slates on the grass.

Elizabeth stared after him for a moment, then continued to give her message to Mrs. Pascoe. After that, she turned to retrace her steps to where Grandmama directed all the festivities from the porch of the church.

Lord Penvenan reached her, likely the reason Rowan had strode away so abruptly.

"You look charming today, my dear." His gaze swept her from the lilac bow on her hat to the white toes of her leather boots. She flinched away as though he'd touched her inappropriately. He didn't yet have the right to look at her as though he were inspecting a new filly.

She dropped a slight curtsy. "Thank you, my lord. Are you enjoying yourself?"

"I just arrived." He sounded annoyed.

Of course he would. She should have known he had just arrived.

"I came for the dancing," he added.

"Oh dear." Elizabeth glanced at the far end of the green where several musicians were gathering. "This isn't like dancing in a ballroom, you know. It's more like a frolic."

She couldn't imagine the staid baron kicking up his heels to hop and skip and whirl village girls around on his arm as Rowan had done at the horse fair. As she had been spun about at the horse fair. As they both had done before he drew her aside and kissed her, proposed to her, claimed he loved her.

Would Penvenan make claims of loving her, or just propose?

"It's rather vigorous dancing." She spoke too quickly.

Penvenan nodded. "I like to watch, so feel free to join in."

Elizabeth looked at the first set forming in the golden light of the lowering sun. "That's all right. I . . ."

The music began with a few tentative notes, then rose to a lilting and joyous melody. The dancers clapped, stomped, and began to move. They whirled past in a shimmering array of blue and crimson skirts and flowing hair, flashing smiles and glimpses of trim ankles.

"Perhaps one set." She started across the green, Penvenan beside her. "If you truly don't mind."

"Not at all. I would enjoy watching you."

She reached the end of the line of dancers. Sam Carn grasped her hands and spun her into the figure of the set. The movement sent her to the brief holds of miners and farmers, sons of the local gentry . . .

And Rowan Curnow.

He clasped her hand harder than necessary. For a moment, almost long enough to disrupt the rhythm of the lines, he held her gaze; then he handed her off to someone else and vanished into the endlessly shifting lines.

Feeling as though her boots had been created for feet twice the size of hers, Elizabeth freed herself from the set the next time she came to the head of the line. Penvenan waited for her. He grasped her hand and strode away from the revelers so swiftly she had to lengthen her stride to keep up with him. With a slight shift of her head, she caught sight of Rowan sauntering away from the dancers, his hands in his pockets, as though he didn't have a care in the world.

Except he raised his head and met her gaze from across the growing greensward between them, and even at the distance, she saw his eyes looked bleak.

Her heart squeezed. She tried to tug her hand free of Penvenan's. "I'd like to find something to drink, my lord."

"In a bit we will." He laced his fingers with hers, decreasing her chances of breaking free without a scene. "Let's rest here a moment." He climbed the steps to the church porch.

Grandmama had vacated the location sometime in the past half an hour.

Penvenan took a seat on a bench and drew Elizabeth down beside him. "We can talk undisturbed here."

"I'm needed to help clean things up."

"Not at all. You've done your share of work for one day."

"But Grandmama—"

"Knows you're here." He smiled. He patted her hand. He dropped onto one knee before her.

Behind him, several people stopped to stare.

"My lord, we have an audience." Her glance darted back to him, to the audience, to his lordship. "Please stand. I cannot accept—"

"I thought to wait a little longer to know one another better," he continued as though she hadn't spoken. "But I believe more time is merely wasting it."

"Please, do not waste your breath on my account. I cannot—" She caught sight of Rowan on the far side of the green in conversation with Sam Carn. Her mouth went dry. Words dried like apples in an oven.

"I would be honored if you will consent to becoming my—"

Elizabeth stood. "My lord, I tried to spare you embarrassment, but I cannot accept your kind offer. I . . . I do not wish to wed anyone." Seeing Rowan striding away from Sam Carn, she added, "Anyone I do not accept loves me."

"Surely you know I do." Penvenan remained on one knee.

Elizabeth edged away. "No, my lord, I have no reason to think or believe it. Now, please excuse me. I need to be alone." She turned and entered the sanctuary.

Behind her the audience to the humiliating scene murmured. A few applauded.

Elizabeth didn't stop inside the church. She continued up the aisle to the door behind the little-used choir stall, drew back the bolts, and descended the steps to a hedgerow-lined lane behind the church. Penvenan did not immediately pursue her. The church, the hall, and a half dozen houses and shops blocked the music and laughter from the lane. The crunch of Elizabeth's boots sounded loud. The lane seemed unnaturally dark after the brightness of the open green. She needed to return there, to light and noise and so many people Penvenan couldn't importune her to marry him again.

She should have nipped it in the bud before it happened. But until that last glimpse of Rowan before Penvenan dragged her onto the porch, she considered the marriage in the way of all arranged marriages—if they got on well enough, it was a good match. But she didn't want good enough. She wanted to be loved. Not for a moment did she believe Penvenan loved her. Admired her perhaps, but not with soul-deep love. She knew she didn't love him.

But he had decided to follow her. The footfalls crunched behind her, swift and heavy. She increased her pace. He mustn't catch her alone, out of sight of the village. Another thirty yards brought the end of the building. She could round the corner to sunlight and air smelling of roasting meat, not damp earth and the scent of her own overly heated skin.

Thirty yards looked like thirty miles with the footfalls drawing near. She grabbed her skirt, ready to outright run. Twenty-five yards. Twenty.

The blow caught her between the shoulder blades. She staggered, emitting a gasping cry. The footfalls ceased. The shrubbery rustled.

She started to run, heard Rowan accusing her of always running, and spun to confront her pursuer, her attacker. Behind her, someone shouted her name. Before her, silver flashed in a shaft of sunlight between two roof peaks. She screamed and flung herself back and to the side—

And the blade merely tore through the sleeve of her spencer.

She sank to her knees, her hands pressed to her middle. If she had eaten all day, she would have been sick. Her stomach roiled as though a thousand gulls fought over one fish. Her head spun. But her gaze remained fixed on the slice of silver gleaming on the dusty track.

"Elys." Rowan was there beside her, kneeling on the ground, his arm encircling her shoulders. "Did it hit you? Where are you hurt?"

"Just my sleeve. Something struck my back, and I lost my balance for a moment. And then—" Her eyes went out of focus, and she laid her head against his broad, solid shoulder, crushing her hat, sending her hair spilling over them both. "Someone threw a knife at me. I forgot I shouldn't be alone and someone—" She began to shake. Her teeth chattered. Her chest heaved. Even the toes of her boots scraped against the ground. "Someone tried to ki-ki-kill—"

"Shh." He shifted his position so he held her in both arms. "Hush, my beloved, hush. You're safe now."

"I'm not. I never will be." She buried her face against the soft wool of his coat, inhaled the scent of the sea and sunshine-dried linen and him. His warmth seeped into her. She nestled closer, seeking shelter.

Except a killer ran free beyond the hedgerow.

"Who?" Her voice was a mere croak. "Why?"

"I don't know who. He wore a hat pulled down too low to show his face. As for why . . ." His arms tightened. "You got yourself engaged to Lord Penvenan."

"But I didn't." She raised her head and met his eyes, nearly black in the shadowy alleyway. "I turned him down. Didn't everyone see me walking away from him?"

"They saw him follow you into the church and thought the two of you were"—he swallowed—"were making wedding plans."

Nearly everyone in the parish had seen and presumed the betrothal was complete. And someone wished to harm those connected too closely with Penmara.

Another tremor ran through her. "It's true, then. These men are serious in their threats. I may never be safe here. My home. My sanctuary. My only ref-refuge—" Tears blurred her vision, and she squeezed her eyes shut.

"Don't cry." He kissed her closed lids. "This will make the riding officers look harder to learn the identities of the local gang." He kissed her cheek. "Maybe you and Morwenna should go away until this is over."

She opened her mouth to protest this notion, and he kissed her.

She forgot about knives, fear, and envy of her cousin's beauty. She forgot about Penvenan's proposal and her need to always be good . . . She remembered how much she loved the warm firmness of Rowan's lips on hers. She nestled against him and raised her hands to cup his face, her palms rasping on the stubble of a day's whisker growth, his hair satin soft in contrast.

I love you. I love you. I must love you, rang in her head, rose to her lips, stopped as he kissed her again.

The revels receded into another world, the rhythm of the music lost beneath the pulse of her heart. Warmth stole through her, though a shiver skimmed over her skin.

"Miss Tre-law-ny?" The drawn out call of her name slammed Elizabeth back to the hard earth of Cornwall, the lane where a knife still lay in the dirt.

Rowan released his hold on her and caught hold of her hands to draw her to her feet. "Constable Carn, you're just the man we need."

"What happened?" The constable looked at Elizabeth. "We heard a scream. Was that you, Miss Trelawny?"

"Yes." She began to fasten the top buttons on her spencer for warmth. "I was—"

Suddenly, the lane filled with more people—Lord Penvenan, Mr. Kitto, and Grandpapa. All but Grandpapa surrounded Rowan and the knife, as well as a fist-sized stone Elizabeth hadn't noticed before.

Grandpapa grasped Elizabeth's elbow with a strength belying his age. "I am sending you home with three of our servants. You will go to your room and stay there." His face softened. "For your safety."

"I need to stay here and help explain—"

"I was looking for Lord Penvenan to tell him I was returning to Penmara," Rowan was explaining. "When I didn't see anyone in the church, I came around back—"

"You can do your explaining to your grandmother and me. Right now, I think you need quiet and rest." Grandpapa's hold compelled her gently forward. "We will send for you when we settle things here."

"But someone tried to hurt me."

"I know." A vein throbbed against Grandpapa's temple as he touched her torn sleeve. "And Rowan Curnow conveniently rescued you."

Elizabeth stiffened. "What are you saying?"

"I'm saying you need to be someplace less public than this.

Now, here are your escorts. Go. Carn and I will question everyone here to learn if they saw anything."

No one would have. No one ever did. If they knew nothing of Conan's murder, they wouldn't risk their lives and families for the Trelawny who had left them for London.

Grandpapa released her to the care of three footmen, none of whom would disobey his order to see she went nowhere but Bastion Point and stayed there.

Bastion Point, her sanctuary, her refuge, had become a prison.

CHAPTER 24

The summons arrived an hour later. Grandmama's maid had arrived to assist Elizabeth in changing into a fresh dress and pin up her hair, then left her without more than a dozen words exchanged. At the end of an hour's wait, a footman arrived to tell Elizabeth the grandparents awaited her on the terrace.

She descended with head high and indifferent mask in place. The long, silver fringe of her shawl hid a trembling in her hands as she stepped onto the terrace.

"Sit down." Grandpapa indicated a chair with the bowl of his unlit pipe.

Elizabeth preferred to stand, but perched on the edge of the chair, her toes drawn beneath the hem of her spangled crepe gown.

"What were you doing in that back lane?" Grandpapa demanded without preamble.

Beside him, Grandmama poured cups of tea as though this were nothing more than a quiet evening at home without guests.

Elizabeth laced her fingers through her fringe and made herself look Grandpapa in the eye. "I slipped out the back door of the church to escape Lord Penvenan."

"You acted as though he were some kind of villain, child," Grandmama gently admonished.

Elizabeth ground her teeth. "He was making a fool of himself and me by proposing so publicly and then not taking my no for an answer."

"But why was no your answer?" Grandpapa lifted a candle from the table and lit his pipe.

A smoke Elizabeth once found comforting and pleasant stung her nostrils and brought tears to her eyes. She blinked and looked away. "I don't love him. Lately I haven't even liked him enough to want to go on a ride with him, let alone spend a lifetime yoked with him."

"Is it still the slave issue?" Grandmama asked.

Elizabeth looked from one grandparent to the other and nodded. "I believe he lied to you all about that. I believe he wants my money to reopen the mines."

Grandmama slid a cup of tea across the table between her and Grandpapa. "Is that what Mr. Curnow says?"

"He does."

"And how do you feel about this young man?" Grandpapa's voice sounded like gravel.

Elizabeth focused on the third teacup. "I find him too attractive to consider marrying another man."

"He seems to have too much interest in you," Grandmama said.

Grandpapa removed his pipe from his mouth. "Penvenan is sending Curnow back to Charleston as soon as he can arrange passage."

Elizabeth gripped her fringe. She froze her features. Nothing must give away the ripping open of her heart going on behind her frosty façade.

"He had his arm around you," Grandpapa said. "And you weren't protesting."

"No, I was not. I was understandably distraught."

And not wanting him to let her go for anything.

"We can all draw conclusions, Elizabeth," Grandpapa said.

Elizabeth said nothing.

"Have you truly decided to overthrow the regard of a good man for an undeniably fine, but otherwise unsuitable young man?" Tears filled Grandmama's green eyes. "Are you going the way of your brother and cousin?"

Elizabeth struggled for breath through her frozen throat, for words to pass her breaking heart. "I've no intention of going either Morwenna's or Drake's way, but I've chosen to overthrow the attentions of a good man, yes."

But the grandparents were more concerned with her moral fiber and refusal of Penvenan's proposal.

Her hands curled into fists on her lap.

"Oh, Elizabeth." Grandmama shook her head.

Grandpapa's teeth ground on the stem of his pipe.

Elizabeth rose and began to pace between terrace rail and the grouping of chairs, her hands clasped at her waist to calm the turmoil inside her. "Since I came home in April and Lord Penvenan decided to court me, I've done nothing but entertain dull matrons, ply my needle, and go for sedate walks or drives around the countryside. I am barely allowed to ride and then, again, only as sedately as someone on a job horse. I've enjoyed only a few gallops on the beach, and been forbidden to swim or go fishing. I may as well have stayed in London." She pounded her fist on the stone balustrade for emphasis.

"I returned here because it is the only place I've ever felt like I do not have to pretend interest in things that bore me to tears. I came home not to be importuned to marry someone in whom I have little interest as a husband other than to please you." Her mask began to slip.

"I came home to be loved because I am your granddaughter, not a social asset with the right connection. Yet I am confined like Bastion Point is Grosvenor Square and being importuned to marry another old man who wants me for my money. Even if Curnow is wrong and Penvenan wants my dowry to free his slaves, I'd rather give him the funds to free those people than sell my s-soul."

She barely managed the last word before her throat closed altogether. Tears scalded her eyes, and she spun away to face the garden's fragrant beauty.

Behind her, chair legs scraped on stone. Fabric rustled. The scent of lilacs flowed around her, though the blossoms had long since faded and fallen from their bushes. Grandmama's hand closed over Elizabeth's on the rail—thin, age-spotted, the knuckles growing thick with rheumatism.

"We couldn't have you continuing your rides with Mr. Curnow," Grandpapa spoke from behind her. "It wasn't seemly, and with Morwenna's trouble, we wanted to protect your reputation in the county. And we never intended for you to think we were insisting you wed Lord Penvenan."

"Did you not?" Elizabeth dashed away her tears with the back of her hand. "An alliance with the neighboring landowner would be so advantageous for all. That was always understood. At least if he offered for me, Conan was young and my friend and knew how to enjoy himself. But I suppose he would have only wed me for my dowry too, since he apparently wanted Morwen—" She slapped her hand over her mouth like closing the stable door after the horse had sought its freedom.

Grandmama's hand gripped with surprising strength, and Grandpapa's pipe dropped to the terrace, the stem separating from the bowl.

"What did you just say?" he demanded in a low, shaking voice. "What do you know?"

Elizabeth shook her head.

"Do you know something of Morwenna's alliance?" Grandpapa asked.

Elizabeth kept her lips tight.

"What did Conan have to do with Morwenna?" Grandpapa persisted.

Elizabeth sighed. "More than he should have."

"Did Conan father Morwenna's baby?" Grandpapa asked.

Elizabeth closed her eyes. "I didn't mean to tell you. If I were not feeling sorry for myself, I never would have broken her confidence."

"But why won't she tell us?" Grandmama sounded hurt and confused. "I admit I'm ashamed of Conan, but at least it wasn't one of the miners."

"She fears the smugglers." Elizabeth faced the grandparents. "Conan warned her to keep their secret or they might go after her and the baby."

The grandparents' faces paled. Grandpapa's hand shook as he reached for Grandmama's.

"She should have told us." He cleared his throat. "We could have been protecting her."

In for a penny. More like in for a pound, in for a pony.

Elizabeth looked her grandfather in the eye. "Perhaps you should have protected her regardless. You wonder why I cannot believe in the unconditional love of God, but love in my life has always been tied to conditions. I do not understand unconditional." She hugged her middle. "But I want to."

"We want you to." Grandpapa touched her cheek with the back of his hand, dry and cool and gentle. "We have done a poor job of showing we love you regardless of what you do."

"You placed conditions on Morwenna." Elizabeth needed their response to her challenge or she wouldn't have dared.

"Not conditions of our love," Grandmama said. "We still

love her. We have taken care of her needs. But we had to think of you and your reputation."

"She only kept quiet about the father of her baby because of the connection to Conan. The smugglers threat and all. Just like—just like Mr. Curnow thinks my connection to Lord Penvenan has caused my . . . incidents of danger."

"Hmph." Grandpapa shoved his hand into his coat pocket, then scowled at his broken pipe. "Penvenan has had nothing to do with the smugglers. Indeed, they've been quiet since his arrival, so there's no credence in that theory. But Morwenna has reason to fear them with that kind of a connection to Conan."

He pulled his hand from his pocket, and it shook. "Even illegitimate and unable to inherit if he's a boy, the baby is still Conan's and worthy of using for a threat to warn others not to try to break away as Conan did." A tick on one side of his mouth belied his calm, analytical words. "Now that we know there's cause for her fear, we will take better care of her. I'll send some men to guard her cottage." Pausing only long enough to gather up the broken pieces of his pipe, he strode toward the house.

Grandmama rested a hand on Elizabeth's shoulder, keeping her from following. "Please forgive us for making our love seem conditional. We have always wanted the best for you, and sometimes perhaps what we thought was the best for you hasn't been."

She looked so old and sad, Elizabeth wrapped her arms around her grandmother, starting a little to feel how frail she'd become in the past six years. Yet she could not resist asking, "Would you still love me if I wed a man beneath my social standing?"

"Of course. That said . . ." Grandmama knit her brows. "If you refer to Mr. Curnow, we wouldn't approve. Even if he agreed to stay here in Cornwall, you know a female is lowered to the rank of her husband, and you would be ostracized by most of your peers. When one is in love, one doesn't think that matters, but isolation wears on a body and has a way of tearing even the strongest bonds of the heart."

Elizabeth laughed. "He has mentioned love, but now that he is returning to America—" She stopped, realizing that he had planned to return to America all along. "Perhaps he has merely been toying with me." She let out a bitter bark of laughter. She had, after all, thrown herself at him.

"Or perhaps he waits to ask you to go with him."

"He did ask. I said no. I couldn't. This"—she swept her arm out to encompass the house and garden—"is my anchor. He will have to stay here, and as you said, if he does, not even local society will accept him, an outsider who marries an heiress."

"And without a name."

Elizabeth gave Grandmama a blank look. "He has an old Cornish name."

"Yes, child, through his mother. She was related to Mrs. Kitto."

"Through his—oh." Sympathy clenched her heart.

No wonder he was so solicitous of Morwenna's welfare. No wonder he felt so much gratitude toward Penvenan for giving him a home and education. "I doubt I'll see him again unless it cannot be avoided."

She wanted to lay her head on Grandmama's frail shoulder and sob like a child who had lost her dearest friend.

Grandmama patted her hand. "As much as I understand why you consider Bastion Point your anchor, it is just stone and mortar and land. The Lord should be your true anchor. Only his love never fails."

A longing to believe Grandmama touched Elizabeth's heart. "I've no idea how to believe that. But I wish—right now I wish I could."

If Grandmama was right, Jesus wouldn't break her heart.

"May I please be excused? I am quite worn to a thread from today."

"Shall I send a tray to your room?" Grandmama stepped back, giving Elizabeth permission to leave.

"Just some soup and tea. Thank you." Elizabeth ambled into the house, her legs suddenly too weak to support her, her heart too heavy to talk anymore. She would only take nourishment because she had eaten nothing all day. Mostly she wanted to sleep. She knew she must call on Morwenna, apologize for spilling her secret, be a friend to her regardless of how the grandparents thought she should abandon her prodigal cousin.

She opened the door of her bedchamber.

A commotion of protests and admonitions rose from the entry hall. Elizabeth released the door handle and rushed to the head of the steps. Other doors opened in the upper corridor. Senara and Miss Pross joined Elizabeth.

"What's amiss?" Grandpapa emerged from his study to address the protesting butler and three burly men in rough laborers' garb, but carrying horse pistols and cutlasses.

"We are being invaded by pirates," Senara whimpered from behind Elizabeth.

"No, they are workmen from the outside staff. But why—"

"'Tis Miss Morwenna, sir." One of the men stepped forward and tugged on his forelock. "We went to her cottage as you said, but she weren't there."

CHAPTER 25

ROWAN LEANED HIS HEAD AGAINST THE BACK OF HIS chair and closed his eyes against the sight of Austell Penvenan's face flushed with temper. If only shutting out the sound of his voice were so simple. Rowan wanted peace and quiet in which he could replay the day, memorize those precious moments in the lane with Elizabeth.

"You did something deliberately. You persuaded her not to accept my proposal." Penvenan's Charlestonian drawl sounded nearly English in the precision he placed on each word.

Rowan forced himself not to smile. She hadn't needed any persuading at all.

"She's a gently bred lady you know will never ally herself to a penniless whelp like you."

Not as penniless as Penvenan wished Rowan were, at least not forever.

"She fears no one wants her for anything but her money. With reason, since you're included in that list." The words slipped out before Rowan thought better of the remark.

"And I suppose you thought to save her?" Penvenan began to pace around the library, his footfalls heavy enough to vibrate the floorboards through the worn carpet. "What did you offer her besides reckless behavior?"

"Nothing, sir." Rowan opened his eyes with reluctance. "Nothing beyond recklessness. She's weary of being treated as though she'll break. Maybe if you and her grandfather didn't hobble her activities, she'd have been more amenable to your suit."

"I can still win her if you're out of the way."

"Sir?" Rowan straightened, all his attention on Penvenan, the boss man, as they said in the islands. "You want rid of me?"

"I've wanted rid of you for ten years."

"Yes, sir, I am more trouble than I'm worth, I know. But you can trust me to be honest, and not many others."

"There is that, which is why I'm sending you back to Charleston as soon as I can arrange passage."

"No, sir, you're not." Rowan rose, stood face-to-face with Penvenan. "You can dismiss me from my post, or I'll save you the trouble and resign, but you cannot force me to return to Charleston before I'm ready to go."

"Do you think you can woo her if you stay—an unemployed, penniless nobody?"

"No, I don't. She won't leave Cornwall, and I don't wish to stay. But I won't leave until I know who has been sending threatening messages, who killed Conan Lord Penvenan, and who has twice tried to kill Miss Trelawny."

"If someone has tried to kill her, it is no doubt smugglers responsible for it all. They'll go away once they know I won't play their games."

"You may be right. Unless Romsford wants revenge for the Trelawnys outwitting him."

He didn't believe for a moment that smugglers would simply give up, nor that Romsford was not to be taken seriously and cautiously.

Penvenan gave him a look of disgust.

Rowan went to the door. "I'm going to my bed now unless you wish for me to vacate tonight."

Penvenan took so long to respond, Rowan thought he might indeed find himself without shelter that night.

He opened the door to the startled faces of a housemaid and footman who had obviously been eavesdropping. He smiled at them and glanced over his shoulder into the library. "Very well, then I'll pack up my things and leave. I expect I can find shelter somewhere close at hand. Miss Morwenna Trelawny has a number of rooms she doesn't need. And the Trelawnys are hospitable to all, even penniless, fatherless whelps like me." He closed the door before Penvenan had made up his mind.

A moment later, something crashed against it with a thud and tinkle of broken glass pattering to the floor.

"I'd wait awhile before going in to ask him anything or cleaning up that glass."

Despite his jaunty tone, his feet dragged up the steps to his chamber. Arguing with the man was useless. All his life, Austell Penvenan had gotten what he wanted, and he'd decided he wanted Elizabeth. No one, not even Rowan, would succeed in winning her instead.

But the friction between Rowan and Penvenan ran deeper than them both wanting the same lady. The conflicts began the summer Rowan turned fifteen and Penvenan found himself in sole charge of Rowan, for he was too old to allow the servants to look after him. He'd gotten himself expelled from school by the simple act of leaving to attend his mother's funeral and not going back. On his own more often than not, he encountered antislavers and the real trouble began.

Rowan didn't want one more argument to end like this. He needed to return, apologize, offer to leave Cornwall even if it meant leaving Elizabeth behind. What did that matter? He didn't want to stay in Cornwall forever. It wasn't home.

But it was home for Elizabeth. He hadn't had the right to ask her to leave the only place where she found herself secure and plunge her into an unknown future. Only if he persuaded her that he loved her and not her fortune would she consider going with him, and as long as he was there, wooing her when and however he could, he could hope.

And maybe the Lord was telling him the time had come to go, to let her go. Wooing her, when he was certain she held him in high regard at the least, if not felt something far deeper, might be unfair to her. He needed to return to America, find a wife who was suited to the uncertainty of his future if Penvenan was setting him free of his promise to work for him until the debt incurred by his education was paid in full.

Slowly, his heart tumbling before him, Rowan retraced his steps to the library. The door stood open to accommodate a maid with dustpan and broom just finishing cleaning up shards of glass. As cool as though he hadn't lost his temper, Penvenan sat behind his desk writing on a piece of vellum.

He glanced up at Rowan's entrance. "You may go, Alis."

"Aye, m'lord." The maid scrambled to gather up dustpan and broom and exit the room.

Rowan closed the door behind her, then leaned against it, his hands shoved into his pockets. "Please forgive me, sir. I was out of line and disrespectful."

"And I was wrong for keeping you here when I knew how you felt about Miss Trelawny. Now I shall keep you no longer." Penvenan picked up the sheet of vellum from his desk. "You're free of any obligation to pay your debt. Go pursue your dreams of ministering to the savages or slaves or whatever you like. You owe me nothing more."

"I'd still like to stay, sir. Your safe—"

"I've a household of servants now. I am quite safe from bogeys or anything else. You may go. Tonight. Here is a bank draught for enough money to get you back to Charleston."

"All right, sir, if you insist." Rowan's throat felt oddly thick. "But I've no intention to leave Cornwall right away. I don't like unfinished business." He swallowed to ease the constriction. "I'll refrain from seeing Miss Trelawny, however, unless she chooses to see me."

"Good. She won't ask to see you. I intend to make her an offer again, you know, once your influence is beyond us."

"Then I wish you happy." The tightness spread from his throat to his chest, as though a draft horse stood on his ribs. "I'll just pack my things and leave then, if I may borrow a horse."

Penvenan rose and moved close enough to Rowan to hand him the bank draught. "Just take what you need for the night and send your whereabouts back with the horse. I'll have your belongings sent to you."

"Of course. The sooner I'm gone, the better for you." Rowan snatched the bank draught and strode from the room.

Rowan was halfway up the steps when pounding on the front door resonated throughout the hall. Though two footmen sprang into action and headed in that direction to answer the urgent-sounding summons, Rowan took the steps down in three strides and reached the door first, one word ringing in his head—Morwenna.

A footman in the Bastion Point dark blue livery stood on the threshold, gloved hand upraised for another go at the knocker.

"What is it?" Now another name rang in Rowan's head—Elizabeth.

"It's Miss Morwenna. She's . . ." The young man gasped for

air as though he had run all the way across the fields. "She's missing. Sir Petrok sent me to ask for help from here to locate her."

"Of course we will." Penvenan spoke from behind Rowan. "Go assure them I will mobilize every man I have."

"Thank you, m'lord." The footman turned and raced back the way he'd come.

Penvenan cleared his throat. "I realize I dismissed you, but maybe you could—"

"Of course I can help." Rowan turned to the footmen. "Jago, Carey, get the outdoor staff and go in pairs so one can run back to Bastion Point to report if you find Miss Morwenna while the other stays with her. Woods. Mines, home farm, and here around the house. Take lanterns. It's nearly dark."

"You're forgetting the beach," Penvenan said.

Rowan shook his head. "Not at all. I'll take the beach myself."

"Alone?" For a beat, concern clouded Penvenan's eyes.

Rowan's gut twisted. He wanted to say something about forgetting their last conversation, but the words stuck in his throat. He simply shrugged. "I know the beach well and doubt she's there anyway."

But she might possibly have been there if something had frightened her, or if her time had come, she might have gone into the caves. Either that or someone had abducted her.

Blood running as cold as the Irish Sea, Rowan charged for the door. Penvenan called something behind him that might have been, "Have a care," but Rowan didn't pause to find out for certain. He hoped so. He hoped Penvenan cared that much about him.

He had spent so much time in the past two months traversing the path from house to beach he needed no light beyond the stars to guide him. Beneath those glimmers, the sand glowed like an irregular ribbon between cliffs and sea. White capped the waves of an incoming tide adding more luminescence to the night, while the roar of surf blotted out any other sound.

No wonder someone had managed to sneak up on an experienced man like Conan and stab him before he could fight. He never should have been on the beach.

Conscious that he shouldn't be there alone himself, Rowan backed against the cliff and moved sideways so he could watch for an intruder or a sign of Morwenna in all directions.

He had reached the point where the cliff had broken away enough for a clear path to rise from beach to headland when he spied the lone figure striding toward the sea with a swift, long-legged gait. Not Morwenna. Not a female at all. He waited in the shadow of tumbled rocks, knife in hand, for the man to draw nearer.

Although the light wasn't bright enough for features to be distinct even when only a yard separated them, the eye patch gave away the man's identity. Thus far, Rowan had met no one else in the district with a patch over one eye.

He stepped into Romsford's path. "What are you doing here?"

Romsford jerked to a halt so abruptly he took half a step back. "You have no business asking that of me, you . . . you— riffraff. What are you doing here, I might ask in return?"

"You won't intimidate me with your bluster, my lord. I have a right to be on Penmara land. You do not."

"I do if I'm seeking Miss Morwenna like everyone else." Romsford's voice softened, and his teeth flashed in a quick smile.

Rowan's fingers tightened on the knife handle, though he kept it at his side. "How did you know she was missing?"

"I was in the village. Came down for the fete and to take a look at the mines again."

Reasonable. Too reasonable.

"And what makes you think she'd come this way?" Rowan smiled as well.

Romsford shrugged. "Every place else seemed to be thoroughly searched."

"With no sign of her?"

"No sign of her. I fear these smugglers have spirited her away."

Rowan took a step closer to the marquess. "Why would you think that?"

"She's a Trelawny and easy to use as a way to get the revenue men to stop harassing them before the next new moon."

Sensible again. Too sensible, too calmly delivered. As though it were practiced?

His heart beating a slow and painful rhythm like a bass drum lodged in his chest, Rowan grasped the marquess's arm and turned him away from the shore. "She's not there. You may as well return to the village or, better still, Truro."

"I'm not going to take your word for it." Romsford yanked out of Rowan's hold. "I'll have a look for myself. The way you spirited Miss Elizabeth away, I wouldn't be surprised if you did the same for Miss Morwenna. Now step aside."

Rowan stepped aside. Save for outright assaulting the man, Rowan couldn't stop him. Not a peer of the realm, he was in too lowly a position to insist the man leave Penmara property. But that didn't mean he didn't have reason to stop the man from going anywhere but the village lockup.

As if anyone would believe Rowan Curnow over the word of a marquess, not without true, physical evidence. He hadn't considered the notion himself until that moment. After all, to anyone's knowledge, Romsford hadn't been anywhere near Bastion Point when any of the "accidents" occurred. He made no secret of his presence in the town, nor of his interest in Penmara's mines and Elizabeth. Today, however, he had been in the village, and Elizabeth had been assaulted. He had been in the neighborhood, and Morwenna had disappeared. Weak evidence, and yet . . .

Rowan turned and followed the marquess down the beach. He strode with that same easy gait as though he owned the stretch of sand between cliff and surf. Twice Romsford paused to look out to sea, to an empty horizon. Twice he looked behind him. Pressed to the shadow of the cliff, Rowan didn't think the marquess saw him. Knowing Romsford would have to stop where the tide already covered the beach and half covered the mouth of the Trelawny caves, Rowan ducked beneath an outcropping of rock and waited to see if the marquess would wade through the surf or turn back.

He turned back. He whistled a jaunty melody. He passed Rowan without breaking stride.

Rowan waited until Romsford had climbed the path to the land before he followed. By the time he reached the top of the cliff, the marquess had turned toward the house. He should follow the man, warn Penvenan. But he needed to find Morwenna or learn if she was in hiding by her own volition or otherwise.

Penvenan was armed. He could take care of himself. Romsford wouldn't harm a peer of the realm when he knew he'd been observed at Penmara.

Rowan circumvented the overgrown gardens and took the woodland path. His steps crunched on gravel and dried vegetation. The musky aromas of loam and moldering leaves rose around him, accompanied by the pure fragrance of wildflowers, scents that would forever remind him of Elizabeth, the lady he should have forgotten two months ago.

She did not love him, at least not enough to leave family and land for a life with him. He understood why, yet it didn't stop her rejection from stabbing through him again and again, as though each step drove the knife deeper into his middle. Added to Penvenan sending him away, he wasn't sure a man could endure such pain.

Surely this isn't your will for me, Lord, he cried out in his head.

And what if it were? What if he needed to go into the little explored territories west and minister to the native peoples there, or take freed men to find and build futures, and he needed to go unfettered by a wife used to luxury. He'd wanted it all six years ago. Now, with his heart bound to Elizabeth, the idea appealed less. But if going into the wilderness was what the Lord wanted for him, all those anchors holding him back from going needed to be removed.

He paused and leaned against the broad trunk of an oak, winded as though he'd been running or carrying a hundredweight burden.

Jesus, I can't go on like this. My heart, my soul, is too burdened for me to take another step. I think I've been going my own way and calling it your will. But I need to know your will. Stay here? Leave? I don't know, and I'm ready to listen and obey, even if it means leaving Elizabeth and my love for her behind.

He leaned his head back against the tree and gazed at the growing canopy of stars through the tree leaves. Wind sighed through those leaves. Nearby, a bird shifted and muttered in its sleep.

And footfalls pounded down the path.

Rowan straightened, his hand going to the knife in its sheath down his back. Starlight glinted off the steel blade.

The footfalls skidded to a halt. "Who's there?"

A female.

Rowan didn't lower the knife. "I could ask the same. This is still Penmara land."

"Mr. Curnow?" The woman, a stout shadow against the pale stone of the path, was panting.

"Who wants to know?"

She clutched at his arm. "Henwyn, Miss Morwenna's companion."

"What are you doing here? It's not safe."

"I'm a village girl on my way home. No one will hurt me. But Miss Morwenna . . ." Her voice trailed off, and she pressed the cold, smooth stone of the carved jade apple into his hand. "She said you'll know what to be doing with this."

Elizabeth paced around her bedchamber too restless to go to bed and pretend she could sleep. She wanted to be wide-awake and dressed in suitable clothing, a sturdy gown and boots, in the event the men hunting her found Morwenna and she needed to go out.

She and her servant were no longer at the cottage. They were no longer anywhere to be found in the gardens or woods around the cottage. After three hours of hunting, they seemed to have disappeared from the countryside.

Voluntarily or involuntarily? Elizabeth paused by the open window facing the sea and clasped her hands over her heart. *Lord, keep her safe, but especially if she didn't go by her own volition.*

She startled at her prayer. She hadn't been in the way of praying since she left Cornwall six years ago. Yet the words slid out without a hitch or hint of self-consciousness. Praying for Morwenna's safety just seemed right.

The rhythmic splash of the waves rose to her window on the clean scent of the salt water and fresh night air. She'd grown up within sight and sound and smell of the sea. It was power and life and beauty.

It was also deadly. Storms had destroyed entire villages over the past century. Ships wrecked on a regular basis, sometimes by accident and sometimes because they had been lured onto the rocks. And dangerous men traded in contraband on the sea—men who would lose their freedom or even their lives if the authorities caught them smuggling. To preserve both, as well as their livelihood, they would stop at nothing—they did stop at nothing—to preserve their way of life.

Even if that meant murdering a peer of the realm and destroying his child as a warning to others to not leave their ranks, nor snitch on them.

"Morwenna, where are you?" Elizabeth leaned far over the sill. Sixty feet below, the sea began the *boom, boom, boom* of the incoming tide reaching the mouth of the cave. "Why didn't you trust the grandparents with your secret? They love you."

But if she, always the favored grandchild because she sought so hard to please them, doubted their love, how much more did Morwenna, the black sheep of the family, doubt how much they cared about her? They loved and they were generous, but they had always seemed to expect something in return.

I do not understand this unconditional love, Lord. Elizabeth rested her palms on the cool, weathered stone of the windowsill's outer edge and fixed her gaze on the horizon, the same silvered black as the sea. *The vicar says it's so. The Bible says it's so, but it makes no sense to me. Will you show—*

A tapping sounded on the other window. Elizabeth jumped.

The tapping came again like a tree branch blowing in a breeze, except the night was nearly calm.

She faced the window. It was locked. Thank God it was locked. No one could enter without breaking one of the leaded diamond panes and flipping the lock free. No one could accomplish that without a great deal of noise—like her screaming and racing from the room.

The tapping sounded a third time. Her heart pounded louder. She lifted a branch of candles from the mantel and tried to peer into the night. But the flames reflected in the glass so she couldn't see out, could only see her fragmented reflection and no doubt giving the would-be intruder a clear view of her.

Intruder. Burglar. Worse . . .

She set down the candle and backed away from the light. She needed a weapon, something with which to stop anyone bent on harming her should he break through the casement.

A poker was too awkward and risky. The knife that had come with her supper tray was too dull. The dagger Drake had given her was lost somewhere. After tonight, if she lived through this night, she'd buy a pistol and learn how to shoot it. Rowan would be willing to teach—

But Rowan was gone. The grandparents said Lord Penvenan had sent him away.

The tapping turned to a rap, quick and impatient and loud enough Miss Pross might hear it from her chamber on the other side of the dressing room. Loud enough to knock sense into Elizabeth.

No one bent on harming her would knock on the window. Only one person would knock on her bedchamber window.

She sprinted across the room and shoved the bolt from its cradle, then pushed open the window.

A hand caught it before she managed to move the casement more than a few inches. An instant later, Rowan Curnow stepped over the sill. "Thank the Lord you're dressed." Speaking in an undertone, he closed the window and clasped her hands. "Elys, don't ask questions. I'll answer them later. Right now I need you to come with me."

"Go with you? I don't believe—"

He touched a finger to her lips. "No questions. We need to go down the secret stair to the cave hidden—"

"How did you learn about that?"

"Morwenna is there." He glanced around the room. "Where's your cloak?"

Elizabeth grabbed a cloak from a hook on the wall inside the dressing room, then closed that door and turned back to Rowan. "Why is Morwenna there?"

Even as she asked the question, she guessed the answer.

"Her lying in," Rowan said.

Cold enough to need a fur-lined winter cloak, Elizabeth snuggled into the light woolen wrap and tried to speak without hysteria coloring her voice. "She needs a midwife, not me."

"Tide's up. We can't get a midwife in there. Besides, Morwenna thinks the midwife is attached to the smugglers."

"All right, but . . ." Elizabeth pressed one hand to her heart in an attempt to slow it down. "We will hope the labor lasts until the tide ebbs and we can get the midwife in and then keep her there until we have Morwenna and the baby to safety."

"We could do that if there's time. But if there isn't, you'll have to play midwife."

"Oh no." Elizabeth shook her head. "I can't do that. Are you forgetting that I'm an unmarried lady? We aren't told anything about childbirth, let alone allowed to see it happen."

"But you have been to a foaling."

"Yes, but—" She gripped the edges of her cloak as though they protected her from participating in what he requested, what Morwenna required.

Rowan grasped her hands and drew her near to the door, nearer to him. "I think you can do this."

"I think," Elizabeth said with resignation, "this will be the final straw to my reputation."

CHAPTER 26

MORWENNA'S CRIES REACHED THEM, FAINT THROUGH A heavy panel, before they attained the bottom of the stairs. With a gasp, Elizabeth thrust the candle into Rowan's hand and dashed down the rest of the steps, calling to her cousin.

Rowan followed with more care, uncertain of the evenness of the hewn descent. In the chamber, Morwenna lay on a cot against one wall and Elizabeth knelt beside her, holding her hands. The faces of both ladies contorted in pain.

"Can you help?" Elizabeth glanced up. "She's crushing my fingers."

"So . . . sorry." Morwenna panted out the words through clenched teeth. "I can't help it. This past hour . . . much worse—" She broke off on a groan.

"Last hour?" Elizabeth's eyes dilated. "How long have you been here?"

"Dawn. I felt a twinge." Morwenna closed her eyes. "Told Henwyn not to fetch Mr. Curnow until dark. Sa-safer."

"You little fool." Elizabeth glared at her cousin. "You thought you could do this alone?"

"For all the help you are . . ." Morwenna ground her teeth together.

Rowan's lips twitched. "Could you two put your differences aside for tonight?"

Elizabeth freed her hands and rose. "We need blankets. Are there any?"

"Here." Rowan fetched the two he'd already brought from Penmara.

Elizabeth spread them over her cousin with a tenderness that belied any of the harsh things she'd spoken of Morwenna. In return, Morwenna's attempt at a smile and outheld hand pronounced how much she appreciated Elizabeth's presence.

"Now what?" Elizabeth gave Rowan a helpless look.

His ears grew hot. "I think you examine her to see if the baby is coming."

"Oh." Her face turned the color of fresh strawberries. "Um, Morwenna, do you know . . . That is . . . I've no idea what to do or what to look for or . . . We need the midwife. Surely she's trustworthy."

"No. I have reason to believe her son is one of the gang." Morwenna's eyes closed. "Trust no one who isn't a Trelawny."

Elizabeth wiped Morwenna's brow with the edge of her cloak. "You trusted Mr. Curnow."

"He's different. He's a—"

Rowan cleared his throat, and she closed her mouth.

"He's a what?" Elizabeth, of course, wouldn't let it go.

"I was Conan's trusted confidant." Rowan crossed the room and poured water from a pail into a basin. "I wish we had a way to heat this."

"Fresh water? Blankets?" Elizabeth set her hands on her hips and sent a frown from Rowan to Morwenna, and back again to Rowan. "I understand why you came here, Wenna, to protect your baby, but how did Mr. Curnow know how to get here, and how could you have all these things ready so quickly?"

"I showed him the way in and he brought things here." Morwenna let out a bark of a laugh. "He must have had a time of collecting cloths for—" She broke off on a cry, as another contraction made her body go rigid.

Rowan took her hands this time. How a female so small could exert such pressure astounded him. How she managed not to outright scream astounded him more.

He gazed at Elizabeth wringing her hands in the flickering candle and lantern light in the cave room. If not for those twisting fingers, one would never know she'd been dragged into the bowels of the earth beneath her home, to the side of a cousin in her lying in, when she was still a maiden, if not one as icy as she'd no doubt like to be.

"Elizabeth," he directed her, "fetch a damp cloth and a glass of water."

Elizabeth dipped a square of linen in the basin and picked up the ewer, but splashed water over the side of the tin cup before managing to half fill it.

He released Morwenna's hands and touched Elizabeth's shoulder. "Don't be anxious."

"I am not anxious." The water in the cup looked as though a hurricane blew through the confines of the tin. "I simply think others are better suited for this than I. I'll make a mistake. I'll hurt her or the baby." She blinked hard, but one tear escaped her efforts and headed down her cheek.

Rowan brushed it away with the pad of his thumb. "I can tell you what to do."

"And what do you know of childbirth?"

He smiled. "More than you, I expect." He took the cup and knelt to half lift Morwenna and press the tin to her lips. "Take a sip or two."

"Thank you." She managed it, but slumped back. "Need to sleep."

"If you can, then you should."

Rowan set the cup beneath the cot, wiped Morwenna's face with the damp cloth, and rose to take it back to the basin. Behind him, Elizabeth had begun to pace. He watched her with her cloak and skirt swinging, her hair drifting behind her in a loose, shining veil, her face so stiff it appeared as though a touch would make it shatter.

He hesitated a moment, then caught up with her and slipped his arms around her. "Shh." He cradled the back of her head with one hand, urging her to lay her cheek against his shoulder. "Don't fret so. I was at the lying in of a runaway once and had to give more aid than I wanted to."

"What if something happens to her?" A shudder ran through her. "I'll be responsible. They'll never forgive me."

"I will." Morwenna spoke in a voice slurred with exhaustion. "Grateful . . ." Her voice trailed off. Her breathing grew even.

For a quarter hour, the cave lay quiet save for the distant rumble of the sea. Rowan and Elizabeth perched on the bench against one wall saying nothing, afraid to wake Morwenna. Another contraction did that soon enough and began a pattern that seemed to go on for an entire night, but was likely less than two hours. Then she half sat up and cried out louder than her previous whimpers and gasps.

Rowan and Elizabeth rose as one and crossed the cave to Morwenna's side. She was doubled up and clutching at her belly.

"Let me fetch Grandmama. She's borne children. She knows what to do. Even Miss Pross must know something. Please, Morwenna. Anyone but me."

"Too . . . late." Morwenna gasped out the two words between gritted teeth. "Pains are closer."

"Then there's time to fetch someone still, isn't there?" Elizabeth's complexion held a greenish hue.

Morwenna clawed at Elizabeth's arm. "Don't leave me. I think . . . soon."

Not soon enough for Rowan's comfort. The pains grew closer together, but what felt like an eternity passed before Morwenna cried, "Now!"

"Now?" Elizabeth's voice squeaked. "I don't think . . . I cannot . . ." She crossed her arms over her chest.

Rowan smoothed her hair back from her face. "Of course you can. Remember who you are."

On the cot, Morwenna laughed through another contraction. "He knows the family motto."

"That doesn't mean I'm a miracle worker." Elizabeth dropped her arms to her sides. "Even Trelawnys have limits."

"Helping a baby into the world is not one, I've no doubt." He kissed her cheek. "Especially when it's another Trelawny and the offspring of a friend."

"For Conan," Morwenna said in more of a whimper, "if not me."

"For you." Elizabeth took a deep breath and sank to her knees beside the low cot and began to murmur, "Remember who you are. Remember who you are."

Rowan wanted to embrace her, take all her burdens from her.

Morwenna let out a low chuckle that rose into a shrieking crescendo.

Elizabeth flipped back the blanket, and Rowan turned his gaze away to study the striations in the stone walls of the cave—gray with flecks of gold from particles of copper.

"I think," Elizabeth said in a voice as cold as the sea roaring at the distant mouth of the cave, "I see the head."

"Can you push, Miss Morwenna?" Rowan dropped to his knees beside the younger Trelawny. He took out his handkerchief and wiped beads of perspiration from her brow. "Just hang on to me as hard as you need to and push."

She clutched his hands like a drowning person caught in a whirlpool and pushed. At the end of the cot, Elizabeth kept up a steady flow of nonsense talk like, "Time to face the world, little one," and, "You're a wee bit lazy, are you not, Coz. Get this over with." She delivered each word in her coolest, crispest voice, a lifetime of training, generations of breeding, taking over her apprehension.

Rowan smiled and kept his eyes fixed on Morwenna's face contorted with pain, wet with tears and sweat. "You can do it, Miss Morwenna. The sooner you get this done, the better you'll feel." He wiped her face, then took her hands. "Hang on to me. You can't hurt me."

Which wasn't quite true. Her grip would surely crush his fingers. Her cries would surely deafen them in the confines of the chamber, echoing off the stone and panels nailed up to disguise the openings, as they did.

Elizabeth's own cry added to the hubbub. Rowan glanced her way to see a wrinkled, red baby slide into Elizabeth's hands.

"What do I do with him?" Panic widened her eyes, darkened her pupils.

"Is it a boy or a girl?" Morwenna demanded.

"Get him to breathe." Rowan tried to remember. "A little smack, I think."

"Smack something this little?" Elizabeth stared at the baby as though he were a new species, but she tapped him on his backside.

The baby released a mewling wail.

"Let me have him," Morwenna commanded. "Please."

"Cut the cord." Rowan produced his knife. "Wait. I think we tie it first. I don't know what—"

Elizabeth tossed aside her cloak and drew the drawstring from her gown. "Will this work?"

It worked well enough. While Elizabeth assisted Morwenna with the no-doubt bloody aftermath of childbirth, taking wet cloths to her and ignoring Morwenna's complaints about cold water, Rowan tied the string around the umbilical cord and severed the connection with his knife. "Now we wash him, except the water is likely too cold."

"Let me have him." Morwenna's tone had become imperious.

"In a minute," Elizabeth snapped in return. "He's too messy."

"He? It is a he?" Morwenna began to laugh and cry and murmur something like, "I did it, Conan, just for you." Then aloud, she said, "I don't care how messy he is."

Childbirth was messier than most men realized, Rowan suspected. Few were given the "luxury" of taking part in the experience. If so, many fewer children might be born. Or perhaps not. Once they rubbed the infant dry and wrapped it in soft cloths, the sight of Elizabeth holding the child, her face aglow with wonder and tenderness, expanded his heart to a soul-deep ache. He wanted to see her holding their baby like that, every vestige of the ice princess warmed by maternal adoration.

"I want my baby." Morwenna sounded surprisingly strong considering what she'd endured.

Slowly, with obvious reluctance, Elizabeth relinquished hold of the infant into his mother's hands. "He's perfect."

He was, in truth, rather ugly with his wrinkled face and pointy head covered in dark, matted fuzz. But he was whole and his cries, more like a kitten mewing, were healthy enough.

"He is perfect." Morwenna peeked beneath the wrappings, then cuddled him close. "Don't let me fall asleep and drop him."

"We'll stay with you." Elizabeth sat on the stone floor and slid her arm beneath her cousin's shoulders. "I need to tell the grandparents so we can get you upstairs, but you can't be moved now."

"Should I feed him, or try?" For all the fatigue bruises beneath her eyes, Morwenna's face glowed.

Elizabeth laughed. "You're asking me? But I do know the calves do it."

Rowan walked away, certain if . . . if the tide would have receded yet, he would have gone through the outer door and wended his way through the tunnels and gotten as far away from these scents and sounds and sights. Except it would have done him no good. Forever he would recall that image of Elizabeth holding a newborn close to her heart.

If only it were theirs.

He rested his brow against the cool paneling and took several long, deep breaths. He must not think that way. She'd made herself clear. Bastion Point came first. Her family came first. He understood her attachment to the land. It was where she'd been happy and carefree. He understood not wanting to abandon her grandparents. Family was important. If he had put his family first, or what was left of it, his life would have become far different. He wouldn't have ended up in England and wouldn't have met Elizabeth. But he had let anger and disdain rule him and now paid the consequences.

For being out of your will, Lord?

Apparently so. He'd accomplished too little that glorified God. Freeing four score of men and women did too little to shift the scales in the direction of freedom for all. In return, he had made enemies that gave him fewer avenues to travel in serving the Lord.

He could leave in the morning, return to South Carolina, and repair as much damage as he possibly could. He was no longer needed in Cornwall. Elizabeth could wed Penvenan or go about her way, whichever would please her grandparents enough to have them give her Bastion Point. Morwenna would be returned to the arms of her family now that the child had been born, especially if she revealed its paternity and let them help her. Penvenan said he needed no help from Rowan. A man couldn't ask for a clearer message from the Lord.

Head and heart clear, he realized how loudly he heard the sea. He must be leaning against the door panel.

Elizabeth was talking to her cousin in low murmurs he couldn't hear. The baby had long since ceased his newborn cries, and eventually, the voices stopped. A glance showed that Morwenna slept and Elizabeth sat cross-legged on the floor, heedless of the cold stone or showing her ankles, in order to hold the baby in her arms. Her head bowed over the infant, her hair a satin curtain around him.

Rowan opened his mouth to speak, but his throat closed on the words, and he simply watched.

Elizabeth must have sensed the intensity of his gaze, for she glanced up and smiled. "I've never held a baby before. He is so . . . alive."

"Yes." It was a mere croak.

"I never thought about wanting children. I knew they would come with marriage, most likely, but it was more a philosophy than a reality to me. But now that I've turned Penvenan down I don't know when or if I'll wed and that will deny me this." She stroked one finger along the baby's smooth cheek.

Rowan held his breath against an onslaught of need for her in his life. "I still want to marry you, Elys. I love you."

"Will you stay in Cornwall?"

"When you and everyone else would think I wed you for your money?"

She bit her lip and turned away.

"If you have any doubts about it, then, no, I can't stay. You need to come to me empty-handed."

"To someone else who is empty-handed? I've seen how poverty stifles any love that might be there."

"My dear, I'm not—" He stopped. She would come to him as he was or not at all.

He looked around the chamber for something they could use as a bed for the child. A small crate stood in one corner. He carried it to the side of the cot and lined it with a blanket and soft cloths. It wasn't the worst place an infant had spent his first few hours of life. Above in the house, no doubt a cradle with satin cushions awaited the next Trelawny offspring. He would enjoy fine clothes and a good education, the opportunity to travel if the war with France ever ended, and the ability to stay on the land or buy his way into a diplomatic or Parliamentary position if he chose that route.

The makeshift bed complete, he returned to the door and leaned his head against it to listen. "The tide has gone out. We should get you home before anyone worries about you."

"Can we leave Morwenna alone?" Elizabeth rose to her knees to set the infant in the box. "She's so worn to a thread."

"I expect your grandparents will send someone down to carry her and the baby up. She'll be all right until then."

"Yes, I'll . . ." Morwenna yawned. "Where is Baby Conan? And may I've some water? I'd give my left arm for some hot tea, but water will do."

Elizabeth hastened to help Morwenna sit and take the baby. Rowan brought her water. For a moment, he rested his hand on her fragile-feeling shoulder.

She reached up and covered his hand with hers. "Thank you, Mr. Curnow. You have been a true friend."

"I'll always be a friend. If your grandparents won't help, I'll find someplace safe for you to go."

"Perhaps America." Elizabeth sounded a bit too sharp. "Her baby needs a father, after all."

Morwenna looked at her cousin and laughed. "Not him. He's yours."

"Don't be a ninnyhammer." Elizabeth spoke more harshly than necessary. "He's no one's." She strode to the outer door. "It's too late for me to go up the inside steps. A maid might be in the study. Shall we go, Mr. Curnow?"

Morwenna made shooing motions. "I doubt I'll be here alone for long, and you need your rest before you return to your work, Mr. Curnow."

"Thank you." Rowan bowed over her hand and kissed it. "But I have no more work." He followed Elizabeth to the door.

Once outside, she turned to him in the flickering light from her candle. "Why do you have no more work?"

"I've been dismissed."

She startled. "Because of yesterday?"

"Mostly. Partly. It's been coming for a long time."

"I'm sorry for any part I played." She started along the first stretch of the maze of tunnels, her back straight, her gait firm and even, her demeanor frosty.

"That's all you have to say for yourself? You've never told me you love me, but I have reason to believe you do."

"I—You've been clear. Our futures go in different directions."

"Is that so?" He closed his hand over her shoulder, halting her forward momentum.

She swung to face him, a protest on her lips, and he snatched her candle out of her hand and tossed it against a rock wall. Brass clanged. The flame died.

He didn't need to see to draw her against him and kiss her. He held her until she relaxed against him and leaned into him. He kissed her until her lips softened and opened. He kissed her until both of them gasped for air and they trembled with response to the closeness.

"I cannot." She wrenched herself free and blundered into the darkness, her boots clattering.

Rowan followed at a more cautious pace, his hands before him to protect his face and head. He shouldn't have extinguished the light. He didn't know his way that well to manage in the dark. Elizabeth's clattering heels acted as a guide as to which way to turn at each junction until a miscalculation smacked his head against an outcropping of stone, sending him reeling back, pain searing through him, blood trickling down his temple. When he recovered, he no longer heard her ahead of him.

He paused at the junction, certain he heard the sea more in one direction than the other, but both remained as black as a moonless night.

Slowly, he headed the way in which the sea hissed and rumbled more loudly. He didn't take more than a pace or two before a scream billowed up the other tunnel.

He spun on his heel and chased down the other passage, hands upraised until his shoulder careened off a bend in the wall. He staggered around the corner to where daylight spilled through the opening. He raced toward it to find Elizabeth.

She stood around the edge of the headland point, gasping and sobbing a yard away from a body stretched out on the sand just above the tide—a body of a man with dark, silver-streaked hair and a knife in his back.

Rowan would have bellowed "Noooo" if he could have breathed, if his knees hadn't turned to boneless lumps.

He dropped beside the man and reached out his hand for a wrist, a pulse, a sign of life. Though the hand still held some human warmth, his spirit had left his body.

"No." Rowan bowed forward under a burden too great to remain upright. He pressed his hands to his face, willing himself to stay calm, to think, to take the right action. He wanted to run before the pain inside him exploded into rage. And anguish. He remained motionless, forcing stillness upon himself.

"Rowan?" Elizabeth pressed her hand against his cheek. "Are you all right?"

"All right? Of course I'm not all right." His face had grown hot and wet with tears beneath her caressing fingers. "How could you think I'm all right with Austell Penvenan lying here dead?"

"Of course. You knew him and worked for him for a long time." She brushed his hair off his brow. "It must be difficult to lose someone who—"

"Elizabeth." He caught her hand and pressed it against his cheek. "Austell Penvenan was my father."

CHAPTER 27

ELIZABETH HAD NEVER SEEN A MAN WEEP. SHE COULDN'T imagine the depth of pain and anguish that drove a self-contained man like Rowan Curnow to release his tears over a man who may have fathered him, but often seemed to be more an adversary than a parent. They hadn't much liked one another. Yet Rowan must have cared deeply to know nothing in their relationship could ever be right.

Tears of her own swelled, and she sank to her knees and slipped her arm around Rowan's shoulders. "I am so sorry."

What inadequate words.

She pressed her cheek against his arm, a hundred questions whirling through her head like why Penvenan had never married Rowan's mother, why Penvenan never acknowledged his relationship to Rowan, or why he treated his own son only a little better than a slave.

She flicked her gaze to the supine body and shuddered. "Who? Why? What's he doing here?"

The clipped queries seemed to snap Rowan out of his silent paralysis. He shot to his feet and drew her up with him. "I don't know what he'd be doing here. You'd think with Conan's murder, he'd have the sense not to come to the beach at night. I told him to be careful. I told him—" His face contorted. He scrubbed his hands over his features, leaving them smoothed out, impassive.

"As to who, I saw Romsford heading toward the house last night before I learned of Morwenna's whereabouts."

"Romsford? You think Romsford killed your—Lord Penvenan?" Elizabeth's stomach rolled. "For the land? For courting me? Rowan, you must tell Grandpapa about seeing Romsford."

"I will, but I could get into a great deal of trouble if he doesn't believe me."

"And he won't, will he? Romsford's a peer. Oh no. Oh no." Elizabeth hugged herself and rocked on her knees. "I need to tell my grandfather about Mor—"

He pressed a finger to his lips. "No, do not. If you can get food and water down to her, do, but she and the baby especially may be in danger."

"But if the grandparents know, they can help protect her."

"Your grandfather is the justice of the peace. He's going to be preoccupied with this, and if anyone learns of the baby's father— What is it?"

The blood drained from Elizabeth's head, and she clung to Rowan for support. "Any number of people may know by now. I told the grandparents last night on the terrace."

The look he gave her was not friendly.

"It wasn't intentional. I was overset . . ." She trailed off under the intensity of his blue eyes.

"You'd better get home before you're missed. Don't go out of the house or say anything to anyone."

"What will you do?"

"What a responsible citizen—er—subject is supposed to do. I'll go fetch the coroner and tell the magistrate what I know."

"Shouldn't someone watch over him?"

"Do you wish to volunteer? Or would you like to ride for the coroner and announce to the world you were with me all night?"

A punch in her middle would have hurt less. She couldn't tell anyone she was with him all night without mentioning Morwenna, and she'd done enough damage there.

"You needn't destroy your reputation over me." He softened his tone. "I'll only be gone long enough to send a Penmara servant for the coroner. Now go before you're discovered out here."

She went. She climbed the path to Bastion Point, each step heavier than the last, each crunch of her boot heels on the rocky ground proclaiming her a coward.

Yet ruining herself, destroying her future, would not bring Lord Penvenan back. He'd been on the beach during the night or in the early morning when he should not have been if he knew he was in danger. She'd already risked a great deal spending the night in the caves with Morwenna and Rowan. Sir Petrok's granddaughter, the elder one by four months, must remain above reproach if she wanted any kind of a future.

Selfish. Selfish. Selfish. Yet she couldn't help the thoughts that ran through her head. Learning of Rowan's illegitimacy rang the death knell on a future between them. Whether material or spiritual, that was no kind of treasure the grandparents wanted for her. He had no future in which a wife fit. Hers lay behind the gray stone walls of Bastion Point, walls he was not welcome to enter as an equal. She certainly never treated him as one in public as though she were shamed of him even before she knew of his low birth. Yet he claimed to love her, had sacrificed his work and his tenuous relationship with his father for her.

How could it be so when she was so free to denounce him? She denounced everyone who claimed to love her. A self-centered prig like her didn't deserve to be loved. Perhaps her self-centered behavior had killed his love for her.

She leaned against the inside of the garden door, inhaling the morning sweetness of dew-drenched herbs along the path.

If she plucked some mint or rosemary, no one would question her presence outside so early if they smelled the herbs and not Morwenna's blood on her gown covered by her cloak.

Her cloak covered the blood like everyone's belief in her goodness covered all her lies of omission. She was undeserving of love.

While we were yet sinners Christ died for us. The verse rang in her head.

If anyone was a sinner, she was. She might not have shamed herself and the family as had Morwenna and Drake, but she'd shamed herself.

You can't possibly love me, Lord.

She believed she didn't deserve for anyone to love her. She must fill in the empty spaces with what she had—Bastion Point, respect, the ability to attract sycophants, if not friends, material things to which she could cling.

After gathering enough mint leaves for a cup of tea, she headed for the kitchen entrance, the only one that would be unlocked that early. A maid building up the fire and a scullion pouring water into the reservoir behind the chimney that provided hot water for the household both startled in surprise at her entrance, but asked no questions. The maid took the leaves and prepared a cup for tea.

"Water'll be hot in the kettle in but a moment, miss."

"Thank you. I'm not feeling well." Elizabeth climbed the back steps to her chamber.

In her room, she flung off her cloak and stared at her gown. It was a ruin from the birth. Somehow she must hide it until she could burn it. With the drawstring gone, it was easy to pull off. She stuffed it beneath her mattress, washed in chilly water, and donned a new nightgown and dressing gown. By the time she finished, the maid had arrived with her tea.

"It's hoping I am that you'll be feeling better, miss." She set the cup on the table beside the bed. "If you need more, you don't be needing to go fetch it yourself."

"Thank you." Elizabeth slipped beneath the covers. "Please tell the household that I'm unwell and need to rest more."

She needed to think, to add things together, consider the notion that Romsford was after more than her, was worse than an aging rake. Surely no one killed for possession of a derelict mine or two. Surely . . .

The maid departed.

Elizabeth sipped at the fragrant tea and was suddenly so weary she could no longer keep her eyes open. And by feigning illness, she'd have a better chance of slipping down to the cave to help Morwenna.

Even Morwenna loved her child enough to sacrifice comfort and privilege and respect to keep him safe. Never again would Elizabeth show disdain for her cousin regardless of the mistakes Morwenna had made. She loved her baby. She must have loved Conan to keep his secret so long.

Lord, show me what is missing in my life. The vague prayer was the last thing she knew until her bedchamber door burst open later enough that the sun streamed through the westward window.

"Elizabeth. Elizabeth, wake up." Senara pounced on the bed and shook her. "You cannot continue sleeping."

"Why ever not?" Yawning, Elizabeth rubbed her eyes. "Tired."

"But you must hear the news." Senara shook her. "Rowan Curnow has been arrested for my cousin's murder."

Elizabeth snapped awake, eyes wide, blood racing. "What? He can't be. He couldn't have. He—" She woke enough to shut her mouth before blurting out she'd been with him. "Lord Penvenan was murdered? When? How? How do you know Rowan has been accused?"

"Mr. Curnow says he found him on Bastion Point beach, dead with a knife in his back. Then I heard Sir Petrok speaking with the constable, Sam Carn, and the coroner about arresting Mr. Curnow." Senara's eyes sparkled with excitement. "Perhaps he killed Conan as well."

"He couldn't have. He was—"

With her then too.

Elizabeth flung back the bedclothes and slid to the floor. "Where's Miss Pross? I must get dressed."

She rang her bell, then dashed into the dressing room to pick out a gown, something sober in memory of the latest man to ask for her hand because of her fortune. *Nothing too somber,* a spiteful voice taunted inside her head.

A somber gown because a man was being falsely accused of murder. A conviction of murder, if the inquest jury found enough evidence to send Rowan to the assizes on the next quarter day, meant hanging, especially once they learned Penvenan was Rowan's father.

His father. A father who had rejected him. A father who had forced him to work for him, had courted the lady Rowan wanted. More than enough motivation to take the case to trial when the circuit judge came around.

Elizabeth yanked a lavender gown from the clothes press and dug for a matching pelisse and slippers.

"When is the inquest?" she called back to Senara.

"This afternoon, as soon as they round up twelve eligible men for the jury."

"Why so quickly?" She emerged from the dressing room with her clothes over her arm.

Senara shrugged. "They want a good reason to lock him up before he flees back to America."

"They can round him up in America and bring him back here."

"Why waste all those months and risk him vanishing into that great wilderness if they can avoid it?"

"But they could hang an innocent man." Elizabeth dropped onto the dressing table stool and began smoothing on her stockings.

She must look nice before speaking with Grandpapa.

"Do you truly believe he's innocent?" Senara asked. "Who else would kill my cousin?"

"The same person or people who killed your brother."

Senara wrinkled her nose. "Like him."

"Senara, he couldn't have killed Conan. That was established at that inquest. Besides, how could two different murderers be roaming Cornwall?"

"Smugglers." Senara shrugged. "Conan wanted to quit, and they needed our caves. Good reason for killing off my cousin if he wouldn't let them."

Elizabeth shuddered. "You sound so bloodthirsty about it."

"I like Mr. Curnow, but I make no secret of not liking Austell Penvenan."

"But now that he's—" Memory of Penvenan lying facedown on the sand, a knife jutting from his back, flashed into Elizabeth's mind, and she covered her face with her hands. "Justice must be served."

But serving up Rowan Curnow to the gallows would not be justice.

Miss Pross bustled into the room. She smoothed a hand over Elizabeth's brow. "So glad to see you feeling better. One of the maids said you'd been ill."

"Of course she's ill," Senara said. "Bastion Point is no longer a bastion." She giggled over her jest, then covered her mouth, her eyes huge above her fingers. "I didn't mean to be laughing. This is horrible. So glad I'm staying here and not at Penmara."

"Histrionics," Miss Pross muttered. Aloud, she said, "Let me help you, Miss Elizabeth. You were never going to dress without your stays."

"Bother. They take so long to lace." But she dared not go into public, even Grandpapa's study, without them.

The library. The secret stairs. Morwenna alone with the baby and scared.

"Hurry." Elizabeth stepped behind the embroidered silk dressing screen and tossed off her dressing gown. She must talk to Grandpapa. She must tell him of Morwenna, even if she didn't want anyone to do so.

She must tell Grandpapa about Morwenna and Rowan?

No, no, she could not admit that Rowan had been in her chamber, through the house, and down those steps alone with her in the middle of the night. Grandpapa might think the worst once he knew she'd been with Morwenna. He might place her in the same class as her cousin. She would lose his regard, she'd lose Grandmama's regard, and she'd lose Bastion Point for certain. Without Bastion Point, she had nothing to offer anyone.

Yet Rowan was certain to tell Grandpapa or the coroner or both of them that he had witnesses to his innocence. People might not believe Morwenna, but they would believe Elizabeth.

"Hurry," she said again. "I must talk to Grandpapa."

If Rowan had said nothing yet, perhaps she could stop the progress of the inquest before anyone needed to testify.

Heart racing, toe tapping, Elizabeth submitted to Miss Pross's slowness in hooking up the back of her gown. All the while, Senara talked about what would happen to Penmara now.

"There are no heirs now. But there's money. My cousin said

he had seen to that—making sure there's money to keep the land going. Wasn't that generous of him?"

"Quite." Elizabeth snatched up a brush and began to work it through her hair. "Is that why you were so much kinder to him of late?"

"He cared about Penmara and continuing the line. A pity—"

"Excuse me, Senara, I cannot wait any longer." Elizabeth tossed the brush onto the dressing table, grabbed her pelisse, and sprinted for the door.

"Your hair," Senara and Miss Pross called together.

Elizabeth let the door slam behind her. She sped down the front stairs and spun around the newel post to the study. "Grandpapa?" She flung open the door.

The room lay empty.

Elizabeth whirled toward the nearest footman on station. "Where is he?"

"Gone to the inquest, Miss Trelawny. Coroner didn't want to be coming out here twice when it's easy enough to get a jury together."

A local jury that could be made up of local men who had conspired to murder.

"But he cannot. I need—" She needed to follow, not talk to an impudent footman. "Thank you." She closed the study door in his face and locked it.

Five minutes later, she entered the cave chamber.

"I wondered when you'd return." Morwenna glanced up from the baby in her arms. "No food? I'm starved. I ate the last of the bread and cheese hours ago."

"I am terribly sorry, Wenna, but I had to tell you about Lord Penvenan."

Morwenna listened with shock whitening her already pale face. "But he's innocent."

"I know. And you know. But if he won't speak up for himself to protect us, they'll hang him."

And he wouldn't speak up for himself. Elizabeth knew it as clearly as she knew he should. But he wouldn't ruin her or risk Morwenna's life because he was a good and kind and loving man she loved. She would love him even if he chose returning to America over staying in Cornwall with her. If he asked her again, she would give up Bastion Point to show him she loved him. Even if he changed his mind about wanting to marry her, even if he turned out to be like the others and wanted only her fortune to ease his lot in life, she would still show him her love in the one way she knew best—she would save his life.

And if a selfish, spoiled creature like her could love like that, how much more could Jesus love without expectation of return?

"Unconditional love," Elizabeth murmured.

"I beg your pardon?" Morwenna arched her perfect brows.

"Jesus' unconditional love is real." Turning toward the outside entrance, she said over her shoulder, "I'll return as soon as I can."

The tide wasn't quite out. Heedless of her kid slippers or muslin gown, Elizabeth splashed through the foot or so of water lingering at the mouth of the tunnel and sped up the beach. She would take a horse from Penmara. Fewer questions asked with the master dead and his secretary the subject of an inquest.

An inquest that wouldn't be taking place if she weren't so worried about her reputation and keeping hold of a house and land. Instead of staying with Rowan and assuring everyone he had been with her—not even Morwenna, but her.

Breathless and perspiring, she reached the Penmara stable. The horses stood in their boxes loose with no sign of a groom. She found a gelding she'd helped choose at the fair, slipped a halter over his head, and led him to the mounting block. She didn't waste time finding a saddle, but swung onto his back with her wet skirts clinging to her calves and her hands buried in the gelding's mane. "Go, lad."

He went, galloping faster than safe on the rutted drive, faster than anyone should ride saddleless. Will, strength, and the grace of God kept the horse from stumbling and Elizabeth on his back until they reached the village.

A crowd gathered outside the church, quiet save for the handful of people repeating what was being said inside so everyone could hear.

"Terrible fight they had," echoed across the square. "His lordship were shouting and throwed a decanter after Mr. Rowan."

Condemnatory words, more reason for Rowan to lose his own temper and get revenge.

Elizabeth slid to the ground and began to push through the crowd. People muttered in protest. Others hushed them.

"'Tis Miss Trelawny."

Soon, "Make way for Miss Trelawny" all but drowned out those repeating the proceedings inside.

"And what did Mr. Curnow do once he was dismissed?" Likely the speaker inside now was the coroner.

"He left, sir."

Elizabeth reached the church door. The constable tried to bar her way; then his eyes widened as he realized who she was.

At the front of the church, a dozen businessmen and freehold farmers sat like a row of carven images upon the Penvenan and Trelawny pews. Grandpapa sat behind this jury, and Rowan stood before them, his clothes disheveled, his face stony, his eyes bleak.

An apothecary from Truro who served as coroner stood before him not even reaching Rowan's shoulder in height, but surpassing imagination in rotundity. "Do you have anything to say for yourself, Mr. Curnow?"

Rowan said nothing.

"Mr. Curnow?"

"I will say nothing in my defense." His voice rang out strong and determined.

Elizabeth ducked under Sam Carn's arm. "He may not say anything out of honor," Elizabeth cried, "but I've a great deal to say."

The church erupted in exclamations and enquiries.

"Elizabeth, no." Rowan's voice rose above the hubbub as he lunged forward.

The coroner's bulk blocked his way. "Constable."

Sam plowed forward.

Elizabeth followed. "Quiet, everyone. I've something to say."

"I thought women weren't supposed to speak in church." From one of the box pews stepped the Marquess of Romsford. "Miss Trelawny, you look deranged. Perhaps we should remove you to—"

"What is it?" Grandpapa stepped between Elizabeth and Romsford and grasped her arm. "You look like you just climbed from your bed."

"My looks aren't important." She pulled away from him. "This is."

"Then you may speak to me in private."

"No . . . sir." She spun to face the packed church and raised her arms for silence.

The dull roar of voices died to a rumble.

Elizabeth raised her voice to be heard above it. "This man is innocent. I am a witness."

The growling murmurs inside swelled to a cacophony outside as word spread. Elizabeth waited for the constable and others to bring order and quiet. They would. They did, for she had already made one shocking pronouncement. She intended to say more, though perspiration ran down her hairline and between her shoulder blades at the sight of two hundred pairs of eyes upon her, Grandpapa's dark and troubled ones close at hand, and Romsford's one good eye gleaming like a black beacon from beneath a lowered lid.

Behind her in the growing stillness, Rowan spoke in a near groan, "Don't do this to yourself, my love. It'll ruin you."

She smiled at him over her shoulder. "What does my reputation matter when Jesus loves me?"

Rowan's lips parted and his eyes widened. He shook his head. His lips moved as though he were about to say something.

"Miss Trelawny." The coroner, face red, wheezed with each breath. "This is highly irregular to interrupt the proceedings. I really must ask— Oh, fiddle." He raised his voice above a renewal of the hubbub. "Quiet, everyone, or I'll have Sir Petrok order the constable to arrest you all."

It was an empty threat, but the tumult died down to a low murmur like distant surf.

"Will you repeat what you just said, Elys?" Rowan asked.

Elizabeth let out a shaky laugh. "I realized that Jesus does love me. And because I realized that—"

"Miss Trelawny." The coroner bellowed out her name, though quiet had fallen once more. "Please be seated. This is an official proceeding of the Crown."

"I know." She smiled down at him. "I do apologize for the disruption, sir, but you're about to send an innocent man to the assizes and likely hanging." She raised her gaze to Rowan, then shifted it to Grandpapa, who stood not a yard away gripping the back of a pew, his face taut. "I was with Mr. Curnow when we found his lordship's—his lordship. I'd been with him since the tide was in, so the—his lordship could not have been—"

The church and square burst into raucous shouts again, this

time some name calling interspersed with the shock and horror. They were names she'd called her cousin and worse. They stung like swarming bees, leaving their stingers behind. She stood straight and tall through it all.

Grandpapa looked old and tired. "You're coming home with me, young lady."

"Not so fast." The coroner gripped her other arm. "Why should I believe you, a female, and apparently not a respectable one at that? You'd say anything to protect your . . . er . . . lover."

"You doubt the word of a Trelawny?" Grandpapa demanded.

"I doubt the word of an unwise female."

"What about two unwise females?" Morwenna's contralto, though quiet, cut through the remaining racket.

Elizabeth caught her breath.

Supported between Grandmama and Senara, Miss Pross close behind holding a shawl-wrapped bundle, Morwenna stood in the sanctuary doorway looking too frail to be alive, let alone upright.

"He was with me too." Her voice was strong enough to be heard in the now utter stillness of the throng. "They were protecting me and helping me give birth to Conan Lord Penvenan's baby." As the noise rose again, she raised her voice. "My son is the true heir to Penmara. Conan and I were married on Guernsey a year ago."

CHAPTER 28

A SILENCE SO PROFOUND FELL OVER CHURCH AND SQUARE. The coroner's wheezing breaths sounded like a Newcomen engine pumping water from a mine. Then the baby began to cry, the mewling wail of a newborn yanking the crowd to their feet, necks craning for a glimpse to the true heir to Penmara. Murmurs rose like an incoming storm.

"It can't be true."

"Sensible to wed a Trelawny."

"I don't believe her."

"Neither do I." Senara's voice rose in a crescendo above the others. "Can you prove it, you lying, cheating, little—"

"Senara," Grandmama snapped.

"Well, can she?" Senara grasped Morwenna's shoulders and shook her.

Morwenna wobbled as though she'd fall if Senara released her. "I can." She spoke decisively, if somewhat breathlessly. "I've my marriage lines." She reached into a pocket of her now too-big gown.

And Senara screamed. "You can't have wed him. Penmara is mine, mine, mine. You won't have it. You won't—" She lunged for the baby.

"Stop her," someone shouted.

Rowan and Grandpapa surged toward Senara.

Rowan caught her, wrapping her in his arms with her arms at her sides, but her feet lashing out at his shins. "Stop it, Cousin."

Senara shrieked. "I've seen the letters to Conan. You're not my legitimate cousin. You'd be dead too if you were."

Elizabeth pressed her hands to her middle. She would not be sick. She would not faint. *Remember who you are.*

Yes, a woman who didn't have to be strong on her own.

She stepped forward and grasped Senara's shoulders. "Calm yourself, Senara. This will all work out."

"Work out?" Senara began to weep with deep, racking sobs. "It never can if that baby is still alive."

Behind Rowan, the coroner, looking apoplectic, called for the constable to restore order. Grandpapa gathered Morwenna to his chest.

"Even if you destroyed your nephew too," Rowan said in a gentle voice, "it wouldn't change matters for you."

"It would. It would." Senara's voice rasped between sobs.

"Calm yourself, Miss Penvenan." Romsford stepped forward.

Rowan stepped back, still holding Senara. "I'll take care of her, my lord. She's my kin."

Romsford's upper lip curled. "She's a lady, and you are a—"

"Gentleman." Elizabeth stepped between Romsford and Rowan, facing the former. "You should leave. This is none of your affair. Cornwall has nothing for you, not me, not Penmara's mines, not—" She stared at the marquess, the coldness of his eye, the sneer of his lip as he looked at her, and she tried to scuttle backward, came up short against a pew door. "It was Bastion Point all along."

"It was Penmara all along." Senara's voice rose to a shriek. She brought the heel of her boot onto Rowan's toes and heaved herself out of his hold. "Penmara should be mine. He promised if I helped him—"

"She's mad." As cool as his countenance, Romsford's voice nonetheless rang through the church as though the building were empty, so quiet and still had the onlookers become. "She should be put in the lockup."

"She will be if she's done anything wrong," Grandpapa said. "But we need to know what she's talking about. If you helped whom, Senara?"

"Him." Senara pointed her finger at Romsford. "He wanted the beach, he wanted the caves. He—"

He lunged for Elizabeth. She grasped the top of the pew door and vaulted over it. Romsford sprang after her.

Rowan caught hold of the back of the marquess's coat collar in one fist and planted him a facer with the other. Romsford sagged. Rowan released him to fall in a heap onto the stone floor.

Elizabeth sank to her knees and clung to the side of the pew with shaking hands, an entirely shaking body. "He was going to attack me." She doubted anyone heard her above the tumult once again filling the church and square.

Nor could they hear her above Senara shrieking as she applied the toes of her sturdy boots to Romsford's ribs. "You promised Penmara would be mine if they died. Promised. Promised."

Grandmama slapped Senara. The blow stopped the histrionics and quieted the throng.

Sam Carn glanced from Senara, to Romsford, then to Grandpapa and the coroner. "I don't know what I should be doing here. Take 'em both in?"

"I'm afraid so." Grandpapa's face worked. His eyes turned suspiciously bright.

Elizabeth hauled herself to her feet to go to him.

"Miss Penvenan." Kindly Sam Carn laid a hand on her arm.

Senara shook off his grip. "Don't touch me."

"I must, miss." Sam looked at Rowan this time. "I'm not sure I understand what's afoot here, but—"

"You should." Senara shot a murderous glare at Morwenna, who sagged against a pew, Miss Pross and the baby beside her. "Penmara would be mine if that doxy hadn't lured my brother into marriage."

"No, Cousin, it wouldn't." Rowan spoke in a low, carrying tone. "My parents were married more than a year before I was born."

A storm wind of voices rolled from the front of the church and back to spill out the door.

"Legitimate son."

"Another heir."

Shocked faces. Lots of tears.

Elizabeth expected her own face mirrored those of many in the crowd, betrayal added to the astonishment. *Remember who you are—a lady Jesus loves.* She slipped out of the pew so she could lean against Grandpapa's shoulder. If she hadn't, she never would have heard Senara's sobbing murmur.

"I helped him kill them for nothing."

Elizabeth pressed the back of her hand to her mouth to hold back a cry. Her throat burned with bile. Her eyes burned with tears. "Senara, not just for Penmara." She didn't speak loud enough for anyone to hear.

"Who did you help, Miss Penvenan?" The coroner bustled forward. "Tell us so we can bring this inquest to a close."

"The inquest," Grandpapa said over the shouts from the onlookers to know what was happening, "will reconvene at a later date. Sam, take her to the jail."

"And him." Elizabeth followed Rowan's gaze down to where Romsford lay on the floor, just beginning to stir. "I know as a Christian I should abhor violence, but right now—" His hands fisted at his sides.

"We'll see to him, Mr. Curnow." Sam shouted for two men to come forward and help. "He's a marquess so we gotta take him to London." His nostrils pinched as though he smelled something foul. "His kind get took care of by their own kind."

Elizabeth swallowed against the lump in her throat and reached a hand toward Sam. "Take care of Senara. She's not right in the head."

"We'll treat her gentle." Sam's dark eyes were clouded with his own grief. "She were good to us, and she were his lordship's sister." He took Senara's hand, and she went with him as docile as an obedient child.

Two miners picked up Romsford and followed. He tried to struggle. He mumbled curses that sounded almost obligatory. His jaw swelling and darkening, he, too, looked defeated.

The crowd parted before the cavalcade, and for the first time in her life, Elizabeth covered her face with her hands and wept in public.

❧

The Trelawnys gathered around Morwenna's bedside where Grandmama had tucked up her younger granddaughter as soon as they all managed to extricate themselves from the coroner and the church. On the far side of the room, Miss Pross sang a lullaby to a sleeping infant, her face aglow as though the baby were hers.

The sight was the first thing Elizabeth found to smile about since discovering Penvenan's body at sunrise. Now, at sunset, she needed something to lift her spirits, for everything her cousin said increased her sense of betrayal.

"Conan didn't want to waste a fortune restoring the house," Morwenna was explaining. "He wanted to sell the land to someone who would reopen the mines and then get us far away from the smugglers. He even talked about America."

"Was that why he contacted the American Penvenans?" Grandpapa asked.

"To break the entail, yes."

Which was one more blow to Elizabeth's heart. "You knew all along that Row—Mr. Penvenan was Austell Penvenan's legitimate son?"

"I did." Morwenna's eyes conveyed sympathy. "But we kept up the pretense of him being a mere secretary for his safety."

"Why safety?" Grandpapa's face wrinkled into lines of fatigue and disappointment.

Morwenna plucked at embroidery on the edge of the coverlet. "There were threats. Conan was trying to get the smugglers to stop so he could get free of the business, and the threats began—a scrawled message, a dead bird . . . little things."

"And you couldn't think to tell me as the magistrate, let alone your grandfather?" Hurt added more lines to his face.

"We couldn't." Morwenna flashed a look at him, then down to the coverlet. "If Drake was involved, it could endanger you and Grandmama."

"You think Drake would betray Conan?" Elizabeth scowled at Morwenna.

She shrugged. "He was still thick as thieves with the gang. He seemed to know every time the revenue officers intended a raid. He didn't want Conan to stop. Do I need more reasons?" Her dark eyes held a challenge.

"He's my brother. He's your cousin. He's a Trelawny."

"And you kept more than a few secrets yourself, young lady." Grandmama patted Elizabeth's hand. "So get off your high ropes. When people are frightened of one or two people, they tend to trust no one."

"More like a hundred people we didn't trust." Morwenna shuddered. "Conan didn't tell Senara anything. She flew into a rage once when he mentioned breaking the entail if he could. So he never mentioned bringing the American Penvenans to Cornwall. And by the time they arrived in England, he feared for his life enough he didn't want them to admit who they were."

"But Austell Penvenan was too arrogant to hide his chance to be a lord." Elizabeth rubbed her arms, cold despite her woolen shawl.

"Someone had to have the right to oversee Penmara," Morwenna pointed out. "But with only one person in the lineage. Rowan needed to be free to roam around. He's quite intelligent." Morwenna shot a smile in Elizabeth's direction. "About some things."

Grandpapa cleared his throat. "So when did the threats begin? After you two wed?"

"About a week or two when we would, um"—Morwenna blushed—"meet at night."

"About the same time Romsford started paying court to me." Elizabeth rose to shovel more coal onto the fire and build up the blaze. "Was he paying court to Senara too, to persuade her to go along with him?"

"She says it was strictly business." Grandpapa sighed.

He had spent several hours in the jail with Senara and Romsford. The latter refused to talk other than demanding he be taken to London at once, his right as a peer. Peers were tried in Parliament. He neither declared his innocence nor admitted any guilt. Senara, on the other hand, seemed resigned to whatever fate the circuit judge meted out to her—most likely transportation to New South Wales, Grandpapa had told them earlier—and was talking freely.

"Romsford," Grandpapa continued, "promised her a Penmara all her own out of the haul if she would help him take over the smugglers. She claims she had no idea he meant murder until she lured Conan down to the beach on some pretense of the smugglers leaving something behind, and Romsford—" He broke off as Morwenna snatched a pillow and buried her face in it. "I am sorry, child. You must have loved him dearly."

Morwenna nodded, still holding the pillow to muffle her sobs.

"She thought Penmara was hers then, so she didn't turn Romsford in for fear he'd incriminate her," Grandpapa continued. "And then Penvenan came along. When he and Morwenna received threats, Rowan worked out how anyone connected with the Penvenans was in danger."

"Then why didn't he tell the coroner?" Elizabeth demanded.

Grandpapa sighed. "He did mention we should look at Romsford as a suspect, but no one believed him, not a mere—" Grandpapa hesitated.

"He referred to himself as a scrub one day." Elizabeth smiled for the second time as she remembered that first glorious gallop. "But I wouldn't have believed it. Romsford being here to court me or even buy land is one thing. Murdering a fellow peer is quite something else." She gripped the poker as though she could wield it against those who could no longer harm her. "And the accident Senara had was just to muddle things. Though I think that makes it no accident at all. She must have thrown herself down the stairs or only pretended to fall."

"No one," Grandmama said, "would call Lord Romsford stupid."

Elizabeth let the poker slide back into its stand. "Intelligent evil is more frightening than the ordinary criminal."

They all sat in silence for several minutes, then Elizabeth

returned to her chair. "And you let us treat you badly about your
condition to protect your baby, Wenna, in case it was a boy and
the heir." She took a deep breath. "I think you're the bravest
woman I know. I hope I can be half so much in my life."

Morwenna smoothed a ribbon on her dressing gown. "You
seem to have forgotten you don't like me much."

"I haven't forgotten." Elizabeth rose and kissed her cousin's
cheek. "And you didn't like me much either. Envy, pure and
simple. You are so small and pretty." Elizabeth emitted a bark
of mirth. "Other than that, though, I liked you. I remembered
how much pleasure all of us had together, you and Drake and
Conan . . . and Senara." Her chest ached. "Why didn't we see
Senara's troubles? She was Conan's sister."

"And we loved her even if she annoyed us much of the time."
Morwenna wiped her eyes on a corner of the pillow slip and
tossed it aside.

Elizabeth gave her a handkerchief. "I'm just working out
how Jesus loves us when we must annoy him a great deal more."

"Oh, that." Morwenna ducked behind the handkerchief.

Elizabeth started to say something, but Grandmama shook
her head. "Just love her and let her grieve."

Elizabeth switched her gaze to the window and the sea
beyond, sparkling slate blue beneath the dropping sun. Far out
along the horizon, a boat caught the wind, its sails billowing like
the skirt of a graceful dancer. She tracked the boat's progress
over the waves while the conversation flowed around her.

"We were wrong to exile you," Grandmama was saying to
Morwenna. "We had the best of intentions, wanting you secure
in a marriage, as well as your child safe with a father, but you
should have been able to trust us."

"I should have done more about the smugglers," Grandpapa
added.

"And have them making a target of you?" Morwenna sounded horrified. "I didn't want that."

Bedclothes rustled. The chairs creaked. From the corner of her eye, Elizabeth saw the grandparents and Morwenna embracing. Good. She needed them now more than ever.

Elizabeth rose and crossed the room to the window. Now she could see a bank of clouds rolling in from the east as though chasing the sun out of the sky.

She wanted to chase the sun out of the sky, mount Grisette without benefit of a sidesaddle, and fly along the beach. Except it wouldn't be as much pleasure without Rowan racing beside her. She'd saved his neck, only to learn he had been keeping yet more secrets from her—secrets he had shared with her cousin.

"No wonder Senara was so against me marrying Austell Penvenan," Elizabeth mused aloud. "Or was most of the time. She tried to muddle matters there too. She thought Romsford had to kill me to stop me from producing another heir since he couldn't marry me himself. Who could want a house and lands that much?"

"Are you not willing to sacrifice everything for Bastion Point?" Grandpapa asked.

Elizabeth whirled to face him. "I beg your pardon?"

The baby began to cry, and Miss Pross picked him up from the cradle. "He's hungry."

A beatific smile crossed Morwenna's face, and she held out her arms.

The grandparents and Elizabeth left Morwenna to see to her baby and descended the steps to the blue sitting room. A footman hastened ahead of them to light candles. With light plentiful, Grandmama settled herself with her needlework.

Grandpapa halted Elizabeth in the center of the room, a hand on her shoulder. "I was proud of you today, Elizabeth. Shocked and appalled at your behavior in spending the night in the company of a gentleman, however innocently, but proud you came forward and saved a fine young man from his own destruction."

"I had no choice. He didn't save himself to save me." She rested her head on Grandpapa's shoulder wanting to weep, but drained of tears for one day. "He thought keeping my reputation intact and inheriting Bastion Point was more important to me than his life."

"Obviously they're not." Grandpapa set her at arm's length and looked into her eyes. "How do you feel about Bastion Point now? You know it's yours."

Elizabeth shook her head. "I never earned it the way you asked. I never worked out what you meant by treasure."

"But you did. You found the treasure of learning what is more important in life than a house and land and the security they bring—your faith in Jesus and willingness to put others before yourself. Those are the treasures worth having."

"They are." Elizabeth started to wring her fingers together at her waist, but stilled them and found something else to smile about. "I'd rather you save it for Morwenna. She needs a clear path to follow."

"She'll have Penmara now," Grandpapa said. "It belongs to that infant upstairs, but she's his natural guardian."

"And Penmara will need more money than Austell Penvenan left behind. It's why he wanted my dowry. Morwenna needs money to build Penmara into a true inheritance for her son. I'll give up as much as I must, even all of it, so she can do that. I made Bastion Point too important to accept it. I nearly let Rowan hang rather than admit I was with him last night."

"And the night you arrived in Cornwall." Grandmother's mouth was stern, but her eyes twinkled.

Elizabeth jerked back in surprise. "You knew?"

"We're old, child, not unobservant." Grandpapa patted her cheek. "My powers of reason haven't all fled me."

"Oh, well, um." Elizabeth rubbed the back of her neck. "I'm appalled that I put property before honor."

"And love?" Grandmama asked.

Elizabeth bowed her head.

From the corner of her eye, she noticed the grandparents exchange one of those glances that spoke volumes between them, then her grandfather turned back to Elizabeth. "I thought you might say that. And in that event, there's someone cooling his heels in the garden, waiting to see you."

"See me?" Elizabeth shoved her fingers into the tangled mass of her hair. She'd changed her dress, but scissors might be the only solution for her hair. "I look terrible."

"I don't think he cares what you look like," Grandmama said.

"Go." Grandpapa gave her a gentle push toward the door.

Knees wobbling like a newborn foal's, Elizabeth made her way to the garden parlor and door onto the terrace. A dozen questions, accusations, and proclamations jostled one another through her head until she couldn't think of two coherent words to put together. She halted on the top step of the terrace and glanced around to find him.

He glided from the shadows of the oak outside her bedchamber window, a stranger, a friend, the man she loved. He paused on the step below her so they stood at eye level. "Rowan Curnow Penvenan at your service, Miss Trelawny."

The absurdity of the introduction after all they'd been through together loosened Elizabeth's tongue. "Why didn't you tell me? I was keeping enough other secrets well enough. Did you think I couldn't keep yours?"

"I knew you could keep mine well enough." He took her hand in his and led her down the steps. With her fingers pressed beneath his on the crook of his elbow, he began to stroll along a graveled path between beds of fragrant roses and flowering rhododendrons. "And will you hold it against me that I wanted you to love simple Rowan Curnow, secretary, rather than the son of, as you thought at the time, a peer of the realm?"

Elizabeth winced. "You thought I needed a lesson in humility."

"I thought you needed to know your own heart free of debris like titles and money."

She paused at the edge of the herb garden and faced him. "I've loved you for weeks."

"I suspected you did, but nothing told me so clearly as you did when you walked into that church looking like a wanton to everyone there, but an angel to me." He smoothed his thumb across her cheek.

A frisson of pleasure shivered through her. "As soon as I learned you'd been arrested I knew I had to do it. I didn't care if you still wanted me as your wife or not. But of course I knew you did. Only a man who loved would be willing to sacrifice himself to protect others." She tilted her head and peeked at him from beneath her lashes. "Of course, you might have been protecting Morwenna."

"Only until she was safe." He reclaimed her hand and resumed their promenade. "I'd have protected your name forever so you could have what you want."

"Morwenna's word alone might not have saved you. She may have married Conan a year ago, but her reputation hasn't been the best since she was fifteen." She squeezed the hard muscle of his forearm. "And if you'd hanged, I'd have lost what I want—you."

"Are you sure? Really, really sure?" He stopped in the shadow of a peach tree this time and scrutinized her face. "Penvenan really did disinherit me, from the plantation anyway. It will be sold and the proceeds used to free and relocate the slaves, according to my father's will. There is, however, a horse farm in Virginia, a house in Alexandria, another house in Philadelphia, and shares in a shipping interest out of New York. None are terribly prosperous, but together they do well enough by me."

"I still have a substantial dowry, I suppose, but I gave up my claim to Bastion Point."

He smiled. "I know."

"You do?" She drew her brows together. "How? I just told Grandpapa."

"I told him not to send you out to me unless you did."

"Indeed." She crossed her arms over her chest.

He laughed. "I didn't want a wife tied to Cornwall by land and people she'd be responsible for."

A wife.

Her knees nearly gave way, and her arms fell limply at her sides. There it was—the message she needed to make a momentous decision—the most momentous decision after giving her heart to the Lord.

She gulped. "You . . . you're going back to America, then."

"I am." He took her hands in his. "Will you go with me, Elys? Will you marry me and start a life with me in America?"

She didn't even have to think about it. "I will." She kissed him, not at all like that desperate girl at the ball. Once and for all melting the ice-blue ice maiden he had called her.

"Your grandparents can see us, you know," he murmured against her lips.

"Good. I hope all the servants can as well. It's past time I stopped hiding my love for you." And she drew him out of the shadows to kiss him in the light.

AUTHOR'S NOTE

Today, a movement is afoot in Cornwall to renew the Cornish-English language. In the Regency, however, it was considered dead, though a few words lingered amongst the country folk. I've chosen not to include those words despite having searched high and low—and finally locating—a Cornish-English dictionary. Spelling and pronunciation are just too difficult.

I have also taken the liberty to change the spelling of the hero's name from the Cornish spelling, which is rightfully Ruan or Rouan. Those spellings, when spoken aloud by most English speakers, sound like "ruin." Since that won't do, I have chosen to spell the hero's name in the more familiar English form of Rowan.

Why not simply change his name? When I ran several groupings of other Cornish names through a test group, they said they sounded like something they would find in a science fiction or fantasy novel, with the exception of the popular name Tristan. Tristan is a name I personally love . . . but so much so that I've already used it in another Regency romance.

As for the smugglers, they are romanticized in dozens of books, but they were anything but romantic. They were vicious, cruel, and intolerant of even a hint of treachery against them. Secrecy was of utmost importance. Their lives depended on anonymity and honor among thieves.

DISCUSSION QUESTIONS

1. Obedience is a theme in *A Lady's Honor*, and in the beginning, Elizabeth is acting against her parents' wishes for her life. How does she justify this act of disobedience? How is she right? How is she wrong?
2. Elizabeth's grandparents want her to earn her inheritance. How does this challenge contribute to her belief that love must be earned?
3. In what way, if any, are Elizabeth's grandparents justified in how they treat her cousins Morwenna and Drake?
4. In the beginning, Rowan justifies his deception by omission. If he is right, how? Or do you think nothing justifies deceit? If you have ever had to mislead someone for a "good" reason, are you willing to share why and how?
5. What are the consequences of Rowan's deception? How could he have behaved otherwise?
6. Why is believing in the unconditional love of Jesus difficult for Elizabeth?
7. What has helped you believe in unconditional love? Or what makes that belief difficult for you?
8. Why does Elizabeth cling to the material treasures of the world?

9. How do Rowan's actions at the end of the story help Elizabeth to believe that Jesus loves her without reservation? What about Morwenna's actions?

10. What wishes for their lives do Senara and Elizabeth have in common? How are they different?

ACKNOWLEDGMENTS

CONTRARY TO WHAT PEOPLE SAY, WRITING IS NOT A solitary profession. Without a host of people, I would never get through a novel. For this one, a horde of the usual and a few suspects held my sanity intact while I wrote this around a major move and a few other minor crises.

My thanks to Gina Welborn and Patty Smith Hall for reading early chapters to ensure I was on track, as well as taking my slightly panicked phone calls asking, "Does this make sense to you?" They weren't afraid to say, "No, it doesn't." Kathleen Y'Barbo Turner read the entire manuscript and made some great suggestions for clarifying and tightening. The crew on the writer's accountability Facebook group kept me working because when I reported I intended to finish no less than two thousand words in a specific time period, I knew they were watching to see if I would. They were also encouraging.

Closer to home, I cannot go without expressing my appreciation for my family, even if four of the members have four paws instead of only two. Nick, the crazy golden, gave me great excuses to get out of the house for walks. Bess, the obedient black Labrador, just makes me laugh, which is good for the soul. And the cats . . . Well, my husband says I talk about them far too much, but who can avoid talking about a pile of purring fur lying on one's desk?

As for the two-legged member of my family, without my husband's encouragement, I wouldn't have started writing at all; therefore, he deserves the most thanks.

Introducing Sarah E. Ladd, another fresh voice in Regency romance.

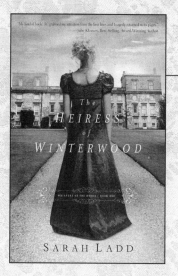

"If you are a fan of Jane Austen and Jane Eyre, you will love Sarah E. Ladd's debut."

—USAToday.com

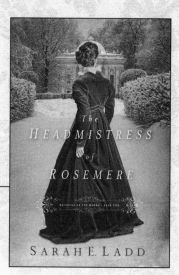

"Sarah E. Ladd has written a story sure to warm your heart even on the coldest day."

—Laurie Alice Eakes, author of *A Lady's Honor*

A Lady at Willowgrove Hall, available October 2014

9780310332060-A

ABOUT THE AUTHOR

RECIPIENT OF THE NATIONAL READERS Choice Award, Laurie Alice Eakes is the author of nine books and a novella, with four more books and two novellas scheduled for release. She is a writing teacher and speaker and has her master's degree in creative writing. She also writes articles on writing, including "Writing from the Heart While Writing for the Market" for *The ACFW Journal*.